Homosexuality in the Priesthood and the Religious Life

EDITED BY
JEANNINE GRAMICK

CROSSROAD • NEW YORK

1990

The Crossroad Publishing Company
370 Lexington Avenue, New York, N.Y. 10017

Printed in the United States of America

Library of Congress Cataloging-in-Publication Data

Homosexuality, the priesthood, and the religious life / edited by
    Jeannine Gramick.
        p.   cm.
    ISBN 0-8245-0963-3
        1. Homosexuality—Religious aspects—Catholic Church.
    2. Catholic Church—Clergy—Sexual behavior.   3. Gay clergy—
    United States.   4. Lesbian nuns—United States.   I. Gramick,
    Jeannine.
    BX1795.H66H67   1989
    253'.2—dc20   89-33997
                                                                    CIP

Contents

example, when Francis Schulte, then bishop of Wheeling, West Virginia, proposed that Harvey be invited to establish a ministry group in the diocese, an advisory board who listened to Harvey's approach rejected the proposal.

In contrast, the basic philosophy of another group, Communication Ministry, assumed that homosexual persons were not essentially disordered and could grow spiritually by mutual sharing and support. Communication Ministry began as a network mainly of priests and brothers who exchanged views on particular themes, such as celibacy and relationships, through the medium of a monthly newsletter. The organization has since offered annual retreats in various regions of the U.S. and has devoted two issues of its journal to AIDS and to seminary and religious formation.

A third group founded in 1977, New Ways Ministry, also began to work with priests and religious as one part of its educational and pastoral ministry regarding homosexuality. In response to requests from women religious who had experienced a disproportionate number of males at retreats for homosexual religious, New Ways Ministry sponsored a retreat for lesbian nuns in 1979. In 1984-85, New Ways conducted a series of regional workshops for women religious who were exploring their sexual orientation. The first three articles in this anthology are based on keynote addresses delivered at a series of symposiums for religious congregational leadership sponsored by New Ways Ministry in 1985-86. One of the essays in the second section together with the contributions of John Hilgeman and Jo Louise Pecoraro in the third are likewise based on presentations made at these symposiums.

Articles and books devoted to issues of lesbian and gay clergy and religious communities, such as Maryknoll, the National Sisters Vocation Conference, the Religious Formation Conference, and the newly formed National Religious Vocation Conference, addressed the topic in their respective journals or newletters. Increasingly the issue surfaced in the public forum of more mainline publications such as *The Priest, Review for Religious, Sisters Today*, and *Commonweal*. Portions of books or anthologies on homosexuality invariably contained chapters or contributions on religious life and priesthood. By 1983, a discussion document on sexuality from the Committee on Priestly Life and Ministry of the National Conference of Catholic Bishops even contained a case study about a homosexual priest.

Initially most of the literature discussing homosexual religious and clergy, as well as pastoral ministry to these individuals, was directed toward priests and brothers. Women religious were usually an afterthought. But by 1985 lesbian nuns had gained widespread interest and attention not only in Catholic circles but in the world at large because of the heavy publicity surrounding the publication of the book *Lesbian Nuns: Breaking Silence*. The title was somewhat misleading since most of the essays were contributed by former nuns. Although this collective work received less than enthusiastic reviews from the *National Catholic Reporter* and *Sisters Today*, its real value lay in drawing public attention to this neglected women's issue. Another book, *Immodest Acts*, a carefully researched historical account of a seventeenth-century lesbian nun, appealed to scholars and students of history. An article that appeared in *Women and Therapy* in 1986, titled "Counseling Lesbian Women Religious," was helpful to the religious professional. However, neither the historical work nor the counseling article had as significant an effect on the general public as the much ballyhooed trade book.

Public awareness of homosexual priests has been aroused recently by a plethora of print media accounts and TV talk shows on the problem of clerical pedophilia. Although adult homosexuality and pedophilia are distinct clinical categories, gay priests have unfortunately been linked to this dysfunctional behavior in the public's mind. However, some sensitive articles dealing with gay clergy have appeared in Catholic newspapers beginning with a 1976 interview with an anonymous gay priest in the *National Catholic Reporter*. Since then this newspaper has periodically published opinion pieces and news items on gay priests and brothers in a generally balanced manner.

The present volume is intended to contribute to the further opening of the doors of silence that have blocked a healthy discussion of sexuality and homosexuality in some church circles. An ecclesial community that fears to probe delicate issues is like a neurotic individual locked in a world of fantasy. A faithful community trusts in the guidance of God's Spirit and accepts the challenge of difficult issues in an honest and caring fashion. A loving Christian community makes the concerns of all its members, even the most hidden and marginal, its own. Hence the need for this book.

The book itself is divided into three parts: ecclesial, personal, and ministerial perspectives. The first part sets the homosexual debate in its theological and historical context. The groundwork is laid in Maguire's article, which argues that before a healthy debate on sexual issues can be undertaken, unresolved issues of ecclesiology, celibacy, and the nature of friendship and community must be addressed. Reuther then offers a specific critique asserting that the roots of homophobia lie in a traditional Christian view that sees sex itself as debasing and allowable only for reproduction. This section concludes with Boswell's more focused essay which documents the admiration and encouragement of romantic attachments among secular clergy and religious communities prior to the thirteenth century.

The second and major section of the book presents the personal stories, experiences, and reflections of homosexually oriented religious and priests. These essays will strike a resonant chord among lesbian and gay clergy and religious, and will invoke in the non-gay reader sympathy for the struggles that the homosexually oriented have endured and admiration for the rich spirituality they possess.

The fact that most of the personal accounts use pseudonyms indicates that most gay brothers, sisters, and priests are not yet comfortable with being completely public about their sexual orientation. These anonymous authors wonder if their "going public" at any future time may entail effects similar to those experienced by Sister Eileen Brady, whose article here recounts the reactions of her community and friends to her coming out publicly in the book *Lesbian Nuns: Breaking Silence.*

Nuns generally come to an awareness of their sexual identity at a much later age than priests and brothers. This is illustrated, for example, by William Hart McNichols who states, "I knew I was a priest around the age of five, not too much earlier than the time I began to experience a glimmer of my given sexual orientation."

On the other hand, for Sisters Mary and Vickie, this realization was obviously more gradual and evolved after many years in religious life.

A wide range of ages is represented by the contributions here. Some, such as Richard John Cardarelli and Father Francis, have been in religious life for about a dozen years, while the contemplative Matthew Kelty uses his vantage of seventy-odd years to state: "My life as a priest, as monk, as gay, is not in what I say or even in what I do, but in what I am. And I think that is really all that matters." Sister Raphaela, a very creative and exuberant woman who describes herself as "at the edge of old age" and who has "made many weary detours" in life, believes that "she who directs herself is directed by a fool."

The lesbian sisters, gay priests, and gay brothers who have courageously told their stories in this anthology have been engaged in a diversity of ministries, especially education and promoting justice-seeking work. Sisters Linda, Mary, Raphaela, and Judith Whitacre and Brother Jonathan and Father Aelred have served the church in leadership positions in their religious congregations or dioceses.

While there is much diversity in the background of the writers and in their essays, there are also common themes and experiences. Many, such as Father Paul and Sister Mary Louise St. John, write about the integration of sexuality, celibacy, and spirituality. Others, like Brother Amos, tell of the feelings of isolation they experienced during their journeys to self-acceptance. The Paschal mystery of suffering-death and joy-resurrection is clearly evident in the essays of William Hart McNichols and Brother Jonathan, both of whom seem to be intimately immersed in God.

The third and final section of the book has been written by those who have ministered to homosexually oriented priests and religious in the professional capacity of counselor, spiritual director, or formation director. John Hilgeman's and Jo Louise Pecoraro's articles are companion pieces. One written from a male and the other from a female viewpoint, they suggest concrete ways that church personnel can provide support and assistance.

Robert Nugent analyzes several relevant church documents dealing with gay candidates, delineates what he sees as the beginnings of a more restrictive attitude, and offers some positive directions for the future. My essay explores questions frequently raised by women religious: How can I know if I am a lesbian? How can we support our lesbian sisters institutionally? And what are the differences, in terms of experiences and needs, between lesbian sisters and gay priests and religious? Jeanne Schweickert concludes this section and the book with an analysis of the portion of a study undertaken by the National Conference of Religious Vocation Directors in 1985, that dealt with the incorporation of lesbian women and gay men into community life.

I believe this book is timely. It comes at a time when many in the church are suspecting that the great resistance to and suppression of any development regarding sexual issues within some segments of the hierarchical church is due to its unwillingness to face homosexuality within its own ranks. It comes at a time when lesbian nuns and gay priests and brothers are claiming their own pride and goodness and following the Gospel mandate to let their lights shine instead of hiding them under a bushel or in a closet. It comes at a time when the faith community may be ready and willing to listen to and to actually hear the voices of the lesbian and gay ministers in our midst.

Jeannine Gramick, SSND

ECCLESIAL PERSPECTIVES

1 Homosexuality and Religious Life: A Historical Approach
JOHN BOSWELL

INVISIBILITY AND MARGINALIZATION

One of the most difficult aspects of being a lesbian or gay person is the phenomenon of pervasive invisibility: exclusion from any generally recognizable category. This usually happens with persons considered "outsiders" in some way by their contemporaries. Most societies distinguish, consciously or unconsciously, degrees of "acceptability" among persons who are perceived to diverge from the norm, often in three categories: "distinguishable insider," "inferior insider," and "outsider."

"Distinguishable insiders" are, to paraphrase a familiar modern concept, different but equal. They are persons who could be recognized as distinctive if someone had the desire to discriminate, but whose divergence from the norm is viewed in the society at issue as part of the ordinary range of human variation. They are therefore not disadvantaged or segregated, socially or conceptually. Eye color marks such a category in most Western societies; someone might be able to remember which of his or her friends and acquaintances had blue and which brown eyes, but it would hardly make any difference. In the United States the classic example is Protestant church affiliation; though a Presbyterian genetic "trait," a psychological "state," an "inclination," or a "preference." Though these terms vary in their implications of permanence and mutability, all suggest an essential, internal characteristic of a person rather than an external, voluntary activity.

The importance of the difference between the modern view and preceding systems of conceptualizing sexuality can scarcely be exaggerated. Contemporary concepts have drastically altered social views of sexual behavior and its significance by focusing on sexual object choice and correlating it with an inherent, defining personal characteristic. The majority supposes itself to have the trait, condition, or preference of heterosexuality, which is "healthy" and "normal," and believes that a minority of persons have the "opposite" trait, condition, or preference, which is "unhealthy" and "not normal." The difference is rendered more profound and alienating by the fact that the "normal" or "healthy" state is generally considered (as were all forms of sexuality in the past) to be primarily behavioral. Because "heterosexual" is conceived to be the norm, it is unmarked and unnoticed. "Heterosexual person" is unnecessary. "Person" implies heterosexual without indication to the contrary. But the normal person is not "heterosexual" in any defining sense; he or she engages in heterosexual activity from time to time, but hardly any information about his or her character, behavior, life-style or interest is inferable from this fact. "Homosexual," on the other hand, is understood as a primary and permanent category, a constant and defining characteristic that implies a great deal beyond occasional sexual behavior about the person to whom the term is applied. Not only, it is imagined, does his or her sexuality define all other aspects of personality and life-style, which are implicitly subordinate to sex in the case of homosexuals but not heterosexuals, but the connotations of the term and its place in the modern construction of sexuality suggest that homosexuals are much more sexual than heterosexuals. That is, in the case of a "normal" person, heterosexuality is assumed to be one part of his or her personality; in the case of a "homosexual" person, sexuality is thought to be the primary constituent of his or her (abnormal) personality.

This partly explains why the very idea of lesbian sisters and gay brothers and priests shocks many people. How could there be gay religious persons? The controlling influence in the lives of religious is presumed to be the absence of sexuality,[2] a sexuality assumed by the majority to be always and everywhere heterosexual; whereas the controlling influence in the lives of gay people is assumed to be overt, abnormal sexuality. Since gay people are not a permitted category, the average person has so little information about them and so little opportunity to consider their lives that the possibility of *sacrificing*, channeling, or dedicating homosexual desire simply is not entertained.

Being outsiders in this way, morally and conceptually invisible to the majority, is one of the greatest problems gay people encounter in modern society. It is especially difficult for gay religious, who are doubly marginalized. They are "outsiders" to other Christians because they are gay, and "outsiders" to most gay people because they are religious. This is a poignant irony on both counts. Not only is homosexual eroticism the oldest and most persistent strand in the Christian theology of romantic love, but Christian religious life was the most prominent gay life-style in Western Europe from the early Middle Ages to the Reformation, about two-thirds of the period since Europe became Christian.

Celibacy and the Appeal of Religious Life

One of many transformations in the nature of marriage effected during late antiquity and the early Middle Ages was the gradual narrowing of the concept of marriage from an institution filling a variety of needs—such as dynastic, emotional, sexual, or political —to one designed and fit (in the minds of ascetic theologians) for a single purpose, that is, for procreation. Although progeny and the continuation of family lines were prominent in Roman and Jewish ideals of marriage, both of which were influential on early Christians, matrimony also included, in both traditions, aspects of affection, sexual satisfaction, and companionship. For Roman males, moreover, marriage was not expected to constitute the sole outlet for eroticism; sexual interaction with other women, other males, or both was acceptable in Roman society and not considered adultery, although jealous wives were free to object if it displeased them.

Because marriage filled a variety of needs, was conceptualized as a civic duty, and did not limit other possibilities for erotic fulfillment, gay men and women in the ancient world would have had little reason to resist matrimony and much reason to undertake it. But late antique social and philosophical movements, including but not limited to Christianity, increasingly insisted not only that procreation was the sole justification for marriage, but also that it was gravely sinful to engage in any sexual activity outside marriage, or in any acts between spouses not directed at procreation. This made marriage a much less attractive option for most people, both male and female, since it was presented exclusively as a duty to the race, and the role of eroticism and pleasure even within legitimate matrimony was severely disparaged by theologians. "Any love for someone else's spouse or very much for one's own is adultery," warned Jerome,[3] and Augustine urged wives to direct their husbands to prostitutes if they wished to indulge in any sexual activity that was not procreative.[4]

The Christian alternative to marriage, something unheard of and disapproved among Jews and rare among Romans, was celibacy. Although it was not a rule for the secular clergy until the twelfth century, and then only in the West, and although the superiority of the state of celibacy to the married state would not be defined until the Council of Trent in the sixteenth century, from the very beginning of Christian religious life celibacy was a much admired and common ideal.

Gay and Lesbian People and Religious Life

Many men and women entered religious life or undertook celibacy on their own, in response to personal convictions about the superiority of celibacy, reaction against the new and ascetic view of marriage, or both. For obvious reasons, gay people would find the more rigid institution of marriage even less satisfying than heterosexuals, since they would find *no* erotic satisfaction in it, whereas the latter might, incidentally, enjoy procreative activity although such enjoyment was probably sinful in the view of many.[5]

Celibate religious life offered women escape from the consequences of marriage—for example, having to sleep with a husband and bear children—which might not only be unwanted but even life threatening. It afforded both genders a means of avoiding stereotypical gender roles.[6] Women could exercise power in religious communities, among other women, without being subordinated to the male head of a household. Men could become part of a community of equals, all male, without the responsibilities of fatherhood or ruling a household; or they could exercise through the priesthood skills of nurturing and serving otherwise associated with women and considered shameful for men. Men could avoid obligations of warfare and devote themselves to study; women could become literate and learned, an opportunity rare for their sex outside religious communities after the decline of Rome.

It is reasonable, under these circumstances, to believe that the priesthood and religious communities would have exercised a particular appeal for gay people, especially in those societies that treated them as "outsiders" and in which there was no other alternative to heterosexual marriage. Indeed, lesbian and gay people would hardly have needed a spiritual motivation to join a same-sex community of equals. Joining a religious community from about 500 c. e. to about 1300 was probably the surest way of meeting other gay people.

Many non-Christian observers of the Catholic clergy believed that it was disproportionately gay. The Germanic invaders of Roman Europe, Muslims who came into contact with Christians in medieval Spain, and Protestants from the time of the Reformation all charged that Catholic religious tended to be gay. There is doubtless a considerable element of mudslinging in this, but it may also be evidence of ways in which the atypical gender roles of the clergy and religious, and the relation of these to homosexuality, are noticeable even to outsiders. Many clerical observers, with no intention of denigrating their own vocation, also complained about the prevalence of homosexuality in their ranks. Saint Peter Damian in the eleventh century wrote a long treatise, "The Book of Gomorrha," about homosexuality in the priesthood and claimed that gay clergy confessed to one another to avoid detection. He tried to persuade Pope Leo IX to expel gay people from orders, but in a famous reply, "We More Humanely,"[7] the pontiff refused to do so, arguing that disciplinary action should be taken only against flagrant, very longstanding violations of clerical celibacy.

During the eleventh and twelfth centuries there was, in fact, an enormous struggle over the efforts of the institutional church to enforce the ideal of clerical celibacy. As part of the propaganda warfare that accompanied it, there were frequent charges that homosexuality was playing a large role. An apparently heterosexual priest attacked his bishop for promoting celibacy by claiming that this was a gay-straight conflict. "The man who occupies this [episcopal] seat is gayer[8] than Ganymede.[9] Consider why he excludes the married from the clergy: He does not care for the pleasures of a wife."[10]

Religious Life and Romantic Attachment: The Secular Clergy

It should not be imagined, however, that gay people were attracted to religious life for subliminal sexual reasons, or that they took ideals of celibacy less seriously than others. For the secular clergy, as noted, celibacy was not binding before the High Middle Ages, and many clerics left records of passionate involvement with persons of their own gender. Some of these may have been purely emotional relationships; others were clearly sexual. The love poetry between Ausonius and Saint Paulinus, bishop of Nola, helped to establish a tradition of explicitly Christian same-sex erotic lyricism that would have a profound impact on Western literature through the time of the Reformation.

> Through all that life may allot
> Or assign to mortals,
> As long as I am held within this prison body,
> In whatever world I am found,
> I shall hold you fast,
> Grafted onto my being,
> Not divided by distant shores or suns.

> Everywhere you shall be with me,
> I will see with my heart
> And embrace you with my loving spirit.
> . . . And when, freed from my body's jail
> I fly from earth,
> Wherever in heaven our Father shall direct me,
> There also shall I bear you in my heart.
> Nor will that end,
> That frees me from my flesh,
> Release me from your love.[11]

Like most residents of the ancient world, Ausonius and Paulinus accepted love between men as a normal variety of human affection, but unlike their pagan contemporaries, they invested it with Christian moral and spiritual significance. The author intends to pursue his love in heaven.

Gay clerics apparently took part in homosexual marriage ceremonies, which were widely known in the Catholic world from the fifth century on. Such ceremonies were performed in Catholic churches by priests and either established what the community regarded as marriages, or commemorated special friendships, in both cases in devoutly Christian terms.[12]

Romantic Love in Communities

Monks, too, appear to have taken part in these gay marriages, although most monastic communities required a commitment to celibacy, and this obviously created a conflict. In the Greco-Roman world in which monasticism originated, homosexuality was regarded as a perfectly ordinary aspect of human eroticism, and early religious communities had to come to grips with the possibility of erotic attachment between sisters or monks.

Two basic approaches developed. One, probably influenced by the increasing tendency of Christian thought to reduce human eroticism to the purely functional role of child production, a role it could not properly play in a monastery, condemned human attachments within religious communities and insisted that religious avoid them altogether. This attitude was not specifically antigay. Because homosexuality was not "outside" human eroticism or invisible in the ancient world, it was included along with other forms of sexuality as being improper for those committed to a life of celibacy. It was no worse or better, although perhaps a little more worrisome, because more available in same-sex communities. (Heterosexual religious have, however, in most times and places found it possible to violate rules of celibacy when they wished to.)

Saint Basil's writings are a clear indication of this trend. He expresses both the anxiety of the ascetic that human sexuality not disrupt the sober purity of monastic life, and the assumption that any male might naturally find another male sexually exciting.

> It is frequently the case with young men that, even when rigorous self-restraint is exercised, the glowing complexion of youth still blossoms forth and becomes a source of desire to those around them. If, therefore, anyone in the monastery is youthful and physically beautiful, let him keep his attractiveness hidden, and you sit in a chair far from such a person. Whenever he speaks to you, look down when you respond to him, so that when you gaze at his face you do not take the seed of desire from the enemy sower. Do not be found with him either indoors or where no one can see outdoors, either for studying the prophesies of Scripture or for any other purpose, no matter how necessary.[13]

Basil does not believe that *experiencing* homosexual desire is abnormal or even reprehensible. He simply expects celibate religious to make efforts to maintain their vows, and he thinks that doing so is a worthy struggle. It is not clear from his writings that such eroticism would be wrong for those who have not vowed to give them up, any more than talking is inherently evil because some orders observe silence as a form of monastic discipline.

Another strand of spirituality in religious communities, however, not only accepted but idealized love between persons of the same sex, both in and out of religious life. This approach could find clear precedent in numerous New Testament passages and examples, which it often cited. The ceremony for same-sex union, for example, cited many same-gender couples from Christian history.

O Lord our God, dwelling in heaven but looking down on that which is below, you who for the salvation of the human race sent your only begotten son, Jesus, and took Peter and Paul and made them brothers by consecration, make also these your servants —— and —— like those two apostles. Keep them blameless all the days of their lives. Lord of all and maker of humankind in your image and likeness, who gave humans eternal life, consider as worthy of union these two, joined not by nature but by the holy spirit of fidelity and unity of mind, just as you united Serge and Bacchus, Cosmas and Damian, and Cyrus and John.[14]

In the early Middle Ages Walahfrid Strabo, the abbot of the Benedictine monastery of Reichenau, wrote poetry to his friend Liutger evocative of the love sonnets of the Brownings:

When the splendor of the moon shines from the clear heaven,
Stand in the open air, and see in the wondrous mirror
How it grows light in the pure brightness from the moon
And with its splendor embraces two lovers,
Divided in body, but linked in spirit by one love.
If we cannot see each other face to loving face,
At least let this light be our pledge of love. . . .[15]

This particular monastery, in fact, produced a great deal of love poetry, as did a number of others, including communities of women. The longest and most beautiful examples of premodern lesbian poetry surviving from anywhere in Europe were composed by nuns for each other in southern Germany in the twelfth century.

To G., her unique rose,
A. sends the bond of precious love.
What strength have I that I may bear it,
That I may endure your absence?
Is my strength the strength of stones
That I can wait for your return?
I never cease from aching, night and day,
Like someone missing a hand and foot.
Without you anything happy or delightful

Seems like mud trod underfoot.
Instead of rejoicing I weep;
My spirit never seems joyful.
When I remember the kisses you gave me,
The way you refreshed my little breasts with sweet words,
I would like to die
Since I cannot see you.
. . . O if my body had been committed to earth
Until your longed-for return,
Or if I could go on a journey like Habakkuk's,
So that just once I could come to where
I saw the face of my lover,
Then I would not care if I died that very hour.
For there is no one who has been born in this world
Who is so lovable and dear,
No one who without feigning
Loves me with so deep a love.
Therefore, I ache without end
Until I am allowed to see you.[16]

Three things are particularly noteworthy about this poem: (1) Although it is uncertain whether the reference to physical interaction describes something real or is a metaphor in the tradition of the Song of Songs, in either event it is clear that carnal love between two women was part of the conceptual framework of the nuns. (2) The love involved, whether physically embodied or not, is clearly a particular erotic passion, and not simply general charity. (3) It is a Christian love, and understood to be incorporated into a Christian, religious life. It is not presented as pagan, or in contrast to virtue, or as an impediment to a holy life. On the contrary, the poem is filled with biblical allusions and references, and is wholly unabashed and unapologetic.

Aelred, the abbot of the Cistercian monastery of Rievaulx, had led quite a wild gay life in his youth, involving multiple partners and passions, but when he entered religious life he took his vow of chastity very seriously. He would bathe in any icy pool to quell his libido—the original cold shower approach. It did not seem to him, however, that he had to give up passionate attachments. On the contrary, he fell in love with several members of his order and wrote candidly about his feelings: "We had but one mind and one soul, to will and not to will alike. . . . For I deemed my heart in a fashion his, and his mine, and he felt in like manner towards me. . . . He was the refuge of my spirit, the sweet solace of my griefs, whose heart of love received me when fatigued from labors, whose counsel refreshed me when plunged in sadness and grief. . . . Was it not a foretaste of blessedness thus to love and thus to be loved?"[17] Such passions did not seem to Aelred a departure from a spiritual life, but a part of it, based on the example of Jesus himself.

> We can enjoy this [kind of love] in the present with those whom we love not merely with our minds but with our hearts; for some are joined to us more intimately and passionately than others in the lovely bond of spiritual friendship. And lest this sort of sacred love should seem improper to anyone, Jesus himself, in everything like us, patient and compassionate with us in every matter, transfigured it through the expression of his own love: for he allowed one, not all, to recline on his breast as a sign of his special love, so that the virgin head was supported in the flowers [*sic*] of the virgin breast, and the closer they were, the more copiously did the fragrant secrets of the heavenly marriage impart the sweet smell of spiritual chrism to their virgin love.[18]

Although part of a long tradition, Aelred's views were not universal. His biographer expressed astonishment that Aelred encouraged his monks to hold hands, and noted that many other abbots expelled those who did so from the monastery.

Changing Times: The Rise of Hostility

Disparagement of personal attachments in religious life eventually triumphed over the tradition of admiration for them, in part because European society grew increasingly hostile to gay people and their feelings from about 1250, and began to treat them as "outsiders" rather than as ordinary sinners. The kind of gay romance that had been so common in religious life since the beginnings of Christianity became not only suspect, but dangerous. Homosexual infractions of rules of celibacy came to seem much worse than heterosexual failings.

The change is evident in the case of Benedetta Carlini, an Italian Theatine nun of the seventeenth century. Given to a convent at age nine, Benedetta hardly had a choice about celibacy. Her parents had decided she was to be a nun; so she was a nun. Quite brilliant and capable, she rose to be the abbess by the age of thirty, at which time she began having ecstatic visions of Jesus. During these she was transformed into a male angel named Splenditello. The other nuns testified that when she was Splenditello she actually spoke and acted in a more masculine manner. As Splenditello, Benedetta had for two years a vibrantly sexual relationship with her companion, Bartolomea, who shared her room.

> At least three times a week, in the evening after disrobing and going to bed, Sister Benedetta would wait for her companion to disrobe and . . . pretending to need her, would call. When Bartolomea would come over, Benedetta would grab her by the arm and throw her by force on the bed. Embracing her, she would put her under herself and kissing her as if she were a man, she would speak words of love to her. And she would stir so much on top of her that both of them corrupted themselves. . . . Splenditello asked her many times to pledge that she would always be his beloved and promised that he would be hers.[19]

Benedetta was deposed and tried when her activities came to light, and ultimately imprisoned in the convent for thirty-five years. She died in confinement. This makes quite a contrast to the tolerance of the High Middle Ages, when prominent bishops published gay love poetry and clerics composed arguments about whether gay or straight sexuality was preferable.[20]

Benedetta's case also suggests, however, that despite increasing hostility and intolerance, homosexuality continued to form a part of religious life. Exactly what the feelings of Benedetta and Bartolomea were remains a mystery. The fact that the former pretended to be, or believed she was, a male while making love to the latter poses difficult questions about "homosexual orientation," but the acts and passions were clearly homosexual, and freedom from or variations on traditional gender roles are in fact an ancient aspect of religious life, as noted above.

It is striking, moreover, that both Benedetta and Bartolomea would accept the idea of a permanent, committed love relationship, regardless of gender, for a nun. Even granting that both believed it was an angel's union with a nun, the idea of a committed erotic relationship for a cloistered nun is an arresting one.

Conclusion

The relationship between homosexuality and religious life is a deep and rich one, complicated by shifting patterns of majority attitudes toward gay people and celibacy. Many authors have suggested that gay people have a special gift for religious life not only in the Christian tradition, but in religion generally. Shamans in many cultures seem to be gay, as were the *berdaches* among American Indians, thought to have extraordinary spiritual and religious insights and gifts.[21] Some biologists have argued that gay people tend, for evolutionary reasons, to be particularly altruistic. If such connections are real, they may offer an additional explanation for the traditional attraction of Catholic religious life for gay people.

Gay and lesbian people have contributed much to the human family and to religious life; for example, patterns of selfless devotion not inspired by natural relation, archetypes of love outside the confines of procreative matrimony, compassion for "outsiders," sensitivity to the limits of stereotypical notions of gender. And religious life has given much in return to gay people. Without having entered communities or the priesthood, many would never have discovered their feelings or been able to share them with others. Women especially, who would have been confined to fairly rigid patterns of existence under the control of a husband, have managed to find meaningful relationships with other women, whether sexual or not, and nonsexual relationships, as partners, with religious men. For both women and men, religious life has afforded an opportunity to establish an identity outside the nuclear family, beyond being simply the complement of the opposite gender.

Religious life enabled gay and lesbian people with a vocation to transform their "outsider" status into an advantage. Instead of simply being excluded, they formed part of a group whose "outside" quality was revered and admired by society, because its members devoted themselves to the service of the community and could offer a critique of heterosexual, conjugal society from a disinterested vantage. The superior moral position of the celibate would not have been possible in Judaism or even in pagan Rome, where heterosexual marriage was essential to social standing. It was a Christian innovation to admire those who dedicated their sexuality to something other than pleasure or procreation.

On the other hand, there have been some tragic aspects to the intersection of homosexuality and religious life. Especially in modern times, most gays and lesbians in religious life have been terribly alone. The efforts of early modern and modern Christian societies to make gay people "outsiders" have largely effaced the large and well-developed literary tradition of gay eroticism among the clergy, consigned to oblivion such institutions as the same-sex union, and fostered the illusion that all religious have given up heterosexuality, if, indeed, they ever had any sexuality at all.

Lesbian and gay religious need to reclaim their tradition, publicize it, rejoice in it, and share it with other Christians and gay people. Models of gay Christian religious life embrace nearly every possibility of service to the Lord, from absolute chastity enriched by passionate attachment to another person, to open enjoyment and celebration of eroticism, to permanent unions, with or without physical sexuality. These models should be discussed and utilized as archetypes of Christian love. They are ancient, authentic, and as fundamental to the Christian tradition as heterosexual marriage.

Religious life has probably been the most consistent, widespread, institutionalized, and constructive gay life-style in the West during most of the Christian era. It is poignantly ironic that a group as marginalized and despised as gay people should have exerted such an influence on Christian society within the ranks of its spiritual elite, but that the lowly should be glorified and the last become first is, in fact, appropriate to the religion in question. Instead of experiencing their lives as doubly marginalized, as gays among religious and as religious among gays, lesbian and gay people in religious life and the priesthood should recognize and rejoice in the centrality of their position, the importance of religious life to gay culture throughout Christian history, and the prominence of gay people and their feelings and sensitivities within Christian religious life. The intersection is not only an important key to understanding the history of the church and the gay community, but an ongoing, fruitful, and creative one, enriching both traditions today as it has for nearly two thousand years.

Notes

1. It is worth noting that the ideology of "separate but equal" may be maintained by a society even when the group in question would have a different perception. Most right-handed people are completely unaware of the many difficulties the left-handed encounter in American society, which disadvantages them precisely because it *does not take account* of their variance from the norm and provide for it.

2. This is in itself a misprision in most cases. Most religious sacrifice or channel their sexuality; it is not "absent." But the discomfort most Catholics evince about the subject of sexuality in the lives of religious suggests very strongly that they prefer to believe that priests and brothers and nuns simply do not experience eroticism.

3. "Adulter est in sua uxore ardentior amator. In aliena quippe uxore omnis amor turpis est, et in sua nimis. Sapiens iudicio debet amare coniugem, non affectu." This was widely cited throughout the Middle Ages (for example, by Vincent of Beauvais, *Speculum doctrinale* 10.45), and quoted by the present pontiff, to the consternation of many modern Catholics.

4. *De bono conjugali,* 11.

5. See, e.g., ibid., 13.

6. On this see Elaine Pagels, *Adam, Eve and the Serpent* (New York: Random House, 1988).

7. "Nos humanius agentes"; discussed in J. Boswell, *Christianity, Social Tolerance, and Homosexuality: Gay People in Western Europe from the Beginning of the Christian Era to the Fourteenth Century* (Chicago: University of Chicago Press, 1980), 211–12.

8. Literally, "Ganymedier"; see discussion in Boswell, *Christianity*, 245, 253.

9. A frequent symbol of gay males; see ibid.

10. Ibid., 217.

11. Paulinus of Nola, *Carmen* 11, lines 49ss; text in *Oxford Book of Medieval Latin Verse*, ed. F. J. E. Raby (Oxford: Oxford University Press, 1959), 24; trans. in Boswell, *Christianity*, 133–34.

12. These ceremonies, evident as early as the fifth century and observed by anthropologists in the twentieth, constitute the subject of my forthcoming book, *What God Has Joined Together: Same-sex Unions in the Christian Tradition*.

13. *De renuntiatione saeculi*, 6; *Sermo asceticus*, 323; see commentary in Boswell, *Christianity*, 159–60.

14. From an Italian manuscript of the early Middle Ages, to appear in Boswell, *What God Has Joined Together*.

15. Boswell, *Christianity*, see notes, ibid.

16. Translated in Thomas Stehling, *Medieval Latin Poems of Male Love and Friendship* (New York: Garland Publishing, 1984), 102–5, no. 113; cf. Boswell, *Christianity*, 220–21.

17. Boswell, *Christianity*, 224.

18. Ibid., 225–26.

19. Judith P. Brown, *Immodest Acts: The Life of a Lesbian Nun in Renaissance Italy* (Oxford: Oxford University Press, 1986), 162.

20. Discussed at length in Boswell, *Christianity*, 8 and 9.

21. This point was probably first argued by Plato (*Symposium* 182, 192); in more recent times it has been made by Edward Carpenter, "On the Connexion between Homosexuality and Divination, and the Importance of the Intermediate Sexes Generally in Early Civilizations," *Revue d'ethnographie et de sociologie* 11–12 (1910): 310–16, and *Intermediate Types among Primitive Folk* (London, 1914). On the *berdache*, see the classic study by Walter Williams, *The Spirit and the Flesh: Sexual Diversity in American Indian Culture* (Boston: Beacon Press, 1986).

2 Homophobia, Heterosexism, and Pastoral Practice

ROSEMARY RADFORD RUETHER

Homosexuality is the scare issue in the Christian churches today. It is being used as the stalking horse of all the current social fears concerning the disintegration of moral and social structures. We should see antigay fear and hatred as part of a cultural offensive against liberal egalitarian social principles generally. Homophobia is a vehicle for the conservative ideology that links the defense of the patriarchal family with the maintenance of class, race, and gender hierarchy throughout the society. Such a view of society is typically tied with militarism and superpatriotism. The subordination of women and the hierarchy of social classes is seen as part of the "natural order." Since religion is used as the prime support of this social ideology, it is necessary to develop a sustained theological and ethical critique of it and a pastoral practice based on a correct identification of the problem. Although gay people particularly suffer the consequences of it, they are not the cause of the problem. Patriarchal heterosexism is the cause of the problem.

I shall begin with an analysis of the traditional arguments for judging homosexuality as wrong. This lies in three interlocking views of homosexuality as sin, crime, and disease. The Christian tradition that views homosexuality as a sin rests on a view of sexuality as legitimate only within monogamous marriage with reproduction as its primary purpose. As developed by Saint Augustine in the late fourth and early fifth century, this view disregards the relational purpose of sexuality as an expression and means of creating love. Sexuality is seen as inherently debasing to the soul. Even reproductive sexuality within marriage is seen as spiritually debasing. The optimal Christian life-style was that of celibacy (Augustine 1974). The celibate anticipated the heavenly order of redemption by renouncing sexuality for the "angelic life." Underlying this view of redemption is a quasi-Gnostic anthropology that sees finitude and mortality, and hence the need for reproduction, as characteristics of a fallen order. In the original and future heavenly order, sex, sin, and death were and will be absent.

Saint Augustine sees the blessings on procreation in Genesis as pertaining only to the Old Testament. But this era of the Old Adam has been superseded by Christ, a virgin born of virginal marriage. Although sex and reproduction within marriage are allowable in the Christian era, they are now of inferior value (Augustine 1887b). Married people belong to a moral lower class in the church the members of which are unable to attain the fullness of the gospel, as do the celibates, who imitate the virginity of Christ and Mary and anticipate the eschatological age.

We see from the above that the traditional view that reproduction is the only legitimate purpose of sex sprang not from a high valuing of children, but from a negative valuing of sex. Sex was the epitome of the sinful, death-prone instinct. Original sin was transmitted from generation to generation through concupiscence, the orgasmic feeling of sexual release. The enjoyment of this experience was regarded with horror as a thing to be restricted as much as possible. It was venially sinful in marriage even when used for procreation, and mortally sinful in every other case. Thus even heterosexual married couples "fornicated," or sinned mortally, when they had sex solely for "pleasure" and avoided reproduction (Augustine 1887a; Ruether 1974, 164).

In this view, contraceptive, oral, and anal sex, between heterosexuals or homosexuals, were sinful for the same reason. Thus, in much of classical Catholic penitential literature, the sin of sodomy refers not only to homosexual sex, but to any nonprocreative sex. This view is still reflected in the American laws recently upheld by the Supreme Court. These laws make oral or anal sex between heterosexuals or homosexuals illegal. The root of this tradition lies in a view of all sex as sinful, although allowable or venially sinful within procreative marriage. This view sees no autonomous purpose of sex as a means of creating and expressing a love relationship.

These views of nonreproductive sex as sin flow into the condemnation of them as crime. Sexual deviance of all kinds was regarded as a deliberate flouting of the natural order, which, in turn, undermined the social order. Sexual deviants were subversive to the proper order of society and hence a public danger. To flout the natural order was to rebel against God as well, and so sexual deviance was closely linked with heresy. Heretics were typically seen as sexual deviants who practiced "unnatural sex" in the general sense previously defined. Homosexuality was, therefore, seen as an expression of a general spiritual and moral subversion that sought to undermine the established social order. This subversive attitude was typically described as like a disease in Christian literature. It is contagious and spreads through contact.

Although heresy is no longer an official category of crime, contemporary views of homosexuality still preserve much of this classic Christian paranoia. It is seen as contagious, spreading like a disease, and expressing a pernicious subversion of the moral and social fabric of society. The unfortunate development of AIDS, as a disease affecting predominantly, although not solely, male homosexuals, reveals the prevalence of this mentality among North Americans, especially religious conservatives. AIDS is regarded both as a confirmation of the morally diseased condition of homosexuals and as divine retribution against them for their sinfulness. One cannot think of any other medical epidemic in recent times in which the victims have been regarded with such explicitly moralistic hostility. For example, although the link between cancer and smoking has long been established, Americans would hardly dream of regarding cancer as divine retribution for the sinful activity of smoking.

The categorization of homosexuality as disease belongs to an older Christian tradition, but it has been reinforced in recent times by the psychoanalytic profession. Patriarchal psychoanalysis, as developed by Freud, defined homosexuality as a developmental disorder. Freud postulated that infant sexuality is characterized by "polymorphous perversity." That is to say, our original sexuality is nongenital and nongender-specific. As infants we feel sexual all over our bodies and respond sexually to both sexes. But Freud believed that this infantile "perversity" must be overcome by repressing a generalized sexuality in favor of heterosexual genital sexuality, the goal of which is reproduction. Homosexuality is a developmental failure, a "fixation" on an infantile stage of sexuality. Homosexuals are described as "narcissistic." Their attraction to persons of the same gender reflects a self-love that is incapable of loving others. Oddly enough, this view fails to recognize persons of the same gender as distinct other persons from oneself.

Lurking under the charge that homosexuals are narcissistic lies the psychological doctrine of complementarity. Complementarity defines males and females as rigidly opposite personality types. Males must cultivate the "masculine" characteristics of autonomy, force, and rationality; women, the "feminine" characteristics of passivity, nurturance, and auxiliary existence. Only heterosexual sex is directed to the "other half" of this dualism and unites the two sexes in a "whole." Homosexual sex is, therefore, "incomplete," directed toward one's own "half," rather than the other "half."

This condemnation of homosexuality as incomplete and narcissistic is a basic reinforcement of heterosexism. Its doctrine that only heterosexual sex is "whole" is actually based on a truncated human development for both men and women in which both must remain "half" people who need the other "half" in order to be "whole." This truncated personality development reflects patriarchal social roles. The male and female stereotypes are asymmetrical and reflect the dominance-submission, public-private splits of the patriarchal social order (Barth 1961, 116–240).

Against this patriarchal social stereotyping, I would claim that all persons, male and female, possess the capacity for psychological wholeness that transcends the masculine-feminine dichotomy. Once this is recognized, the argument for heterosexuality, based on the genders as complementary opposites, collapses. All sexual relations, all love relations, should be the loving of another person who is complexly both similar and different from oneself. Such relationships should help both to grow into their full wholeness. Complementarity, by contrast, creates a pathological interdependency based on each person remaining in a state of deficiency in relation to the other. The female can't make her own living. The male can't do his own wash or meals. So each "needs" the other to supply these lacks in themselves. The relationship is set up to reinforce this deficiency in each.

To sum up our argument so far: the traditional condemnation of homosexuality has been based on three assumptions: (1) The sexual instinct is lower and bestial, sinful in itself. It is something that can be cut off from higher human spiritual development. (2) The only "natural" and licit purpose of sex is reproduction. Reproductive sex is also seen as a "remedy" of concupiscence— that is, it prevents the male from seducing other women to whom he is not married—but even this is licit only in marriage when the procreative purpose of sex is not impeded. Sex is thus seen as either "functional" or sinfully lustful. The relational purpose of sex is disregarded. (3) Sexual attraction promotes "wholeness" only when directed at the other sex, the two genders being seen as opposite personality types.

All three of these presuppositions must be questioned. We should see sexuality as an integral part of our total psychosomatic being, not something that can be separated out and repressed without damage to our fullness of being. We should recognize that the love-relational purpose of sex has its own integrity and goodness as the creation and expression of bonding, affection, and commitment. It is not dependent on procreation for its justification, and indeed today out of many thousands of sexual acts in the lifetime of any person, only a small percentage can be intentionally reproductive. The defense of marriage between sterile people; sex after menopause, and the acceptance of birth control, including the so-called rhythm method—all tacitly accept the autonomous love-relational purpose of sex.

Once one has accepted any nonprocreative sex to be moral for heterosexuals, one can no longer define homosexuality as immoral because it is nonprocreative. One cannot even say that homosexuals avoid the responsibility to raise children, since celibates also do not raise children, while many homosexuals are raising natural or adopted children. Once one has accepted the understanding of humanity in which men and women are complex psychological wholes, not stereotypic opposites, and that the goodness of relationship lies in mutual support of the wholeness of each, not the mutual deficiency of masculine-feminine interdependence, then the difference between loving and bonding with someone of the same sex as yourself or someone of the other sex can no longer be rigidly distinguished. Both are relationships with another person, with all the complex problems of developing a healthy mutuality, rather than pathological dependency and exploitative misuse of each other.

There has emerged among Catholic moral theologians in the last twenty years a comprehensive effort to revise the traditional Catholic view of sexuality, although these moral theologians are currently very much under fire from the Vatican, which recognizes that its system of social and ecclesiastical control rests on the older definitions of sexual sin. The Catholic Theological Society of America (CTSA) report *Human Sexuality*, published in 1977 (Kosnik et al.), represents this alternative tradition of Catholic moral theology. The starting point of the moral system developed in this report is that sexual morality or immorality is an expression of moral or immoral human relationality. Relationships are moral when they are mutual, supportive of the full personal growth of each person, committed, and faithful. Relations are immoral when they are abusive, violent, exploitative, keep people in truncated stages of development, and lead to lying, deceit, and betrayal.

This norm of sexual morality, based on moral relationality, eliminates the neat boundaries between moral and immoral sex defined by heterosexual marriage and procreation. Such a norm makes for much stricter judgments about sexual morality in some cases. Much of the sexuality promoted in patriarchal marriage, which, for example, saw the husband as having a right to force his wife to have sex with him, would be regarded as immoral by such a standard. What is moral or immoral sexually becomes more a question of a scale of values than of clear boundaries. No one achieves perfectly mutual love, and perhaps few relationships are totally evil. Rather, such a norm promotes a developmental goal. We are to grow toward healthy, loving, mutual, and faithful relationships, away from abusive and dishonest ones. The morality of homosexual or heterosexual relations is judged by the same standard, rather than by different standards.

In response to the traditional views of homosexuality as a violation of the natural order, or as a developmental disorder, the CTSA report takes seriously the testimony of gay and lesbian people about their own experience of same-gender attraction as "natural" for themselves. Many gay and lesbian people say that they have experienced themselves as sexually attracted to people of the same gender for as long as they remember being sexually aware. Efforts to repress or change this same-gender attraction, in order to conform to dominant heterosexual norms, distorted and violated their spontaneous feelings. Only when they acknowledged their own homosexuality were they able to feel whole and able to express their own authentic being.

This testimony from gay and lesbian experience leads the CTSA authors to declare that homosexual attraction is the natural sexual orientation of a "normal" minority of persons. It is not a deviance from nature, but rather a part of the natural variety of human nature, much as left-handedness is part of a natural variation in humans. We know that left-handedness occurs in about 12 percent of the population, another 85 percent are dominantly right-handed, and some people are ambidextrous. To force left-handed children to conform to right-handedness causes great difficulty when they are learning to read and write. Some societies have indeed regarded left-handedness as "sinister" (the word *sinister* means "left"), and others have devalued left-handed functions. But we recognize today that left- or right-handedness is part of a natural pluraformity in brain "wiring."

The CTSA report argues that homosexual orientation should be seen as a similar sort of natural diversity. This allows the authors to see homosexuality as part of the divinely created "natural" order, rather than as a violation of the natural order. But it also allows the authors to assume that heterosexuality is the dominant orientation of 85 percent of the population, whereas only 10–12 percent are dominantly homosexual. Homosexuals become a natural minority group whose sexuality is an expression of their natures. But they are a small enough group that their existence need not challenge the majority status of heterosexuality. The CTSA report argues against views of homosexuality as either a handicap or something that can be changed by psychological and social coercion. Like heterosexuals, homosexuals are directed to appropriate their natural sexual orientation in a moral development toward healthy, mutual, loving, and faithful relationships.

This revisionist Catholic moral theology is an enormous improvement over the traditional Christian view of sexuality and homosexuality. It has many elements that I wish to affirm, especially the relational norm of sexual morality. Its effort, however, to make homosexuals a fixed natural minority group of 10–12 percent of the population is questionable. It fails to account for the complexity of human sexuality and the shaping of sexuality by society. It does not explain adequately the fear and dread of homosexuals by heterosexuals. Although many gay and lesbian people say they have always experienced same-gender attraction, and are unable to respond to people of the opposite sex, others do not define their experience in this way.

There is some evidence that notions of rigid sex orientation are less prevalent among women than men. Lesbians are more likely to say that their homosexuality is an expression of their general capacity to be sexual, and that this reflects their general capacity to love, to be attracted to and affectionate toward other people, female or male. These women see their lesbianism less as a fixed biological necessity than as a social choice (Heyward 1984; Hunt 1986). They would say that they have chosen to love women rather than men because, in a patriarchal society, lesbian relations are less violent and coercive and more conducive to loving mutuality than are relations with males. Since patriarchal society sets up heterosexual marriage as a relationship of domination and subordination, fully moral—that is, loving and mutual—relations are possible only between women. Lesbianism is an expression of this social morality.

Such a definition of lesbianism as a social choice opens up in a different way the question of homosexuality as a preference, rather than as an unchangeable expression of one's "nature." For patriarchal conservatives this would again open the question of changing homosexuals by social coercion. For lesbians this is exactly the sort of society they are avoiding by their choice of lesbianism. This diversity in the experience of gay and lesbian people points, I believe, to the complexity of human sexuality as a social, and not just a biological, reality. We need to ask not just how people "become" homosexuals, but, even more, how people "become" heterosexuals.

I suggest that we return to the Freudian insight that we are "originally" bisexual and polymorphously sexual. Instead of seeing this as an infantile "perversity," we should see it as a clue to the nature and potential of human sexuality. Human sexuality is not narrowly programmed toward genital sexuality, heterosexuality, or reproduction. Indeed what makes human sexuality "human" is its tendency to transcend the limits of biological reproduction and to be oriented toward human relationality. This more generalized capacity for sexual attraction is both exciting and frightening. It is the body's basic experience of vital, pleasurable feelings, awakened in sensual contact with other humans. This is frightening since it also suggests vulnerability, loss of control, giving oneself up to others.

Human cultures have reacted to this ambivalence of sexual experience with various social strategies that channel its use. Sexuality is channeled socially toward heterosexuality and toward committed family relationships in order to assure not only reproduction, but also the stable relationship of the generations in child raising, mutual care, and support of the aged. Western cultures particularly have channeled sexual feeling away from general body experience to a functional, genital sexuality. We develop into adults by deadening most of our bodies, and most of our relationships, sexually. This has been done particularly by males so they could carry on with one another in public relationships without experiencing sexual vulnerability. It was traditionally assumed that any relationships of men with women aroused sexual feelings, so women were to be segregated from public affairs. Civilization, as Freud noted, is based on repression, training people (especially males) to be genitally sexual, heterosexual, and to enter into permanent marriages.

If we are originally bisexual and polymorphous, however, this means that we all have the capacity for sexual attraction and response to people of the same sex. We are not born heterosexual. We are taught to become heterosexual. Most of us accept our heterosexual socialization and develop in ways that channel sexual attraction toward approved marital objects. This includes not only persons of the other gender, but also persons of the "right" race, culture, and social class. Indeed as our society sees it, it is as much a "perversity" to be sexually attracted to persons of another race, religion, or social class as to be attracted to persons of the same gender. Most of us have deeply internalized this conditioning. Although we might feel sexually attracted to a person of the "wrong" race or culture, we might also feel a physical loathing and disgust at our own feelings. This indicates how much our sexuality is a social product.

For some people this heterosexual conditioning fails to "take." They grow up feeling themselves attracted primarily to the same sex, although at the same time sinful and perverse because of these feelings. I suggest that we simply don't know why some people resist this conditioning, any more than we know why most people conform to it. As in all human development, the biological and the social are so deeply intertwined as to be inextricable. If we all have some capacity for bisexuality, and we are all socialized to be heterosexual, the most we can say is that, for some, the attraction to the same gender remains stronger than the weight of this heterosexist social conditioning.

If we recognize a general capacity for same-gender sexual attraction, a capacity that has been repressed, but not killed, by social conditioning in those who define themselves as heterosexuals, we also discover the psychological root of homophobia. Homophobia—the fear, revulsion, and hatred of homosexuals—is a projection onto homosexuals of our fears of our own repressed capacity for same-gender sexual attraction. Having been socialized to hate and fear our own capacity for same-gender sexual feeling, to deny that such feelings exist, we respond with hostility to those who represent this repressed capacity in ourselves. The secret that the homophobe wishes to keep from him or herself is that he or she, too, might feel sexually attracted to a person of the same gender.

Heterosexuality represents not only a channeling of polymorphous bisexuality toward heterosexual marriage for the purpose of procreation and child raising, but also a socialization that has taken place historically under conditions of patriarchy—that is, under systems of male, ruling-class (and race) domination. We are conditioned to respond sexually to persons not only of the right gender, but also of the right race and class—that is, people who are "marriageable," according to racial and ethnic endogamy and hierarchy. Although dominant males might have sex with such nonmarriageable people, they are not supposed to form any bonds of affection for such sex objects. What is strictly taboo in patriarchy is not so much sex activity itself, but rather *love* for the person of the wrong sex, race, and gender. Mere "sex" is forgiveable for dominant males as long as it does not involve real love and affection for the unmarriageable person.

Sexual conditioning in patriarchy means that this socialization takes place within a system of gender, class, and race hierarchy. Ruling-class males set themselves apart from dominated women and men. They do this by cultivating certain personality and cultural styles associated with dominance and superiority and relegating devalued cultural traits to women and dominated males. Accents, hair and dress styles, the way one moves one's body—all these have been signals that set apart the genders and social classes. In most societies until recently, cross-dressing across not only gender lines, but also class lines has been severely tabooed.

One key element in male, ruling-class dominance is sexual control over women and dominated men, while the dominant men themselves remain sexually invulnerable. There are two ways to create this system of sexual control and invulnerability. One is to create a celibate elite that is regarded as above sexuality, morally and spiritually superior to the lower class of sexual people. This celibate elite not only holds itself aloof from sexuality, but also defines everyone else's sexuality by strictly delimiting what they

can do, and when and with whom they can do it. In classical
Catholicism, the noncelibate are a spiritual and ecclesiastical lower
class. They are allowed to be sexual, but only within heterosexual
marriage, only for procreation, and never for pleasure "for its own
sake."

The second way to be invulnerable and to control other people's
sexuality has characterized aristocratic male ruling classes. The
ruling-class male allows himself a broad latitude of sexual relations not only with his legal wife, but with mistresses, prostitutes,
maids, male paramours, and male servants. But he does so within
a framework of strictly defined roles. His legal wife is to be chaste
at marriage and strictly faithful after marriage. Since her children
must be his legal heirs, any sexual promiscuity on her part is
severely proscribed. His other sexual liaisons should be people to
whom he has no commitment, usable and discardable at will.
Often slaves and servants were not allowed legal marriage to each
other at all. They were not allowed to form autonomous bonds
with each other that conflicted with the master's use of them.

When we look at this practice of sexuality among ruling-class
males, in, say, British upper-class society, it becomes apparent that
patriarchy does not rule out either promiscuity or homosexuality
for these males. Both are winked at as long as they remain discreet
within a public system of heterosexual marriage that will produce
legitimate offspring. In patriarchal aristocracy, the homosexual
activity of the dominant male does not define him as a "homosexual." This status is reserved for the subordinate male in the
relationship. The dominant male typically remains the "pene-
trator" of both women and subordinate males. To be the "penetrated" one defines sexually one's inferior status. This is the
meaning of the Levitical proscription against "lying with another
man as you would with a woman. It is an abomination" (Lev.
18:22). What this law presumes is that the male who is "penetrated" is reduced to the inferior status of the female. The law
defends the equal masculine status of all males at the expense of all
women.

Thus we can say that in heterosexist patriarchal society homophobia reveals two interconnected forms of social and psychological dread. It reveals the dread of recognizing one's own capacity

for homosexual attraction in a culture that teaches us to repress and reject this capacity. It also reveals the dread of vulnerability and loss of control by those who define their masculinity as dominance and invulnerability and fear that, in the homosexual relation, they may be flung into the "penetrated" and hence the demeaned and dominated position. For this reason homophobia also tends to be more virulent in males than in females. Once women have gotten over the denial of their capacity for same-sex attraction, they do not have the same fears of being demeaned and dominated by other women that men have toward other men.

This analysis of homophobia as rooted in a patriarchal social system of dominance and repression makes questionable any pastoral strategy that regards homosexuals as the primary problem, who are to be helped by counseling or therapy. First, it is essential to correctly name the problem as lodged in the system of heterosexist domination, rather than in its victims. We need, then, to ask how all of us, men and women, homosexual or heterosexual, celibate or noncelibate, have been damaged in our fullness of spiritual, moral, and psychosomatic development by this system. The correct naming of the issue is itself enormously therapeutic, taking the burden of fear and self-hatred from individuals and allowing them to claim the complexity of their own experience (Task Force on Gay/Lesbian Issues 1982).

There is a need not only for ways of thinking and communicating that correctly name the problem, but also for ways of ritualizing and celebrating this claiming of our experience. We need rites of "coming out" by which lesbians and gay men can heal themselves of their internalized self-hatred and affirm and be affirmed in their authentic personhood in community. There is also a need for covenanting celebrations by which lesbian and gay male couples can affirm and be supported in committed relationships. In my book *Women-church: Theory and Practice of Feminist Liturgical Communities* (Ruether 1986), two lesbian couples have developed such coming-out and covenanting rites out of their own experience and religious traditions.

Perhaps as more of us acknowledge the complexity of our sexual potential, it will become less necessary for some to identify themselves as homosexual over against a heterosexual majority.

As we recognize the pluraformity of our sexual potential and experience, and the way we have been shaped in our identities by conformity to or reaction against the dominant social conditioning, we can begin to explore a new sexual and social ethic of moral development toward mutual, loving, and committed relationships. Such moral development does not entail a denial of our capacity for many-sided sexual feeling, but it does entail choosing, out of a multiplicity of possibilities, certain particular people with whom we open ourselves to deeper relationship and venerability, with whom we choose to journey into the bonding of committed love and friendship. In the context of such a committed relationship we can then appropriate our sexuality not as something biologically necessitated, or as socially coerced, but as a freely chosen way of expressing our authentic humanness in relation to the special others with whom we wish to share our lives.

References

Augustine. 1887a. *De bono conj.* 3. In *Nicene and Post-Nicene Fathers,* edited by P. Schaff, 13:400. Buffalo: Christian Literature Company.

Augustine. 1887b. *De nup. et concup.* 1, 14–15. In *Nicene and Post-Nicene Fathers,* edited by P. Schaff, 5:269. Buffalo: Christian Literature Company.

Augustine. 1974. *De sancta virg.* 45. In Misogynism and Virginal Feminism in the Fathers of the Church, *Religion and Sexism: Images of Women in the Jewish and Christian Traditions,* edited by R. Ruether. New York: Simon and Schuster.

Barth, K. 1961. *Church Dogmatics,* vol. 3, no. 4. Edinburgh: T. and T. Clark.

Freud, S. 1961. *Civilization and Its Discontents.* New York: W. W. Norton.

Heyward, C. 1984. *Our Passion for Justice: Images of Power, Sexuality and Liberation.* New York: Pilgrim Press.

Hunt, M. 1986. *Fierce Tenderness: A Feminist Theology of Friendship.* San Francisco: Harper and Row.

Kosnik, A., Carroll, W., Cunningham, A., Modras, R., and Schulte, J. 1977. *Human Sexuality: New Directions in American Catholic Thought.* New York: Paulist Press.

Ruether, R. 1974. Misogynism and Virginal Feminism in the Fathers of the Church. In *Religion and Sexism: Images of Women in the Jewish and Christian Traditions,* edited by R. Ruether. New York: Simon and Schuster.

Ruether, R. 1986. *Women-church: Theory and Practice of Feminist Liturgical Communities.* San Francisco: Harper and Row.

Task Force on Gay/Lesbian Issues. 1982. *Homosexuality and Social Justice.* San Francisco: Archdiocesan Commission on Social Justice.

3 The Shadow Side of the Homosexuality Debate

DANIEL C. MAGUIRE

Homosexuality in the context of the Roman Catholic church is viewed with fervid and defensive concern by church officials. If they have their way, the freedom of the sons and daughters of God will continue to be suspended on this issue. Persons, careers, and vocations have been imperiled in the punitive atmosphere the hierarchy has brought to this mystery of our nature. Fortunately, many theologians have finally begun to stand and pay their dues here as Catholic theology takes its first gingerly steps out of its long-tenured heterosexism.

With that fully acknowledged, a meditative step back is still in order. Homosexuality is important as a matter of justice to gay persons in the church. Yet the kind of primacy it enjoys in the hierarchical mind is a distortion. The intrinsic merits of the subject of homosexuality do not place it at the forefront of Judeo-Christian religion and morality. A healthy church would not need this book. No fixation on the rights of those whom God has made gay would be called for, and we could then attend to the weightier matters of the biblical challenge. In a word, we must attend to the hierarchical fixation on this subject without ourselves becoming fixated. We must courageously address the justice and truthfulness issues regarding homosexuality in the church without losing perspective on the greater mission that is ours.

The grand issue of biblical religion concerns the vision of a world that must sow injustice to reap peace. As biblical people our prime business is always *peace,* which can be biblically defined as *the realization of justice.* As we attend to particular concerns, this overriding and critical concern must never be far from our passionate attention.

Issues of micromorality can blind us to issues of macromorality. There is in the best of us a little bit of those German chaplains who accompanied the *Wehrmacht* on its ruthless invasion of the Netherlands, preaching sermons warning the troops against Dutch prostitutes! Meanwhile, those sermonizers seem to have missed the Second World War and the holocaust of millions of innocents. Their spirit must not be ours.

We live in a time when our world is racked with hunger and militarism. We must not be oblivious to the greater evils that surround us and put our world in terminal peril. Forty-two thousand children a day die on planet earth for lack of minimal food and basic medicine. Meanwhile, the managers of the nations have accumulated the equivalent of four tons of TNT for every human head. World population is estimated to explode to 8.5 billion by the year 2025, with 7 billion of these persons in the famishing Third World. While the United States and the Soviet Union stand in archaic postures of hostility to each other, a new mode of militarism is aborning in the poverty of the other world. The principal military peril of the future is from wars of redistribution. Current terrorism is a dim portent of what the poor of the world will do when they tire of going off to die peacefully and hopelessly in the bush. Still, our own nation, so fastidious in its concern about such things as pornography, spends $35 million an hour, twenty-four hours a day, on military preparations, even though 1 percent of its current arsenal would be enough to deter or destroy any possible aggressor. Meanwhile, over 50 percent of black children in militaristic United States are born into poverty. If the Catholic church is not relevant to these problems, and if these problems are not our primary concern, then this book on homosexuality matters little.

I must again call for another kind of step back. I submit that the debate on homosexuality in the Catholic church has nothing to do with homosexuality in any primary sense. Homosexuality fronts for a number of other issues. There is a huge shadow side to the homosexuality debate that must be uncovered if sanity is to come to the issue itself. In the shadows of this discussion we find unresolved issues of (1) ecclesiology, (2) celibacy, (3) sexual ethics, and (4) friendship and community.

Ecclesiology

Jesus was part of a reform movement in Judaism from which the Christian religion evolved. Neither that movement nor the Hebrew Scriptures nor the Christian Scriptures contained a systematic ethics of sexuality. Sex was not a central concern of the early Christian church. Thus, efforts to teach sexual or reproductive ethics on the alleged basis of "what the church has always taught" in these areas are historically naive.

What can be said is that at a certain point the church did evince a marked tendency to define itself and its orthodoxy in terms of what I have called "pelvic theology." This curious obsessional turn is with us yet and profoundly affects church discussion of homosexuality along with the whole of sexual and reproductive ethics. The formal beginnings of this unwholesome trend can be traced to the year 309 at the Synod of Elvira. This council was held in southern Spain in a basilica in what is today the Andalusian town of Granada. The bishops and presbyters at this event had a lot to worry about. Priests of the imperial religion were converting to Christianity and bringing many of their old ways with them. The religious myths of the society had long been in a state of neglect and disarray. There was, in a word, an opportunity for a new religious vision. The elitist assumptions of well-off Christians were blunting the prophetic edges of Christian spirituality. Resistance to militarism was ebbing. Clearly the synod had its work cut out for it. So what did the synod do in this crisis? It concentrated on sex! Almost half of its canons were on sex, and the subject was treated with extraordinary severity. Why?

Samuel Laeuchli (1972) in his book *Power and Sexuality: The Emergence of Canon Law at the Synod of Elvira,* argues that the real issue at Elvira was power. The church was no longer primarily defined by its resistance to the claims of the imperial cult. Clerical power in the church could no longer be ensured by this project at the dawning of the Constantinian age. In Laeuchli's words, "The clergy no longer controlled its subordinates primarily by means of the external conflicts with imperial ideology, but by controlling the sexual behavior of believers" (p. 60–61). The Christian elite sought to carve out a clerical image of the church, and sexual control was a tool in that project. In Laeuchli's judgment, the sexual obsession served two related synodal purposes: "the establishment of social coherence in the church's search for identity, and the creation of a clerical image which was to strengthen the clerical hold on the faithful" (p. 90).

The church was moving from prophetic to establishment status. In so doing it turned to sex to define orthodoxy and authority. I have called this "the Elvira syndrome," and it is with us yet (Maguire 1986a).

Contrary to popular myth, Constantine did not convert to Christianity. Christianity converted to Constantine, and Elvira signals the first symptoms of this perversion (Kee 1982). The canons of Elvira are windows to the soul of fourth-century Christianity. What they reveal is not edifying. The objections to soldiering are softened (p. 85). There is what Laeuchli calls "astonishing callousness about the lives of human beings who happened to be of a low social order" (p. 76). There is shocking anti-Semitism (p. 82). The synod was also distinctly negative to women (pp. 98–100, 104). And with all of this, sex became a prime zone for orthodoxy testing.

We see the Elvira syndrome operating today. The Vatican sought to crush the twenty-four nuns who defended a legitimate diversity of opinion on abortion and wanted to silence Catholic theologian Charles Curran for his gentle differences with them on sex. Sex is so central that the entire Second Vatican Council was allowed to touch any topic *except contraception*. Catholic campuses ban scholars from speaking on any topic if they have dared to reach judgments not approved by the hierarchy on reproductive ethics (Academic Freedom and the Abortion Issue 1986). Meanwhile, scholars such as Michael Novak, with his preferential option for the rich, are respected presences on Catholic campuses and have nothing to fear from the Vatican. It is in this church, with these obsessions and misplaced emphases, that we are discussing homosexuality—a subject, by the way, that also did not escape the attention of the fathers of Elvira (Kee 1982, 134).

The Elvira syndrome with its pelvic obsessions has not been a univocal presence in the history of the church. Other issues might at other times have been more likely to bring one to the stake. It could have been physics and astrology at the time of Galileo. Twelve popes and three ecumenical councils declared with utmost seriousness that all interest taking was mortally sinful. Pope Boniface VIII "defined" the divine right of the church to "invest" and dominate political power, and dissent on this issue was not tolerated. At the time of the modernist witch and warlock hunt, a defense of the ineffable quality of religious experience ended the careers of many theologians. Other issues from the "Deus vult!" slaying of heathens to the denial of religious liberty to other faiths have at times taken center stage in the muscular definition of orthodoxy. (Interestingly, in each of these examples cited, the hierarchical position has been proved wrong. It does show that truth and the keepers of orthodoxy are not, in the providence of God, necessarily at one.)

Today, however, the Elvira preoccupation is urgently present and blocking open and honest discussion of sexual and reproductive issues in a Catholic context. The real crisis here is in the model of the church being used by the Vatican and the hierarchy. These men are claiming a divine right to lord it over the minds of those who disagree with them in selected areas of debate. They are acting against the obvious meaning of the words of Jesus: "You know that in the world the recognized rulers lord it over their subjects, and their great men make them feel the weight of authority. This is not to be the way with you. Among you, whoever wants to be great must be your servant, and whoever wants to be first must be the willing slave of all" (Mark 10:42–43). As the biblical scholar C. H. Dodd (1970) says, this condemnation of authoritarianism "recurs with striking frequency. Evidently it was, in the mind of Jesus, fundamental to the whole idea of the divine commonwealth" (p. 93).

In contrast to the way authority was used in his time, Jesus offers the ideal of children, lackeys, and slaves to those who would be "greatest" among his followers. As John L. McKenzie (1966) says, "Children, lackeys, and slaves in ancient society were not the bearers of authority; indeed under most prevailing law they were not even persons. . . . [Jesus] compares his group expressly with the authoritarian structure of existing civil society, and he prohibits the introduction of this authoritarian structure into the community of his disciples" (pp. 30–31). What model of the church are Pope John Paul II, Cardinal Ratzinger, and Cardinal Hamer using when they banish, harass, threaten, and insult religious and theologians who dare to probe for the truth in debated areas? In what sense are they acting as children, lackeys, and slaves? Have they not decided that they are "the greatest" among the disciples and do not the "recognized rulers" of the world easily see this authoritarian model as their own? History hardly commends the view that compliance with lording and dominating church rulers is the better part of piety. It has been pointed out, for only one example, that "if St. Thomas More had taken direction from the majority of the English hierarchy, he would have accepted the Act of Supremacy" (p. 132). Dissent in and for the church has always been a dangerous but worthy work. The homosexuality debate must proceed courageously and in a spirit of service to the church.

Celibacy

Celibacy is not an aboriginal tradition in the church. Paul wrote: "Do we not have the right to be accompanied by a wife, as the other apostles and the brothers of the Lord and Cephas?" (1 Cor. 9:5). The author(s) of Timothy and Titus have similar views: "Now a bishop must be above reproach, the husband of one wife. . . . Let deacons be the husband of one wife, and let them manage their children and their households well." As for the elders in the towns, "If any man is blameless, the husband of one wife, and his children are believers and not open to the charge of being profligate or insubordinate," he is qualified (1 Tim. 3:2, 12; Titus 1:6).

Indeed, at times celibacy is seen as something to be disdained:

"Now the Spirit expressly says that in later times some will depart from the faith by giving heed to the deceitful spirits and doctrines of demons, through the pretensions of liars whose consciences are seared, who forbid marriage and enjoin abstinence from foods which God created to be received with thanksgiving by those who believe and know the truth. For everything created by God is good, and nothing is to be rejected if it is received with thanksgiving" (1 Tim. 4:1–4). This is not a surprising attitude in a Jewish setting. As the Jewish scholar Geza Vermes (1984) says of this period, "Celibacy, or even a lengthy separation of the sexes is alien to the Jewish way of life" (p. 121). As late as the end of the first century C. E., Eliezer ben Hyrcanus even equated abstinence from procreation with murder. (Indeed the assumption that Jesus was and always had been celibate bears a burden of proof.)

The Christian Scriptures did esteem celibacy, but with a kind of hedged earthy realism. Being a "eunuch" for the Kingdom of Heaven was all right, but "not all can receive this word, but only those to whom it is given" (Matt. 19:10–12). Paul too preferred celibacy, but saw it as a "special gift from God" (1 Cor. 7). (Interestingly, he did not argue from the example of Jesus, which would seem to have strengthened his case, but from his own experience.) At any rate, the Christian Scriptures did not dictate a celibate ministry. As R. J. Bunnik (1965) writes, "The conclusion must be that Scripture does not give a single indication about the state of life of the ecclesiastical minister. . . . Accordingly it can be expected that in most cases he [sic] will do what every man does: he will seek 'a helper fit for him' (Gen. 2:18)" (p. 414).

Subsequent history confirms this exegesis. Most clergy seem to have been married when Elvira urged them not to have intercourse with their wives. The Council of Nicaea in 325, although forbidding marriage after ordination, did not bless the rigor of Elvira. As a result, in the period after Nicaea, most priests and many bishops were married, including Saint Hilary of Poitiers (315–67; Bunnik 1965, 417). Various efforts to return to Elviran standards for the clergy intermittently recurred, but practice did not fall in line. Pope Felix II (483–92) was the son of a priest, as was Pope Agapitus in the sixth century. And it seems that Pope

Hadrianus II (867–72) was married himself (p. 419). Poisons of negativity toward all sexuality crept into the church early on. Groups such as the second- and third-century Encratites and Montanists and later the Manicheans were attracted by stark antisexual asceticism. This negativism, however, was not limited to the sectarians. It found its way into the mainstream wrapped in a florid antiwoman bias. Jerome, Ambrose, and Augustine could not be looked to for wholesome and salutary views on human sexuality.

The Second Lateran Council in 1139 ruled that ecclesiastical ministers could not contract a valid marriage. It is fair to say, however, that the legislation was not a successful graft onto the tissue of church life. Subsequent popes and councils struggled on with the failed discipline until Trent (1545–63) reasserted the rigor of Lateran II in the face of the Protestant Reformation. Still, even the enforcement of Trent had an uneven success. Obviously, mandatory celibacy for all ministers and religious was an idea whose time had never and has never come. The concept labors under too many intrinsic contradictions. Look to the arguments.

It is loosely claimed that the ideal of ministerial celibacy is biblically grounded. As we have seen, however, the Christian Scriptures do not tie ministry to celibacy.

History also foils the defenders of canonical celibacy because it shows variety and contradictions on the subject. It also reveals that the church did without mandatory celibacy for most of its history.

It has often been argued that celibacy gives freedom to the minister. This is a pragmatic, consequentialist argument susceptible to contrary proof, and the contrary proof is there. Clearly the vow or promise of obedience (not an evangelical ideal) took away what freedom celibacy might have given. It is strange too, in an authoritarian church, that this argument from freedom should be put forth. If freedom is perceived as a basic value for ministry and religious life, why does the hierarchy harass and intimidate clergy and religious who speak their convictions on issues such as homosexuality and liberation theology? Why are married lay people so much freeer in the church?

It has also been argued that religious life and ministry are holy

works and that therefore they require celibacy, which is a holier
state. This view, which found expression in the Council of Trent,
does not have scriptural or traditional warranty. Also, Vatican II
abandoned this pejorative comparison of virginity to marriage and
saluted the true holiness of sacramental married life.

It has been further argued that celibacy is an eschatological sign.
It signals the "not yet" of the reign of God and bears witness to
deeper spiritual realities. That may be so, but signals and signs are
ambiguous. Often in the history of the church celibacy has been a
sign of disparagement of human sexuality and of marriage.
Moreover, must everyone offer this sign? Are there no other
messages to be delivered? What of the value of ministers knit
together in agapic marital love, showing the possibility of fidelity
and reconciling love in a cynical world? In many cultures, celibacy
is observed often in the breach and thus is a sign of dishonesty.
This is an old and persistent story. When the Council of Constance
(1414–18) met to consider celibacy, among other things, some
seven hundred prostitutes hastened to the town (Bunnik 1965,
419)! The history of mandatory celibacy has not been an edifying
chronicle.

Some arguments for mandatory celibacy have been almost
embarrassingly weak. It has been argued that ministry should
reflect heaven, where "men and women do not marry" but rather
"are like the angels in heaven" (Matt. 22:30). Aside from the
meaning-giving context from which these words are plucked, it
could also be said that in heaven men and women will not eat
pizza, but one would be hard-pressed to draw conclusions from
that for the diets of ministers.

Finally, it has been argued that celibacy is a sacrifice and that
sacrifice befits the heroic lives of clergy and religious. The notion of
sacrifice underlying this argument is curious at best. A true story
illustrates the deficiency of this theological argument.

At Catholic University in 1969 a lecture was delivered on the
theology of celibacy. It was said that celibacy did not imply that
marriage is not a great good, but rather, precisely because marriage
is so highly valued, the sacrifice of it is noble. A new Japanese
convert to Catholicism was puzzled by this logic, which was

stunningly new to her. She asked the professor, "Do you value celibacy?" "Oh, yes," the priest-professor replied. "Well, then," pressed Katsuko, "why not sacrifice that?" The question was not answered then or later.

The problem that Katsuko sensed, of course, was that the negation of a valued good was being seen as a good in and of itself. The argument, then, easily imploded. Sacrifice, of course, is not good unless the context makes it good. The sacrifice of one's life for no reason is immoral; the sacrifice of one's life to save someone else's life is another matter. As to sacrifice itself, I might add from experience, that eating breakfast while feeding Cheerios to two toddlers may be more sacrificial than a meal in a celibate rectory.

Sacrifice is good if it is conducive to something positive. Otherwise it is an idol. For a Daniel Berrigan, celibacy was good for the freedom it gave him to pursue justice in a special way. He would not have been morally free to leave young children or an unwilling spouse to go to jail for many years. Celibacy might give mobility or, for some, it might be, at least for a time, a useful discipline. A group of celibates might form an enriching kind of community of the sort that could not exist with families. But celibacy is only one of many ministerial and religious options. It is good or bad according to the circumstances that give it meaning.

In summary, the discussion of homosexuality in the Catholic church must be seen in the context of that church's strained and late commitment to celibacy. Once that subject is reevaluated we are freed for a realistic discussion of homosexuality in religious and clerical life. I have discussed elsewhere the possibility of valid and sacramental marriage between two homosexual persons (Maguire 1983). In a church liberated from its arbitrary linking of celibacy to ministry and religious life, the suitability of homosexual married couples in ministry and religious life could be addressed. Given the oppression in these matters in the church today, we are far from free discussion of this possibility, although clandestine solutions along these lines are being realized. The increasing numbers of gay seminarians and gay men and lesbians in religious life will create pressures for further theological reevaluation.

Sexual Ethics

Christianity did not inherit a systematic sex ethic. Of course sex was there and early Christians had to think about it, but they did not develop a sex ethic that was biblically rooted and methodically composed. Instead, they absorbed from here and there, and the best was not always absorbed, as we have seen. What modern Catholicism inherited was a hodgepodge heavily marked by taboo thinking. Taboo is not concerned with the two marks of sin: *real unnecessary harm* and *unreasonableness* (Maguire 1979). It doesn't look to harm or reason as criteria. Taboo says that something is wrong because it is forbidden by the powers that be, regardless of whether it is harmful or unreasonable. It was taboo to touch the ark in ancient Israel. There was no question of whether it would be harmful to touch it; it was just forbidden. In some tribes studied by anthropologists, it is taboo to see the person you are betrothed to. Again, there is no question of whether it would be good for you or not. This was the spirit of much of the older Catholic theology of sexual sin still plied by the Catholic hierarchy. The pleasure of sex was taboo, and the question therefore was "Did you take pleasure?" not "Did you do harm?" The taboo theology divided the body into "decent, less decent, and indecent parts." If you touched an indecent or less decent part, you were in moral trouble, all thoughts of reasonableness aside. This kind of uncontextualized thinking was far from our modern realization that even touching the so-called "decent parts of the body" could be a form of sexual harassment and very morally offensive.

A sexual ethic is best founded on justice, not taboo. *Justice is the virtue whereby we render to each his or her own with an eye to the common good.* Sexual activity is good if it is just. And justice, by definition, does not look only to the participants in sex. It has a permanent eye on the common good. What are the effects on the common good? Justice is concerned with the *minimal essential good* for those immediately involved and for the community. Does a sexual relationship enhance the good of the parties and does it enhance their contribution to their common good context? These considerations alone are an excellent beginning for answering questions of right and wrong regarding sexual activity and sexually charged relationships in any human situation.

Sex is a powerful force and that is a central factor in its moral status. Sex has a binding power that affects one's relationships with others and not just with the beloved. I think sex is best defined as a natural liturgy. I speak of sex here not as confined to coitus, but as a pervasive vitality that looks to periodic coital refreshment in a relationship. Such sex is symbolic and liturgical language.

Symbol comes from the Greek *ballo* (throw) and *syn* (with, together with). A symbol throws together levels of meaning that cannot be simply or verbally expressed. It's hard to *say* what a sigh can mean, or to *say* what one means by a smile. Such is the power of symbol over mere word. Sighs and smiles symbolize and encapsulate in intense eloquence what would be lost in tedious telling.

A liturgy is a coordinated series of symbols that communicates and celebrates meaning. Some are natural liturgies, found, not contrived, such as sex and a meal. Other liturgies are conventional. Coronations of queens, presidents, and popes, and patriotic feast days are conventional liturgies that consist of liturgical rituals contrived for the meanings of the event. As contrivance, they vary from place to place. Natural liturgies, like sex and dining, are substantially similar for all of humankind.

Let me illustrate the nature of a natural liturgy first by showing the liturgical nature of human dining. Obviously, there can be paraliturgical eating as when someone "grabs a bite" on the run to meet biological needs. When a meal is allowed to be itself at leisure, however, its liturgical power blooms.

The table, after all, is not a trough. People who dine together are not just consuming proteins and carbohydrates. Guests are not chosen for their hunger. A meal is a friendship event that, like a sacrament, both symbolizes and effects friendship. (It is not surprising that the Christian religion and other religions favored the meal as a symbolic matrix and principal liturgy.) Witness the exquisite attention to detail that goes into the making of a meal. We are not just feeding our friends when we invite them; we are expressing our respect and love. The dinner table is prepared like an altar. Precious vessels of crystal, silver, and china are brought forth. The lighting is changed. Music is readied. Appropriate vestments are worn. The atmosphere is one of giving and is as splendid as we can make it. An old Irish saying advises: "When you come for a meal, don't come with one arm as long as the other." Carry a gift. It is gifting time for guest and host. So much more than ingestion is going on.

Even the food is prepared symbolically. It would not be a meal if we fed people intravenously or from a vat, though they would be fully nourished. The preparation and arrangement of the food is heavily symbolic. Not all meals can become fully symbolic, but the urgency toward sociality and friendship is always there. The busy househusband or housewife who has gotten the children off to school, and sits for a bit of breakfast, reaches for the phone or the television or a magazine to ward off the aloneness that offends human eating. And if all this stress on sociality, love, and respect as essential ingredients of a meal seems too lyrical, think of what happens when you are forced to eat with someone whom you seriously dislike. The consequent indigestion will bear witness to the fact that mere foodstuffs and a table do not a meal make. If you ate beside a stranger every day at a diner counter, it would be very difficult to ward off the intimations of communication and conviviality that go with personal eating. You would have to become friends of a sort.

Sex is a natural liturgy that meets physical needs such as distraction, relaxation, and nervous release. Sometimes when the personal dimensions are minimal, as when sex is commercialized, there may be little more to it than this. But there is symbolic power in sex that, given due chance, will assert itself. Sex has a power to engender and express endearing emotions and intense personal expectations. It is an intense form of sharing that invites more sharing. In the sexual encounter, the parties are not just physically enveloping and interpenetrating each other; there is psychological envelopment and penetration as well. One is personally as well as physically naked in shared orgasmic experience. The event is truly a *revelatio*, an unveiling. The usual cosmetic defenses with which we gird ourselves do not easily survive such liturgy. The force of the encounter is unitive. The lover may remain only an experience, but she or he tends to become a way of life. The lovers have shared a secret together: they have shared a powerful symbolic event that both signifies and effects friendship. "Getting involved" is a corollary of, if not a prelude to, "having sex."

This is not to say that the symbolic aspects of sex cannot be repressed or almost extinguished in certain cauterized personalities or at lower stages of personality development. But without some manifestation of cherishing and affection, the sexual meeting is not even going to be a sensual success. And if depersonalized sex is repeated, the personal and unitive dimensions are likely to emerge. It is ironic to note that the romantic sexual encounter, which is certainly a high form of fun, has such a lugubrious legacy in terms of songs of broken hearts, the blues, and literary tragedies. Its unitive potential explains this to some degree. The unitive power is felt by one of the parties and not by the other, or circumstances prevent the union that is so commandingly required by the relationship. "A pity beyond all telling is hid in the heart of love," wrote Yeats, and many persons who move into a sexual encounter learn the poignant adaptations that the poet's words can have.

Sometimes the power of sex can only be seen in its pathology. When sexually animated passion is frustrated, the results can be violent or psychologically devastating. Police officers note a peculiar level of violence in sex-related crimes. The urgencies and expectations generated in the sexual encounter are not feeble. Their roots are deep in the human spirit. Their assigned roles are serious in the unfolding of human life. Psychologist Dorothy Tennov (1980) studies the power of sexually involved love in her book *Love and Limerence: The Experience of Being in Love.* She had to coin the word *limerence* to describe the experience of being in love since our language has so specific term for it. That, in itself, suggests neglect of a most fundamental phenomenon. The book is a useful study of the force that lies in sexually nourished love. It is highly illustrative of the unitive aspects of sex.

Sex between persons, then, is not merely physical. It has a meaning we do not give it and a power that never ceases to surprise. Truncated sex, which does not flower into personal meaning, provides neither a basis for marriage nor a stable relationship. Our vulnerabilities, hopes, and secrets come out in the sexual encounter, and if they are not received into reverent friendship, pain comes to the lovers (Maguire 1986b).

Sexual relationships are powerful realities. Of course, they change; their early intensity does not survive. But they remain important and they do not take their meaning only from their impact on the couple but from the full human context in which these relationships unfold.

Friendship and Community

Modern theology and philosophy are virtually illiterate on the subject of friendship, and yet that is what every relationship and every community is all about. A community is ultimately a successful experience of extended friendship. Friendship is also the context for any discussion of sexual ethics and homosexuality, and so I cannot end without a word on it (Maguire 1986b). Sexual ethics should not be discussed as though it were a study of organs. It must be a study of *persons*, with all of their vulnerability, sensitivity, and need. Since the greatest need of persons is for friendship, a theology of friendship should environ a theology of sex.

The first principle of friendship is that it is a process. Friendship and community are processes, not states. The word *state* comes from *stare* in Latin: to stand, to be still, static. Friendship is not static. We now realize through modern science that nothing is static. Even the paper on which this is written, though apparently static, is at the molecular level utterly dynamic and changing. Friendship and community are dynamic processes in movement from more to less or less to more. If a married couple involved in a marital-friendship process were asked if they are married, they could reply: "Not very much," or "Very much," or "Scarcely." If you live in a religious community, a fair question to ask is: How communitarian is the community? It could be the dry bones of former community, or it could be enfleshed with loving, shared communal friendship. As the married are more or less married, so communities are more or less communitarian. In each case the question is: How deeply are the couple and the community into friendship? Process is the first principle of friendship.

The second principle is this: the more a friendship (community) meets the growth needs of the friends, the more friendly (communitarian) it is. This does not suggest that any friendship or community should meet all our growth needs. To expect too much from a friendship or a community is worse than expecting too little.

What, then, are the growth needs of persons? The delineation of some of these needs (the mystery of personhood is too great for anyone to list them all) provides criteria for morally testing sexual or other relationships.

The first of these needs, respect, is the only one I list in order of importance. Respect, the primatial need for all friendship or community, is the opposite of insult, and insult is the root of all rebellion. Respect is the acknowledgment that someone is a person, with all the glories and mysteries thereof. Many persons have done without freedom and been happy. Most people have done without affluence and found peace. But no one can do without respect. Sexism, heterosexism, and hierarchicalism are all disrespectful and dominative of persons. They are all failures in mutuality and shared respect.

Next, we have an aesthetic need. We need massive doses of beauty just as we need massive doses of oxygen. As the sharing of beauty is bonding, friendship grows in shared appreciation. Time for the sharing of beauty is not optional in any friendship or community.

In spite of what we do in education to make learning painful and demeaning, the hunger for new experiences of truth survives unto death. Friendship is, among other things, a shared growth in truth to satisfy an intellectual need.

Apollo and Dionysus have become modern symbols of personality types. Apollo can be seen as a god of order who commands discipline, work, precision, and efficiency from his devotees. For Dionysus the prime value is in celebration, not in order. The Dionysian worshipers are called to dance and merriment and the ecstatic blurring of lines between mine and thine, the human and the divine. Friendship needs a blending of these two gods. The

American Apollonian culture (we sent the Maypole dancers back to England in chains) is maimed in its Dionysian capacity. We are better at doing than at dancing. Our inability to pause for ecstasy hurts our communities, our friendship, and our appreciation of both religion and sexuality.

G. K. Chesterton (1958) said, "Life is serious all of the time, but living cannot be. You may have all the solemnity you wish in your neckties, but in anything important (such as sex, death, and religion), you must have mirth or you will have madness" (p. 97). Since laughter purifies friendship and community, religious communities should reinstitute the office of jester. Laughter is a grace that dissipates hostile illusions. There is no relationship that does not need its savor, humor.

Since humans also need the sacred, shared commitment to sacred values, whether religiously identified or not, is essential to serious friendship. Shared commitment to the sacredness that is discoverable in our midst is a most "intimitizing" communion.

We need the talent of reconciliation because no two of us are similarly socialized. Although union brings collision, differences can be harmonized in mutuality or they can be repressed by domination. Friendship and community are the children of gentleness, and reconciliation is the genius of the gentle.

True love, as the French say, is always a bit crazy. The Hebrew *hesed* and the Greek Christian *agape* knew that the American concept of love is overly romantic and unreal. One of the most neglected truths of sexual ethics is that erotic love promises divinity and delivers humanity. The moral challenge is to respond to that humanity with divine enthusiasm without confusing the beloved with God.

Permit me a story. My uncle Dan had some hard years in his marriage. His wife suffered from profound melancholia for many years, and they knew many tensions relating to this. With my uncle I visited her as she lay dying in a hospital ward. They could not afford a private room. And yet as this man ended a gentle visit with his wife, he paused at the end of the ward with a look of helplessness on his face. He wanted to do more for her. Suddenly an old orderly came by. Uncle Dan went up to him and put five dollars (a fortune for him at the time) into his hand and said,

"Would you keep an eye on the lady in the fourth bed? See if there are things she needs, like water, or just stop and say a word sometimes." It had probably been years since Dan and Annie had said "I love you" to each other, and yet the caring of that moment was an epic. Love can mean so many things, such as fleeting infatuation or impersonal sexual ardor. Or love can mean old Dan and Annie and the orderly. To love like that, beyond prospect of gain or calculation, is human love of divine proportions. It is the consummation of friendship and community.

Space is another friendship need. True union, says Teilhard de Chardin, differentiates; it does not blur. It does not make you less of what you are, but makes all the buds in you blossom. A cloying need to banish all diversity, individuation, and separation is self-defeating for friends or communities. It brings the separation it seeks to bar and breeds control and resentment. True mutuality is untroubled by intermittent distance and different interests.

Love diffuses itself (*Amor diffusivus sui*). Erotic friendships especially can become a form of *egoisme à deux*. Early love may retreat from its accustomed community of persons in the rapture of early discovery and in the insecurity of early and precarious limerence. Good friendship, however, is a social event. The community is better for the loves within it. Good love is marked by outreach, not isolation and disintegration; it threatens no one.

And finally, in this list of human friendship needs are dreams. Engraved over the lintel of any friendship or any community could be the words of Yeats (1956):

> I, being poor, have only my dreams;
> I have spread my dreams under your feet;
> Tread softly because you tread on my dreams. (p. 70)

Made in the image of the infinite, we are bored with the given and are bred of dreams. A matrix for dreaming, true love, true friendship, and true community awaken the dreamer in us and nourish the dreamer's divine pretensions. Reality chastens dreamers but friendship should warm and cherish this hope-filled talent of humankind.

Conclusion

The subject of homosexuality as it relates to religious and clergy in the Catholic church today cannot be approached narrowly. The discrete issue of the morality of homosexual acts is caught in an ecclesiological drama in which the Vatican has chosen sexual and reproductive ethics to reassert its authority and power in pre–Vatican II terms. The debate on homosexuality is caught in a power struggle, but in spite of the risks, the debate goes on, needing a broader theological environment of theology of justice and a theology of friendship. The old simplisms of taboo sex ethics will not be found in this approach. Their loss is the price of maturity in a renewing church.

References

Academic Freedom and the Abortion Issue. 1986. Four Incidents at Catholic Institutions: Report of a Special Committee. *Academe* (July-August): 1a–13a.

Bunnik, R. J. 1965. The Question of Married Priests. *Cross Currents* 15 (Fall): 414.

Chesterton, G. K. 1958. In *Lunacy and Letters,* edited by D. Collins. New York: Sheed and Ward.

Dodd, C. H. 1970. *The Founder of Christianity.* New York: Macmillan.

Kee, A. 1982. *Constantine vs. Christ: The Triumph of Ideology.* London: S.C.M. Press.

Laeuchli, S. 1972. *Power and Sexuality: The Emergence of Canon Law at the Synod of Elvira.* Philadelphia: Temple University Press.

McKenzie, J. L. 1966. *Authority in the Church.* New York: Sheed and Ward.

Maguire, D. 1979. *The Moral Choice.* Minneapolis: Winston.

———. 1983. The Morality of Homosexual Marriage. In *A Challenge to Love: Gay and Lesbian Catholics in the Church,* edited by R. Nugent. New York: Crossroad.

———. 1986a. Catholicism and Modernity. *Horizons* 13, no. 2 (Fall): 355–70.

———. 1986b. *The Moral Revolution.* San Francisco: Harper and Row.

Tennov, D. 1980. *Love and Limerence: The Experience of Being in Love.* New York: Stein and Day.

Vermes, G. 1984. *Jesus and the World of Judaism.* Philadelphia: Fortress Press.

Yeats, W. B. 1956. He Wishes for the Clothes of Heaven. In *The Collected Poems of W. B. Yeats.* New York: Macmillan.

PERSONAL
PERSPECTIVES

4 The Lost Coin

SISTER MARY

What woman, if she has ten silver pieces and loses one, does not light a lamp and sweep the house in a diligent search until she has retrieved what she lost? And when she finds it, she calls in her friends and neighbors to say, "Rejoice with me! I have found the silver piece I lost."

Luke 15:8–9

I find in myself much of that urgency and joyfulness of the woman in the gospel. In coming to understand and accept my sexual identity, I have experienced the good news in my life in a way so powerful that I find myself saying and doing things I would never have dreamed of saying or doing a few short years ago. It is as if the words of Jesus to the possessed man have been personally spoken to me: "Go home to your people and tell them all that the Lord in his mercy has done for you" (Mark 5:19). What follows is an attempt to do just that, to tell of my own experience, and in the course of that story to touch on some questions and issues about homosexuality in religious life.

At the outset I wish to state a few things about my experience. First, my sexual identity is a part of my whole self. My experience in coming to grips with this identity has impressed me deeply with

59

the connectedness of all aspects of my life: my relationship with God, others, myself; my ministry and community life; my physical and psychological health; and so on. So, if these pages sound more like a brief autobiography than an essay on lesbian nuns, in a very real sense that is what they are. Second, coming to understand and accept my sexual identity, though not without much pain and darkness, has been and still is for me at once a religious experience; an integrating experience; a joyful, freeing, and opening experience. The positive aspects of this self-discovery far outweigh the negative ones. At this time I am happy to be and to know that I am a lesbian woman. Finally, I consider myself still very much in process, still exploring questions rather than announcing answers.

Where to begin? I am the daughter of an Italian immigrant father and first-generation French mother. I am the third of four children, two boys and two girls. I was raised in a lower-middle-class family, attended Catholic grammar school and an all-girls Catholic high school, and it seems to me I always knew I wanted to be a sister. I was a good student and very active in school activities in high school. I dated a little, just enough not to stand out as odd or different in my circle of girl friends. The summer after high school in 1956 I entered the convent.

To help the reader focus more clearly on what I have to say, I have divided my life in religion into three time periods. The first period covers my first twelve years in the convent, the second spans the next fourteen years, and the third and shortest is from late 1982 until the present.

If I chose an image to describe the first period, which extends from 1956 until 1968, when I was about thirty-one, it would be the image of a foggy night. Though I entered, like most eighteen-year-olds in the 1950s, full of idealism and enthusiasm, things inside me soon seemed to change. Always a responsible and obedient girl, I tried to be a responsible and obedient sister, and fell easily into the expected and formalized patterns of behavior characteristic of "good sisters" in the 1950s. Externally, I went through all the right motions, was professed, taught for a couple of years in elementary school, then moved to secondary school teaching and did fairly well. I was seen as a good, responsible, hardworking sister, though perhaps a bit too shy and retiring.

I did not realize then, or for a long time to come, how much of my still-developing affectivity, sexuality, and sense of myself as an embodied person were being buried and repressed in the process. What I *did* begin to experience was an overwhelming sense of personal inadequacy, a growing lack of belief in my own love-ableness and ability to love, a sort of holding back and lack of initiative in my relationships with others, a constant state of depression. Such feelings, coupled with an overwhelming sense of guilt about occasional masturbation, served to confirm my assessment of myself as a sick and sinful person beyond all proportion to reality. My feelings of loneliness, occasional attractions to other sisters, struggles to know how to communicate and relate to different people, to express the love and affection I often felt—by a crazy twist of thinking, all of these things became for me not normal challenges to growth, but signs and symptoms of illness and inadequacy. What I was blindly repressing was demanding to be heard in these symptoms, but I was unable then to deal with it. During this time I do not think I was at all conscious of my sexuality, except as a frightening something that needed to be hidden or somehow controlled. I would never have dreamed then of the possibility of homosexuality in myself or in anyone else in religious life. And so for a long time I tended my symptoms, felt very alone and vaguely different, sought counseling, and prayed to a God who seemed infinitely distant from such a weak and sinful person as I. I was constantly looking and longing for something I could not even articulate then.

The second period of my religious life extends from around 1968 until 1982. It is a time I would image as a kind of dawn. In this period more than in any other, I can now see what I believe is God's wonderful providence, timing, and planning of the events of my life so that I could be gradually readied to accept myself and my sexual identity more fully. There is also at about this time a sense of the mysteriousness of how it all happened. What I *can* say about these years is that gradually healing began to occur in me, healing that was the result of grace, a certain readiness in me, and perhaps the right mix of people and circumstances. Little by little the depression lifted and I began to actively engage in my life, to take risks, to care about people, and, more importantly, to express that care.

As for all of us in the late 1960s and early 1970s, religious life as we had known it was turned upside down. Old structures were dropped;habits were modified; sisters were leaving in large numbers. The world quite literally came crashing in on us. Life during those years became something I could no longer hold at a distance. The loves, the joys, the sorrows, the departures of many sisters, some of them longtime companions or close friends, deeply touched and affected me, and uncovered long-buried feelings of love, tenderness, care, outrage, grief—feelings that for so long had been repressed. Through this "best and worst of times" it gradually dawned on me that I could love and was lovable, that I was capable, that though I might be sinful, that was not the overriding reality about me. I began to feel well again, and happy and excited to be so!

I believe this getting well served to set the stage for me to take the next more direct steps in coming to deal with my sexuality. During these turbulent years, I had three very powerful experiences of loving or falling in love with other women in my community that led me to consider more directly the issue of my sexuality. Through these experiences I learned invaluable truths. I discovered something of what intimacy meant: sharing myself as I was, allowing myself to be vulnerable and weak in the presence of another person. I explored the intimacy of touch: holding another person, embracing, physical closeness. Finally, I discovered the intimacy of loving expression of my feelings, of saying in a hundred different ways, "I love you." All of these relationships unfolded in the midst of fairly large communities. None of these women was a lesbian; I did not have genital experiences with any of them. Two of them are no longer in my congregation; two of them are still very close friends. Both at the time they occurred and now, I have seen these relationships as wonderfully positive, precious gifts that have been the source of rich blessings for me.

By the second experience, around 1970, when I was thirty-two, I began to wonder about my own sexual orientation. Notice the tentativeness, fear, and inability to name my feelings clearly in a journal entry of this time:

> During these past few months I have become involved in what has proved to be a highly significant and frighteningly "feeling filled"

relationship with another sister. At first I was almost in a state of panic about this, fearful of the abnormality it seemed to indicate in me. Perhaps now, with even a little more insight into it, I can see that it isn't that abnormal . . . what is so frightening is facing all the feelings I have here directly rather than changing them into other things . . . as I've tended to do in the past.

It was only during the third experience that I could recognize and describe what I was experiencing as falling in love, as erotic feelings for another woman. By this time the specter of homosexuality(and it was a specter then) was looming larger. Such a deeply felt love, delightful as it was, raised questions and fears in me. I instinctively knew that this love was somehow different and tried at one point to articulate that still vague reality to the woman I loved: "I know I do love and care about other people in my life but the way I feel about you seems to have something distinctly different about it, something that has to do with the constancy of your presence to me and the intensity of my feeling for you." Following a conversation about homosexuality with several sisters, I wrote in my journal:

Last night's conversation left me feeling . . . unsettled. I guess this is because it touched on a vulnerable and, in some ways, still very uncertain spot in me. . . . The conversation made me wonder again about the possibility that my own tendencies are more homosexual than heterosexual. I suppose I always wonder how people would react if I said this. Maybe the deeper wonder is in me though—what does or what might the fact mean in terms of my life? What if it is true and I admit and accept it? What are the implications of that for my life here and now?

At this time I began therapy to try to "integrate" into my life my relationship with the woman I loved. During the course of a year or so in therapy, I concluded that my orientation was homosexual. Another journal entry captures a kind of conviction, though still entirely intellectual, still mixed with fear and ambivalence:

I feel more clearly convinced of my own pretty definite and permanent homosexual orientation. It's funny how my understanding and acceptance of that fact comes, it seems, in such a gradual way, or with ever new degrees of depth. Maybe that's part of God's goodness to me, a way of revealing about myself only as much as I am able to take at any given moment. A part of the difficulty in accepting this reality in myself is the fact that I believe the things that are said about homosexuality being in some way wrong, pathological, a sign of stunted growth. I believe these things superficially, but way down deep I sense that this is not true, that this has been my orientation all of my life as far as I can consciously remember, and that it is not the result of something wrong in my childhood or development.

November 1982 marks the beginning of the third period of my religious life, and this period extends to the present time. This is a time in which the fog finally clears and the dawn brightens into day for me. In 1981 I was elected to the leadership team of my congregation. By this time some of the intensity of the relationships I have referred to had in fact been integrated. Yes, in my mind I did think I was homosexual, but I felt no need to think or talk about this. It was a reality I had carefully noted in my journal, then tucked it neatly and ironically into the closet!

Then in November of 1982 a sister in our congregation came to talk to the council about her discovery and acceptance of her homosexual orientation. She wanted to attend a retreat sponsored by Dignity, the organization of gay and lesbian Catholics and their supporters, but wanted us to know what she was doing and why. That afternoon as she spoke to us, I felt a little like Saul being knocked off his horse. I knew with blinding clarity that I needed to take the next steps in dealing affectively, not just intellectually, with my own sexual identity.

The next several months were very painful and lonely ones. I realized how shallow my so-called "acceptance" of my homosexuality had been. I engaged in an intense "review of life." I reread journals and letters I had kept for more than twenty years, trying to piece things together, to see connections and patterns, to understand and accept what the words written in my journal really meant. I felt obsessed by sex, a very unsettling way to feel. I read furtively all kinds of materials about homosexuality from scholarly articles to explicit descriptions of lesbian lovemaking. It was as if the floodgates were finally opened and all the thoughts, fantasies, and feelings I had never admitted or been able to articulate tumbled out. I came close to knowing panic, experienced sleeplessness and physical as well as emotional pain, struggling to face the big decisions that arose as I began to consider the implications of anything more than a detached intellectual understanding of being lesbian.

At this time I again began a year of therapy, this time with a woman therapist. Before my first session, I noted in my journal the following as the issues I needed to address:

> To articulate my experience of myself as homosexual to someone who will understand and affirm that experience for me;
> To get some assistance in trusting my own experience to be true;
> To integrate the fact that I am homosexual into my understanding of my own sexuality, my relationship with others, with God;
> To explore with whom and how I share this;
> To learn how to deal with strong sexual feelings in the light of a more conscious acceptance of homosexual orientation;
> To decide how I will deal with the Church's position on homosexuality and other sexual issues;
> To in some sense choose again a celibate lifestyle in the light of this more complete and conscious understanding of my sexuality.

With the encouragement of the therapist, I was able to trust and accept my own experience as true, perhaps the hardest hurdle of all for women who have been taught for so long to distrust themselves and to look to others, usually men, for the validation of their experiences. For the past several years I have continued to explore these issues and have taken steps in a number of directions, learning more by my experience than anything else.

Because I was and still am a member of our congregation's leadership team, some of the first people I came out to were our major superior and the other members of the council. I have found from them personal affirmation, interest, and a willingness to allow me to become gradually more involved with gay and lesbian activities and groups. In addition, coming out to a number of other sisters in my congregation has been a source of affirmation and support for me and a natural opportunity for education about gay and lesbian issues and people. It has been important for me to come out to people close to me. My reasons touch back to the story of the lost coin. I am happy to have found and embraced this "lost" part of myself, and the natural impulse for me has been to share the good news with people I know and love.

Beyond the circle of close friends, I have also come out to others when the situation seemed right to do so. Having such a broad base of support and understanding enables me to be open and honest about my activities with a wider group of people. This openness is a far healthier situation for them and for me. For the most part, my disclosure has met with acceptance and understanding and not with the backing off or distancing I feared might occur. Coming out, though, is always a risk and the decision to do so requires prudence and good judgment. I know I am not personally ready yet to deal with widespread negative, hostile, or rejecting attitudes, and so I need to continue to be cautious about whom I tell and how.

On the other hand, as I grow more comfortable with who I am, ı find myself more willing to take risks and to be involved with people and groups with whom I can both give and receive support, encouragement, and challenge. For more than two years I have belonged to a small support group of six or eight religious, currently five women and three men. We meet approximately every six or eight weeks to share prayer and life experiences and to socialize. Occasionally we help one another discern decisions that concern our gay or lesbian identity.

Sometimes my friends ask me why I need such a group, why I need to talk about myself as a lesbian. I think if we lived in an ideal world where sexuality was well understood and gay people perfectly integrated in church and society, we would not need separate groups. But as good as I might feel personally to have achieved some insight and integration regarding my sexuality, I cannot ignore the fact that I am part of a marginal and misunderstood group and as such I have some special need for association, support, and bonding with other gay and lesbian people. In addition, as I find myself growing more confident of my own identity, and as I listen to the stories of gay and lesbian men and women in and out of religious life, I feel the need to continue to explore how God is leading me to be involved in ministry in this area.

I have gone regularly to Dignity liturgies in my area. Here I feel I have something to give as well as to receive. Since there are very few women in this group, my presence is a support to the other women, as well as a needed feminine presence in the group as a whole. On many occasions I have brought sisters in my community to mass with the Dignity community. For those who are put off by media stereotypes of gay people, this image of a group of worshiping Christians concerned about community, faithfulness, and service can do much to change one-sided attitudes.

I would like to mention some of the things in my experience in a religious community that have been stressful or difficult for me as a lesbian, as well as some things I have found helpful and supportive. Perhaps most difficult or stressful for me is the great silence on the whole topic of homosexuality and more specifically the silence in the face of the reality of a lesbian religious. Throughout my religious life the presumption has been that everyone is heterosexual. This is evidenced in conversation and behavior, in the lessons of formation, in most of the reading materials to which I was exposed. It creates a situation in which there are no models to look to, no acceptable vocabulary with which to talk about one's experience, few quality written materials to refer to, no forum where it can be discussed except in therapy or the confessional. All this effectively leads a religious to conclude that she is either sick, sinful, or very unusual if she even thinks she might be gay. Perhaps we need to take to heart the subtitle of the book *Lesbian Nuns: Breaking Silence* (Curb and Manahan 1985) and examine whether our silence in this area is unwittingly denying others the right to be freely who they are.

The ignorance and prejudices of people in my community or with whom I associate still have the power to hurt or anger me. This includes people who are repulsed by the very idea of homosexuality, people who will not even use the word *lesbian*, people who even today know nothing but the stereotypes of gay and lesbian people, people who equate the word *gay* with genital activity, people who focus only on the moral issues of being gay, people who make jokes and sarcastic remarks about gay people. I realize that our lack of good education about sexuality, affectivity, and intimacy probably lies at the root of these negative attitudes and fears of gay and lesbian people as well as our fears of our own

natural homosexual feelings. Nevertheless, I often find it difficult
to know how to respond to such attitudes. It is still a challenge for
me to separate myself from people's questions, comments, and
issues regarding homosexuality.

An area of stress for me is in having to lead a "double life," that
is, in having to move back and forth between groups who know I
am lesbian and those who do not. This is especially the case within
my congregation, where I am unable to share some very significant faith and ministry experiences because others do not know I
am lesbian. When this happens I feel pained and less free, yet at
the same time I know I am not ready for unqualified openness and
all that might come with it.

Finally, I think our tendency to be more black and white on
issues of sexuality than on most other issues we deal with in
religious life causes a tension and unease in me. I realize that
sexuality is indeed a delicate issue, but it is one for which centuries
of poor formation need to be gently reversed and all of us probably
need to learn and grow and to be pastoral in our approach to our
own and others' search for greater wholeness and truth. In
mentioning all of these things I do not mean to be unduly critical
of my own congregation. I believe these difficulties and stresses are
experienced to a greater or lesser degree in most congregations
today. Actually I think the kind of support and affirmation I have
received in my congregation is outstanding. I really do not have
personal horror stories to tell. I do, however, think we are at a
point in our history when the time is right to begin to change some
of the misconceptions we have held for so long.

More positively, what has helped me along this sometimes
perilous journey? A significant support was a major superior who,
although she may have been initially surprised by my trembling
announcement that I was lesbian, was willing to trust and respect
me, to allow me to get the help I needed, to continue to support
and dialog with me about my coming out and my growing
involvement in gay and lesbian activities. Another wonderful
support is the fact that I am able to be open with my living
community about my gay and lesbian activities and connections,
that I am not forced to sneak or lie, that I am free to talk about this
part of my life with them. The wide acceptance I have found in my

congregation (more than fifty members know I am lesbian) is a wonderful gift to me and a tribute to the openness of these women.

I have found my congregation willing to take some risks with me, in having gay and lesbian retreats or workshops at our motherhouse, or willing to let me take risks after mutual dialog and discernment about a particular event or situation. I have never felt that those who know about me have "hushed me up" or have been embarrassed by who I am. Indeed it was affirming to be reelected to another term of office by a group of chapter delegates, many of whom knew I was lesbian. In turn, I have felt a great responsibility to continue to move where the Spirit seems to be leading me but to do so within the context of who I am personally and who and where my congregation is.

In this whole process of coming to understand and accept myself as a lesbian religious, I believe I have been powerfully touched by grace. Like the woman who found her lost coin, I am eager to celebrate, not once but many times over, the recovery of the immensely valued lost coin and the action and presence of God in my life. Each new step of my journey is in fact somehow a sacramental reality, a sign that marks and celebrates again the life and wholeness Jesus came to reveal.

There is an incident that reveals concretely the grace of this journey. One Saturday morning in December 1982, at the most painful part of my struggle, I asked God to give me a sign, something the skeptic in me never did and tended to disdain in others. I asked for a clear sign that would not be too subtle for me to recognize. I even suggested to God what the sign might be! I had been reading a part of John Fortunato's book *Embracing the Exile* (1982), in which he speaks about being gay as a gift. "So, God," I suggested, "when I open today's Scriptures, let it be that quote about sharing the gift you've received. Then I will really know that I'm on the right track with all I'm dealing with right now." I really did not know where that quote was in the Gospels, nor had I been looking ahead at the readings for that week. The reading for that day was from chapter 10 of Matthew's Gospel. And there before me was the very sign I had asked for in the words: "The gift you have been given, give as a gift" (Matt. 10:8). How could I doubt

any longer the gift of God given in those words but even more in
the depths of my being!

References

Curb, R., and Manahan, N., eds. 1985. *Lesbian Nuns: Breaking Silence.*
    Tallahassee: Naiad Press.
Fortunato, J. 1982. *Embracing the Exile: Healing Journeys of Gay Christians.*
    New York: Seabury Press.

5 At Home

JUDITH A. WHITACRE, CSJ

Traveling down a city street, I realize that the church to my right is my destination. The main part of the church is a building complete in itself, built of solid stone, possibly fifty years old, standing tall in an established neighborhood. An annex to this building is made of the same stone, yet somewhat incomplete and fashioned in a more modern style than the church—a one-story structure with openings for windows, but no windows; with doorways, but no doors. By a sort of translocation I am in the annex, where there are several men and women, young and old, who are sharing an easy kinship derived not from years of knowing each other, but from the soul and being. I feel at home as I meet and share with these people; superficialities and formalities are nonexistent, though I have never met any of them before. On the other side of each window opening is a woman peering in and quite present in her own way although she does not venture to speak or to come into the rooms. Then, as many dreams abruptly end, the alarm rings to signal the time to begin another day.

The kinfolk in this dream, upon which I have often reflected, were gay and lesbian people like myself whose relationship, deeper than physical presence or blood, was born of pain, growth, and loving. Although I was one of the people gathered in the annex, I was also the woman peering in the window openings.

71

Being a lesbian religious with vows of celibacy, sharing of goods, and obedience in community is symbolized in this dream by the ambiguity of personhoods I assume. Openness and secrecy, joy and pain, confidence and doubt—all mix together to challenge me to be who I am meant to be in my chosen life-style.

Experience and "gut feelings" enable a person to discover who she is and to choose how she will act in minor and major movements of life. Motivated by love, fear, anger, or other emotions, choices are most deeply affected by a person's sense of inner identity and participation in the outer world. Being a lesbian nun is not a deliberate choice on my part. My attraction to women and toward intimacy with my own kind is not a choice for me; rather it is the way I am and is as natural as being left-handed, white-skinned, and brown-eyed. Being lesbian is my inner milieu, from which I relate with the world.

Being a nun *is* a choice I have made for many reasons at different times during my life. My attraction to religious life was simultaneous with the realization of my lesbianism at age eleven! An eleven-year-old can scarcely sort out appropriate times to giggle much less probe the urgings of the inner self. By the grace of a power greater than any of us, I was twenty-one when I came to religious community knowing that I am lesbian, responding to an urging of faith, determined to be the best, the holiest, the most loving nun, and resolved that no one would ever know that I am lesbian. As time went on, the determination to remain "in the closet" became crippling and I needed to make new, deeper choices, truer to my being lesbian and a woman in religious community.

Although my formation in religious life was chronologically post–Vatican II, its style was definitely pre–Vatican II. In the mid-1960s most religious communities wondered what to do with the "new breed" of candidates knocking at the door. Although encouraged to know ourselves, we prayed at the same times and in the same manner. We all did the same things for fun ("forced fun," as some called it). All were expected to grow in the same spiritual style and to fall asleep and awaken at the same time. Living the vows meant asking permission and receiving any material needs for our personal upkeep, doing what the community leadership asked of us and not entertaining any romantic urgings; all this was to keep us free for the fulfillment of our mission.

Renewal in most communities, of course, has changed all this. Maturing as individuals truly committed in faith and action, women religious now recognize and appreciate their gifts and talents and seek to fulfill many social and ecclesial needs.

My own formation really began after the formal training period. Being lesbian became a "monster" for me. I had innumerable painful crushes and experienced lesbian love relationships; yet I remained in religious life feeling as though I was not a good person, not a good nun, and not being true to my inner self. It was then that religious formation really began for me.

Directed retreats, which became popular in the 1970s as a means of growing in our relationship to God, provided valuable opportunities to know that we are lovable, loving, and truly loved. Finally, at a directed retreat the time had come for me to deal with the "monster" of my sexual orientation. As Jesus said to the woman about to be stoned to death, "I do not condemn you," I experienced an acceptance that I could never have asked for since I did not know it was possible and an acceptance from which I could not turn. This gift of freedom enabled me to face my lesbianism in wholesome proportion and even to embrace it. No longer would I be controlled by an overpowering fear that left me feeling utterly helpless and enslaved. For so long tenuous at best, my faith was based on the expectations of parents, the church, and my religious community, but it was now transformed into the raw material from which I prayed, related with others, made life-style decisions, and participated in the church.

I gradually came to realize that, by not sharing my sexual identity, I felt dishonest and untrue to my own faith. I needed to reveal that most important part of myself that makes me "tick." I had heard the anguishing stories from gays and lesbians who, from honesty and trust, shared their sexual identity with family, friends, or religious community and were rejected, lost their jobs, were sent away from their homes, and not permitted to minister in schools or parishes. My decision to begin coming out in my religious community arose from my desire to know more about myself and other lesbians. Needing funds for books and work-shops, I shared my sexual identity with each member of our leadership team with inner quaking as I went from office to office. I had anticipated only rejection, but the acceptance and respect I experienced will never be forgotten. Their support and love have truly been a gift.

Oh, how we were taught that celibacy is a gift, but the gift cannot be realized without the continual unfolding of our inner selves and the making of choices at each discovery. It is natural for an individual to desire a spousal relationship: to love and be loved deeply and totally, to be with someone with whom one is truly home. A lesbian nun has occasion to be with lovely, lively women with whom a spousal relationship would be desirable. In reflecting on my journey, I believe this attraction was part of my reason for choosing religious life. Formation in the vowed life dealt with celibacy in the heterosexual realm; I surely had no difficulty forgoing any heterosexual spousal relationships and all that leads to such relationships! In the gradual unfolding of what it means to be a lesbian who has chosen to be a nun, I have been challenged to discover celibacy as a way for me to be whole. Always living with the tension of being in a same-sex society, I will continue to explore the many facets of celibacy as I relate, pray, and discover more fully who I am.

Regardless of sexual preference, each person has gifts to make this world a better place. Ministry assumes many forms of caring for many kinds of people: ourselves and our own personal growth, members of our religious family, children and families in our local church settings, marginated people in our cities and rural areas, world society, and its quality of life. Gay and lesbian folks have very special gifts to share since the gay and lesbian experience has given us a sense of what it means to be in need of understanding and acceptance. Having been the butts of jokes and the objects of discrimination, having traveled long painful journeys to a sense of wholeness and self-worth, we have within us the gift of sensitivity, which enables us to reach out to others in need. Having had to prove ourselves all our lives, we are intelligent, energetic, re-sourceful, and creative. When we can be ourselves and share our talents as our inner sense moves us, ministry becomes truly a gift.

I am currently involved in administrative ministry within my religious community. My experience of being lesbian and dealing with my lesbianism daily has influenced my ministry with our sisters and our employees; the care, respect, and consideration I have experienced, and hope to continue experiencing, remind me that I cannot treat others with less than that. This realization has freed me from seeking to mold others into what I might want them to be.

I believe that my religious community is a powerful force in affecting change in the Catholic church. The church community is the gathering of all people in the name of Jesus, people who live by faith and a shared experience of God's power in our lives. Although the church must be faithful to its tradition and teachings, dealing in real-life situations according to the gospel is the stuff that gives credibility to the institutional church. Freed of the hierarchical trappings that can remove individuals from the experiences and struggles of living in society, women religious are able to identify with grass-roots people. Since as women we know the pain of structural discrimination that bars women from total participation in the church's life, we are able to teach, counsel, direct, and enable others in their faith journeys through the Spirit rather than through the law.

Because of my felt pain as a lesbian in a church structure that labels my sexual orientation disordered, does not permit my brothers and sisters to gather as Catholics on its property, and discourages honest questioning, I personally cannot be in direct, institutionalized church ministry and remain true to myself. Although I have no desire to work in an ecclesiastical structure characterized by the systematic oppression of women, of gay and lesbian persons, and of married couples, my ministry within my community can enable my sisters to be subversive of those elements in our patriarchal church that are inimical to the authentic discipleship of Jesus.

Currently my faith life bears little reference to church structure but rather revolves about my experience of being lesbian and being loved unconditionally by a very loving God. I remain in religious community because it is the locus of my faith, and a place where women hold power over their lives and where I am encouraged to grow in freedom by reflecting on my life experience. I often recall the church annex, the kinfolk, and the woman in the window, and I know I am at home.

6 Home by Way of Roundabout

SISTER RAPHAELA

The word *home* in the title of this chapter refers to a place where dusky and daring acting out of physical passion is no longer resident and where, instead, a certain sunlit spaciousness waits behind doors open to the green cool of early spring. This is the account of a journeyer who deliberately disregarded maps made by others, drew her own diagrams, and calculated her own distances and positions. By dint of detour and desolation she came at last to the flower-edged neighboring farm she had elected to find on her own. It may be that her tale makes clear that for some the only authentic knowledge of that place must be a slow process, a long meandering through many suburbs, a literally gradual, step-by-step, but ultimately deep, unshakable discovery. The real discovery for me was that celibacy or a certain entirely willful containment of body and soul for the sake of the Kingdom is alone freedom and is practically and concretely a here-and-now universal love.

The First Lap of the Journey

The Christmas I was seven, my mother and I hurried in a southern winter's dawn to early Eucharist. I felt at that moment surrounded by immense peace, which I recognized as God's presence assured and made palpable by my mother's figure as we covered the short distance between our home and church. I was totally content; my senses were open to the morning and to the mockingbirds and visiting robins. Already up, the sun had begun to shoot through the mist with threaded brilliance, laying down near the ground a haze of ecstatic light. I almost drowned in joy; dizzy for a moment, I held tight to my mother's hand lest this ocean carry me away. I received the Body of Jesus, intensely alive to the reality of his presence, feeling again the strange conviction, and making again the same announcement I had made seven months earlier: "When I grow up, I will be a sister."

The goal lay ahead shrouded but real, a certain and absolute harbor. Already I heard in my heart "the hooves of invisible horses" that would carry me there. Why did that conviction arise? What did it mean? I can only say that God was calling me to love Him in a specific way, and He used the only image I knew (being a sister) to catch my attention.

Rilke (1984) says: "Love is at first not anything that means merging, giving over, uniting with another (for what would a union be of something unclarified and unfinished, still subordinate?) It is a high inducement to the individual to open, to become something in herself, to become world, to become world for herself for another's sake, it is a great exacting claim upon her, that chooses her out and calls her to vast things" (pp. 69–70).

Like Francis called to "build my church," I misunderstood the content of my call. I thought I was merely to give my body to God by an absolute separation from every sort of genital imagination or activity and by a practical implementation of that wonderful shibboleth "selfless service of humankind." This dual misunderstanding would lead in the first instance to endless self-recrimination, guilt, shame; and in the second, to entrapment in various unfruitful relationships because "selfless" in my interpretation was dangerously like "victim."

Between my seven-year-old declaration and my actual entrance into a convent lay two other discoveries. Around the age of fifteen I heard in some religion class that the pleasure I had discovered at the age of three or four within "the secret places" of my body was very wicked. Nothing else. Many years and many hours of anguish later I discovered that certain feelings and images are part of human development, have little to do with fidelity to God or fundamental choice of Him, and should not occupy one's time and concern. Indeed, it was not the feelings and images that could necessarily destroy or distort one's sense of God; it was the self-preoccupation and the self-haranguing that held God at a distance.

From the time I had read the life of Catherine of Siena (Curtayne 1942), I had a thirst to think only of God (Garrigou-Lagrange 1949). The problem, of course, is that one cannot maintain this sort of mental concentration and remain sane. Living in a consciousness of God's presence is a gift. Since I did not know this then, I set out to "think always of God." An early admired mentor had shown me how natural things are metaphors for invisible God-things. I determined to discover or devise "spiritual meanings" in everything I touched, saw, dealt with. Church spires became a kind of silence that drew me for a sudden moment into God. Traveling on the bus became a direction of my life more intensely to its goal—God. Scrubbing bathroom walls and toilets was somehow saying to God, "Be thou my rampart, my wall." Rain was and is the image of His grace and His pity. Not very original, since Shakespeare had seen this four hundred years ago! Nevertheless rain always stirred my heart to stillness and to hope.

For many years the struggle went on to empty my head of "vain imaginings," as I characterized the vivid images that rose persistently from the rich storehouse in my memory. By nineteen I had devoured much of the excellent literature that filled our home. Literature and pulp have this in common: both deal with men, women, and their relationships. I failed ten times a day, or twenty; and as many times resolved and began again.

Several things brought a halt to the interior struggle: I was sent to school and my active mind bent itself to learn history and chemistry, theology and Scripture. I acquired a very wise director who taught me a little about the limitations of human nature and urged me "my own heart to have more pity on" (Hopkins 1953, 63).

Three summers before I entered the convent, on a hot summer afternoon as I lay atop the woodshed reading, a sentence from Chesterton (1944) caught fire under my eyes and announced itself with the voice of an apocalyptic angel as the specific answer to a question that had tormented me for seven years: "Why do human beings live? What is life for, really?" The answer: "The purpose of life is the praise of God as the author of life and being" (p. 79). I now had an adult reason to say yes to entering a convent. There I would probably find less distraction from my desired immersion in the adoration of being. I have never been able to find any reason for doing otherwise.

The Second Lap of the Journey

After I had entered religious life, a beloved if ill-listened-to superior gave me a little sermon of three principles that dropped like silent seeds into my consciousness and as silently took root and grew into strong but unobtrusive shade trees. First, God would have to give the ability to "think always of Him." I must become the farmer who "patiently waits for the precious fruit of the ground until it has had the autumn and spring rains! . . . do not lose heart because the Lord's coming is soon" (James 5:7–8).

Second, your desire to think of the Lord is enough! Your heart always leaps toward the Lord. Such assurance was a balm and affirmation to a spirit reared in a dry Puritan herb garden where human nature is regarded as an unfortunate deficiency.

The final principle was the most illuminating: God is leisure; God is delight. An unusual retreat master had said: "We should play with God! When you have done what you must, when your task for the moment is complete, God is your reward, exceedingly great. God is all that you can long for, God is all His creatures' home." This may not be so for every heart, but it would be so for mine. Since God's joy was too much for my little space, I could only enter His.

For me celibacy meant belonging to God in thought. Must one be celibate to come to the shoreless light and to the stretches of green space that are the atmosphere of an inner world bent on God? I am not so silly as to think so. But without the conviction that my celibacy committed me to this laborious effort, perhaps I would never have found God. Celibacy for me was the skein by which the unicorn drew the maiden.

I need to deal as frankly as possible with how celibacy affected

my belonging to God in action. Action for me meant selfless
service of persons, naturally. I held a conviction that no human
being could be totally trusted or relied on and that all human
beings were fragile, limited, needy, and looking for something from
me. Concretely, this meant, "Do not get too close to anyone." This
was not conscious but was powerfully operative. For many years
my endless curiosity, my skill at adjusting or adapting to the
inclinations of others, my early aroused and continuing pity for
human need, my boundless energy to offer myself for any task—
all this served to weave a kind of camouflage garment of charity
and zeal. I plunged with keenest interest into our religious life.

I accepted with immense satisfaction a practical guideline of
Saint Thomas Aquinas: "Love is the effective willing of good to
another." I also accepted what I mistakenly considered its logical
corollary: "Feelings have nothing to do with it." Considering all
strong feelings an unfortunate distraction, I did my best to
suppress or dissipate any strong negative or positive feelings
toward others. The wear and tear of daily life, as well as absorption
in tasks and study, obviated for me any affectional intimacy within
the convent. Outside the convent I ruthlessly and carefully
avoided males and I cannot say I am sorry I did so. Because of the
strength of my passions and my utter naivete, that was probably
the most prudent decision I could have made. As for females, I
listened to them, tried my best to speak to them about God, was
nourished far more than I knew by their appreciation, and
ascribed to the glow of doing good whatever pleasure I felt in their
company. I would have considered myself deficient in proper
detachment and failing against the first commandment if I had
simply enjoyed their company or rather had admitted to such
enjoyment. All this time, of course, I was convinced that I was
indeed "effectively willing good to another."

Because my body and emotions were shared with no one, not
even with God, I was equally certain I was being faithful to my
vow of celibacy. I knew uneasily and dimly that somehow celibacy
really meant an undivided heart, but I did not fully understand
this. Certain phrases, however, no matter when or how often
repeated, stirred me profoundly, seemed like sudden blessed
openings into a place of light, and filled me alternately with

poignant longing and abject guilt. From the bottom of my consciousness a cry arose, begging from God "nothing less than Himself," when in a sermon or text the author quoted Augustine's "You did create us for Yourself, O Lord; and our hearts are restless till they rest in You."

The Desert Experience: The Third and Longest Lap

Just as Vatican II was breaking over the horizon, I embarked on a lengthy desert crossing. The initial days were spent in a brief and dim oasis. I had been a novice mistress for five years when a somewhat older-than-most young woman came to the novitiate. She was widely cultured, knowing far more about music and literature than I. I did not merely love her as I did so many others, well and deeply. I fell in love with her. Whatever physical feelings were involved in this experience were pushed aside with a certain angry embarrassment and were absolutely refused expression. I felt again the wonderful excitement of graduate school, the sharing of ideas and dreams with a responsive, intelligent companion. On her talent, I built plans for the future education of our young sisters. I saw the years stretching before us, filled with the absorbing work of teaching, planning, and creating a small, elite, academic Arcadia. Imperceptibly, I had drifted from my center. The voice from the cloud was silent and the blazing light of a brief new day obscured the morning star.

Six years after my friend's arrival and with no previous word to me, our leadership team dismissed her. I still do not know if they were right or wrong. I do know that all five were good women; I know they tried, with effort and painful searching, to do what they honestly felt was best for our congregation. I did not, however, want to see this at the time. I quite simply hated them because I was suddenly confronted with the loss forever of a close companion and perennial co-worker on whom I had come to rest, though unwittingly, all my joy. I breathed the thin and desolate air left in the void of her going.

So began the passage through the hot sands and arid winds of my desert. When the machinery of church renewal began to hum, the energy that turned the wheels was often from a humanistic psychology that encouraged self-expression, the nurturing of one's gifts (for God, of course), respect for individual differences, and that bright and misleading, many-faceted jewel or bauble, "meaningful relationships." The great sign of modernization, of freedom, and of universal love was to have a "dear friend" outside one's own community. If that "dear friend" could be a layperson, one's emancipation seemed even more authentic. I suppose if that friend could likewise be a layman, one's emancipation would have been considered ideal. I never reached such heights!

I plunged into the cultural life of my city, for which I needed partners, with a passionate vengeance. In truth I had never suffered from cultural deprivation. My superior for nineteen years had been a woman with a pure passion for learning and with an openness to any idea, technique, or information that could enrich us as persons and missionaries. She kept her eyes, ears, and heart open wherever she went and brought back to us absorbing traveler's tales and new friends. She scoured the morning papers for free opportunities, since we were poor, and promptly sent us to listen and learn. We heard anyone who had anything to say or Mother coaxed them to spend an evening at our house, herself so eager to share their special knowledge with us.

Now, however, it was no longer a question of bringing persons into the community, no longer a question of a warm, familial sharing. I ranged and roved alone, indiscriminately inviting whoever was agreeable to be my companion to plays, concerts, and movies. "Renewal" and "friendship" were the excuses; revenge was the real intention.

Then I stopped and for the first time paid deliberate attention to a shy young woman who for years had sought me out for counsel. Together we spent time in languid country drives, listened to music, and studied the works of great artists. She, herself a superb draftswoman, knew I was bitter about the dismissal of the young woman whom I had so deeply loved. She knew also that many sisters were departing their convents. She was ecstatic at the thought that I too would leave and that we would set up a permanent creative duo, she doing her marvelous blueprints, I my rich, original course plans. After a number of years I finally had the honesty to say, "I shall never leave." The relationship died down with no violent leave takings and no angry accusations; just a slow drawing apart, a kind of unraveling. After an intimate relationship of six years, we saw each other occasionally and held brief conversations. She found another companion and, after three years, both were invited two thousand miles away to work on some unusual projects. My blueprint-making friend did not return; I have not seen her since.

I cannot say I was a sadder or wiser woman. I was puzzled, yes. Is human closeness not possible without the necessity of a kind of owning of the other? And I was burdened with doubt. Had I been a coward, selfish not to respond to her need? I knew by now that convent structures were not essential to the service of God. But could I really do without my community's stringent atmosphere of healthy criticism and fundamental support? How could I leave without somehow betraying or blinding myself to my original conviction that life's purpose is God's praise? How could I leave without blurring the witness that "we have not here a lasting city"? I still believed all this dimly, but deeply and stubbornly. If I left, I could not do so without somehow denying in myself these truths. So I stayed. The initial stages of the desert passage had been endured.

Winds of Forgiveness and Reconciliation

New winds were blowing. Like the winds that cooled the children in the fiery furnace, the winds brought dew. What were these winds, these currents at work in my life, my world? There were several.

I was twice elected assistant general of our institute. The duties of this position, the demands of my full-time teaching career, and my intense involvement with renewal movements among women religious kept me occupied with matters of service and objective concern for others. All this weakened the blazing self-concentration that my anger had set up in the center of my consciousness.

The most effective source of healing, however, was the tirelessness with which, despite my unpleasantness, my congregation's leadership had sought to understand and help me. I could not remain blind to their amazing charity, so I was prepared for the winds of forgiveness and reconciliation. When I myself became part of leadership, I began to understand the pressures administrators feel and the endless, wearying responsibility of leading a group such as ours.

I grew to appreciate the particular team responsible for the dismissal of my beloved young friend. I never came to say, "Yes, you were right." Instead I said, "You did what you honestly felt you must. I respect you for that and accept your decision in that light." The letting go of my anger and of my bitter hatred left in its wake a sense of inadequacy and existential failure. But as I had accustomed myself to do from childhood, I carefully camouflaged these wounds and went on.

Meanwhile, two fresh winds came. Despite my sally into "friendship," I was still deeply convinced that other human beings were either a task or a luxury; in either case, somehow objects. I always felt that time given to simply enjoying others was somehow wasted and I found it necessary to have some other reason; helping the other and learning something were my usual excuses. I always felt freer and more at peace when alone. I could rarely feel that it was truly in the company of others we go to God, except in certain community gatherings. There time after time I had experienced, in the midst of my sisters, a sense of God, a contentment, a security, a being-at-home that I do not doubt is a brief and touching flash of heaven. But, generally, others were the distraction or the burden. Furthermore, my body, my feelings, and my emotions were on the one hand suspect, on the other endless sources of delight. I reveled constantly in a banquet of sensations. Externally, however, I managed to convey that "nothing bothers her . . . she does not care." Both statements were the exact reverse of what was true.

I then heard a passionate speech on the essential goodness of creation, the value of emotion, and the beauty and humility of allowing oneself to accept all one's feelings. I had heard all that before, but this time, in a flash, I understood and embraced my body. This I call the west wind. It was the signal for the beginning of an ending, a prelude to a new day.

My companions in leadership sensed a restlessness and a

brooding sadness within me and insisted I ask for at least a half year sabbatical. So in the spring I went to a great midwestern university. There I taught one class to support myself financially. Although it was not a necessity, I insisted on doing so, ostensibly not to be a burden. But why, really? I felt a terrible uneasiness about having too much space. I hungered, unadmittedly, to have some ordered way to fill the time; students seemed safest. I lived in an old building with graduate students and enrolled in three courses, all taught by brilliant young women who liked me. Roaming the frozen lake banks and among the snow-spangled trees, we had several immensely satisfying, deeply significant conversations.

Unaccountably, the students came to count me in as friend. Never intending to do any "selfless serving," I meant simply to keep out of the way, to be pleasant and accommodating when I could. I am not certain what they expected. I do not know why my conduct touched them so profoundly, but when I left, one gave me his favorite Piriette and the beautiful lady professor of early Christian history pronounced me an archetypal Great Mother. At the end of this extraordinary four months, I went home to an astringent program in pastoral counseling.

As I write this, a verse from Psalm 42 leaps into my mind: "By day you will send me your loving kindness. By night I will sing to you, the God of my life." His loving kindness was all around me but my stubbornness held off for seven years the song of night. I refused to listen to the call within, to the roar of deep waters. "God is all that you can long for." "No!" I said. "That is not right! Others are the guise in which God comes. The song is wrong." I looked around once more for a friend but from an entirely different perspective than the one from which I had launched my first plunge into intimacy.

Adventure of Intimacy

Several realities converged. I feared having only God. I freshly discovered that He *means* "What you do unto others you do unto me." I equated loving others with "others will fill my heart and others will be harbor for my small boat's shelter." Further, my defenses were being shattered by the pastoral counseling, which meant learning to read unspoken messages, learning to hear feelings buried in terror, and learning to accept the terror. To understand this language one must come to hear it first within one's own being. Consciously, I fought against allowing the springs of feeling to well up. But where the Holy Spirit patiently breathes and moves, the ice was melting. As feelings rose to the surface, the cool, pleasant, detached facade crumbled.

I wanted desperately to "make up" for my long years of sterile rebellion. Feeling that I had madly clung to my own views for so long, I wanted now to give way, to be open to every suggestion that promised a new vista on life, to be accommodating, merry, affectionate, pleasant, and to be at the service of the other. Finally, I felt restless and needed somehow to come to wholeness and peace. That summer, with my feelings stirred and confused, with longing for a deep, ongoing, intellectually satisfying relationship, and with the partly conscious notion that thus I would expiate all the hatred that had poisoned my heart for so long, I embarked on the adventure of intimacy for a second time with another talented partner.

I met a beautiful and enigmatic girl twenty years my junior. We went occasionally to a movie or concert, or we sat in my room, drinking wine and playing music. I would talk, she would listen.

We traveled and consumed hours driving along beautiful roads, days tramping over ruins and through museums, evenings making exotic meals, nights falling asleep to music. Through her I was introduced to magnificent and outstanding teachers who contributed richly to a growing understanding of my own feelings and to the development and evolution of my inner world. The miasma of guilt, fear, uncertainty, bewilderment, and shadowy longing slowly cleared.

But gradually I became less and less able to adapt my feelings and my conduct to the expectations of my friend. What I really wanted would rise starkly up in my consciousness like a submerged bright rock suddenly revealed by a huge wind that swept away the covering waters. I wanted the freedom to enter without hesitation the wide, bright place of God's gracious presence and to plunge more deeply, more generously, more extensively into the life of my community. I needed not to be torn by expectations of attentiveness and affectionate indwelling directed to another human person, expectations that conflicted painfully with my desire to be oblivious of everything, but the delicate, strong, bright stillness of God's reality. I needed to be able to be entirely engaged in one thing only—praising God as the author of life and being.

For the last three years of this intimate relationship the emotional demands were simply incompatible with my deepest desires. With the help of an intelligent and holy counselor, I finally said clearly, "I need space. I want to be alone." Thus culminated a painful, seven-year experiment that had bound me to a rich and unusual person.

I saw now the meaning of celibacy as having not much to do with the body, but having everything to do with freedom and with the kind of interchange that strengthens, clarifies, and energizes. It does not mesmerize, confuse, or fill with shadowy unease. I came at last to understand my cowardice and my responsibility for clear and unambiguous decision. Often, before this, I would wait for my friend, filled with alternating currents of expectation and revulsion, of deep hope, then of desperate wanting to be elsewhere. Unbidden would come to me lines from a poem by Francis Thompson (1917):

> O lily of the king low lies thy silver wing
> O patience, most sorrowful of daughters . . .
> Lift up thy head and hark what sounds are in the dark
> His feet are coming to thee on the waters. (pp. 254–55)

The reader will say "What arrogance! The poem is about the church." So it is. It expresses, nevertheless, the profound, submerged sense I had of belonging to God and the paradoxical but accurate assessment of the relationship's cramping inappropriateness for me. Finally, the poem states clearly whence deliverance would come; not from myself, surely. I made a decision, molded by the one whose feet unerringly sought me in the dark.

Nearing Home

There is yet no final conclusion of my life's desert journey. There is, however, a kind of coda. I am completing this account in the small sunlit kitchen of my niece's apartment. Business has brought me from the cool, moist woods of a southern spring to the windy plains of western Texas. En route, the bluebonnets were wonderful.

Months have passed since I left my invisible desert. What am I finding in the spirit's border towns? Space, unaccustomed and compassionate perspectives, a fund of stillness, a capacity to wait, an entirely new ability to listen. Or have the hitherto tongue-tied simply learned to speak?

There are brief bouts of sadness because something precious has been left behind. But I have recently seen this friend and all is indeed well with her. Not only have I been freed myself from the necessity of grieving, but I have also somehow obtained freedom for her as well.

I sit quietly, breathing all the ruck and roil into God's tenderness and pity. Much is well; all will be well. There is no other end possible to the passionate, hungry search. I am reminded of the words of Janet Erskine Stuart (1922):

> Through the vastness of creation though your
> restless heart may roam . . .
> God is all that you can long for; God is all
> his creatures' home. (p. 323)

References

Chesterton, G. K. 1933. *St. Thomas Aquinas.* New York: Sheed and Ward.

Curtayne, A. 1942. *St. Catherine of Siena.* London: Sheed and Ward.

Garrigou-Lagrange, R. 1949. Interior Life and Conversation with God. In *The Three Ages of the Interior Life: Prelude to Eternal Life.* Vol. 1. Translated by Sister W. T. Doyle. St. Louis: B. Herder.

Hopkins, G. M. 1953. My Own Heart Let Me Have More Pity On. In *A Selection of His Poems and Prose,* edited by W. A. Gardner. Baltimore: Penguin Books.

Rilke, R. M. 1984. *Letters to a Young Poet.* 1st ed. Translated and with a foreword by Stephen Mitchell. New York: Random House.

Stuart, J. E. 1922. Spirit Seeking Light and Beauty. In *Life and Letters of Janet Erskine Stuart, Superior General of the Sacred Heart, 1857–1914,* by M. Monahan. London: Longmans, Green.

Thompson, F. 1917. *Lilius Regis.* In *Anthology of Catholic Poets,* edited by J. Kilmer. Garden City, N.Y.: Halycon House.

7 Gifts Given

SISTER LINDA

Sitting here in my front yard with the sun warming my back as I look up at my tree guardians, I am surrounded with the peace, joy, and strength that mark my life. This was not always so. Age and experience have brought a certain wisdom, a touchstone of reality.

Tomorrow's celebration of the Transfiguration carries a special message for me. Just a few days from my birthday, this feast calls me to reflect on the impermanence of life. I cannot capture it, nor can I remain forever in one moment of splendor. Life is about movement and change, about growth and development. I cannot pitch my tent or build my house here and stay forever. I must get up and be on with the journey of my life.

For more than a quarter of a century, I have chosen to live with my sisters in our religious community. Just out of high school, I came to live with this group of women, many of whom had been my teachers. I admired them, enjoyed them, respected them, and desired to become one with them. Naive and stubborn, I moved from "my" home to "their" convent.

My German ancestors would be very proud of the tenacious manner with which I found my ground in community and set down deep roots. I came to stay; weathering attempts to send me back, family calls to come home, and even some personal doubts, I persisted. My tenacity seemed far removed from what our spiritual reading called "Holy Perseverance," yet it worked.

My naivete did not serve me as well. Although young and inexperienced, I certainly did not want to appear so, nor to admit it. I was sixteen wanting to pass for forty. This caused more than a few problems.

Two major areas of personal lacunae were interpersonal relationships and psychosexual development. My first years in community were stormy. Jealousy, homesickness, anger, and fear alternated with moments of peace, calm, certitude. Classes both in the formation program and at college addressed many of these feelings. I learned on one level what was expected of me in this life I had determined to pursue. Although I felt attracted to and fond of some of my sisters, I quickly learned the convent term "PF," particular friendship. This caused some confusion, since I was unsure how people could relate as friends in a manner that was not particular. Wasn't this particular person my friend and this one not a friend? Years later in reading about homosexuality, I finally understood the implications of that term. No one directly addressed the issue or the concept of homosexuality. The term *lesbian* was not part of our vow-class vocabulary or of our psychology courses.

Now, a quarter century later, I recognize, name, and accept myself as a lesbian. I choose to remain a member of my religious community. I was called to this particular group at this particular moment in history for a reason. One section of our new constitutions speaks of us as prophetic women. I see myself as very much of a prophet among my own sisters.

My life, as the lives of many others, has been one of pain and growth, of a struggle for self-knowledge and self-acceptance. There is a strength and serenity that grows in me out of that stubborn core. Years of very public—for a community is not unlike a small town—and very private struggle brought me to the knowledge of myself as a lesbian. My naive self became involved with varying intensity with several women. Yet I denied the reality of my attraction to and affection for these women not because anyone said I was a lesbian, but because of some self-protective desire to ward off the truth.

My evident pain and unhappiness brought me to therapy not once, but many times. With the gentle care and persistent honesty of a group of therapists, I slowly learned to trust, to affirm my experience, feelings, and life. Tentatively I moved toward self-knowledge and self-acceptance. From dependence I grew to a more self-reliant independence. Surer and more secure in my own person, I have grown to desire and to act as a more interdependent member of our community. With self-care and self-love, I grow stronger and more open with my sisters. My self-acceptance is my first gift to them as well as my call to them to become more accepting of themselves. None of us measures up to the image of the perfect nun that we interiorized early in our formative process; yet each of us has special gifts with which we contribute to the building up of the whole body.

Another gift I bring to my community from my therapy and from my spiritual development is my firm choice for celibacy. Chastity was but briefly covered in our early study of the vows. No one seemed ready to tackle directly the reality of our own sexuality. We were not induced to make the destructive promise held out to earlier classes: never to touch another person again. What turmoil that has caused!

My teenage years read very like those of my friends; dances, parties, boys, curiosity. My story also included a more secret chapter on my attractions to women and the feelings they stirred in me.

When time for vows arrived, I was eager and ready. I sincerely committed my life to living out these vows, which I understood in a most embryonic form. Soon I was thrown into a teaching career and life in local convents, not exactly the picture I had from my formation years.

Vatican II launched a revolution that affected almost every aspect of my new life. After memorizing and regurgitating all the reasons why Latin would forever remain the language of the mass, within the year our liturgies were in English with the priest facing us. All around me were conversations indicating unrest: we were moving too slowly; the changes were too much; Sister X was spending too much time with Father Q; the vows had no meaning; the superiors should squelch this uproar. The tumult of those early years stirred the unrest within me. A couple of experiences with men and with women further confused the scene. Soon I began the round of therapists in search of clarity in my life.

Part of my identity, part of who I am, is my sexuality. Integrating the reality of my experiences and my feelings, I grew to see and to accept myself as a lesbian, a woman attracted on many levels to other women. As my confidence grew, I recognized the need to reevaluate my vowed commitment in this new light. Fearing a hasty foreclosure, I gave myself five years. During that time I concluded formal therapy; made an effort to meet many different lesbians; became aware of the existence of other lesbian religious; consulted regularly with my spiritual director on my new understanding of the vows; deepened friendships with both men and women; read voraciously about homosexuality, religious life, and women's spirituality; and fell in love.

Just before the ending of therapy, I had formally renewed my vows at a community feast. I promised myself that I would live with my growing understanding of renewed religious life and the vows as I understood them during this period of searching. Toward the end of the five years I spent an Advent retreat pondering all that I had heard and learned, experienced and felt. A deep, peaceful certitude that I belonged—to God, to this religious community, to myself—settled in my whole being. I lived in this serenity weighing the love of a woman who had asked me to leave and live with her. By the end of the week, I knew deeply, and could not deny, the call to live as a religious at this time in this community. I renewed my vows, once again publicly affirming my commitment to live poverty, obedience, and chastity. I also promised to spend the next five years deepening my bonds with the sisters of my congregation.

Thus my second gift to my community is my struggle for sexual identity integrated with my growing understanding of vowed chastity and my choice to live as a chaste lesbian religious. Contending with the notion that if one is lesbian she cannot then be celibate is difficult. Just being lesbian seems to assert a rampantly wild sexual life devoid of any ethical, moral, or spiritual principles. I choose to live my life in defiance of this notion; I choose to live as a caring, responsible, struggling, religious, sexual person.

The next gift I offer my community is honesty. Coming out is an act of honesty, a statement of my reality. Coming out, like most growth, is gradual and consistent. It is also surprising. One day you look out and there are no flowers in the garden; the next day you are greeted with a riot of color as just the right conditions merge for the flowers to open themselves. Coming out begins with self-honesty, looking at my actions, my feelings, my thoughts, my being and saying to myself, "Yes, this is who I am. I am a lesbian." It is not labeling or blaming; it is honest self-acceptance.

As with the flowers, the right conditions come together before self-revelation occurs. Honesty is not a club used to beat ourselves or others into acceptance. Honesty is sensitive acknowledgment and revelation of a truth. A certain degree of fear is present in any risk taking, but it is not debilitating or harmful when the conditions for coming out are present.

For myself I am open and honest with any of my sisters who ask me. I am also aware of those who appear at the fringes of my life with unspoken concerns, giving them opportunities to talk, to connect, to ask, to share. I continue my connections with gay and lesbian friends, invite them to my home, join them, and introduce them to other sisters. I encourage those who show an interest in and openness to ministry with gay and lesbian people. Because of my choice for religious life, I am especially aware of and attentive to the concerns of other gay and lesbian sisters, brothers, and priests. Coming out in so many different contexts and manners helps me to continue developing the gift of honesty that I share with my sisters.

As a lesbian religious, I also bring the blessing of friendship to my community. In my personal struggles, friendship has grown in value. I have suffered the painful loss of a friend who could not cope with me as a lesbian. I have enjoyed the beginnings of trust and connection with new friends. Standing very near me throughout my growth were both men and women. I know the deep love of three very special men in my life. The care and concern of the men in my original Dignity group supported me through the transitional five years to my recommitment to religious life. They listened, challenged, comforted, badgered, persisted, and loved.

Many women, students, former teachers, lesbians, couples, mothers, religious, have been integral to my life. Their friendship teaches me how to be a friend, how to acknowledge myself and still reach out to others. They have demonstrated integration, openness, confrontation, tender caring, anger, prayer, and wisdom.

These men and these women live lessons of friendship and love for me. They gift me and I return gifts of trust and tenderness. Because of my struggle and growth, I bring to my community warmth, joy, pain, concerns: the bases for friendship with them and with others. The open hand of a friend and the open heart of a lover is my gift to them. I am willing to take the risk of being a friend.

Two polarities constitute part of another gift to my sisters. In the past ten years I have seen myself as a dancer moving back and forth, around and round, with certain aspects of life that at times I have seen as dualities and now experience more often as dialectic facets. I dance between the individual and the community and between life and death. Jung once commented that he believed what the world needed for peace was enough people who could hold within themselves the tension of these polarities. My dance is one way I work toward peace.

Who am I as an individual person? Who are we as community? How do all our unique persons become one in unity? What role does solitude play in my life? What position does community hold for me? Often I find myself turning and moving to an inner rhythm. For a time I draw apart, dwell alone, feel the loneliness of life. The more introverted aspects of my being are nourished and refreshed in solitude and quiet. Then I plunge myself headlong into a round of community meetings, conversations with friends, classes, parties, prayer groups. The dance has shifted from a polarized, crack-the-whip furl to an intertwined pas de deux. Both the community and the individual are essential values. Both solitude and communal life are vital aspects of my personal call.

Another polar dance for me is with life and death, with resurrection and rebirth. I remember the time the Scripture invitation to choose life was given to me and I replied, "I can't do that right now. Will you do it for me until I am able to do it for myself?" That time of close consideration of death has passed for me; a time of life-choice is present. My gift to my sisters is to choose life, my life and life for my community. In a time of aging sisters and dwindling numbers, we are called to dance between the death of what we have known and loved and the life being lived into a new reality. Having danced my solo, I am ready to join the chorus line.

Although my generation was the age group torn apart by the Vietnam War, I knew personally no one who died in it. I have known well, however, more than a dozen friends who have died of AIDS. Currently four dear friends are struggling for their lives. We are partners in this dance with death and life. It is my hope in the resurrection and my belief in a new life that sustains me at this time when my friends and my community face this reality of death. I offer to both my gift of a hope that has no reasons.

Here once again is the lesson of the Transfiguration. For one brief moment with shining clarity the splendor and passion of Christ is unveiled. This is reality. Then the pain and strife or the unrelenting ordinariness of existence sets in. This, too, is reality. Neither is false. The Transfiguration was a glimpse meant to provide sustenance for the journey; it was not the whole tour.

Yes, my life as a lesbian religious is a treasure for me and for my community. Through my struggle for life, for self-knowledge, for identity, for love, I have grown richer. From the treasure house of my life, I bring to my religious community, to my sisters, to my friends, many gifts. I bring the courage to greet both life and death. I bring the embrace of solitude and community. I bring the strength to grow in self-acceptance. I bring a considered choice for our vowed life. I bring a knowledge of my own sexuality and a respect for that of others. I bring an honor for deep friendship with women and with men. Where your treasure is, there will your heart be. I bring my jewels to add to the priceless treasure of each of my sisters. With them, that is where my heart is at peace.

8 Speaking My Truth

EILEEN BRADY, RSM

My community, the New Hampshire Sisters of Mercy, Region II, has articulated a feminist vision of life based on the gospel and focused on those most in need. Religious women attempt to identify with the poor as one group of persons in need. The fact that many sisters come from families of poor immigrants, laborers, and farmers strengthens this identity with the poor. When religious women listen to the stories of those of us who are physically or mentally disabled in our communities, there is increased awareness of the best way to reach out to other persons in need of healing. When we listen to those among us who acknowledge being lesbian, we can become sensitive to those who are oppressed by society for being gay.

Hope in the spirit of religious communities led me to believe that speaking the truth can change the horrible reality of prejudice toward lesbians, a reality that keeps women silent for fear of losing jobs, friends, and family ties. It was in this belief that speaking my truth could help eradicate antigay prejudice that I contributed an article to the anthology *Lesbian Nuns: Breaking Silence* (Curb and Manahan 1985). I would like to share some feelings that I experienced before and since the book's publication.

Being part of the groundbreaking experience of *Lesbian Nuns*, while living in an environment of misunderstanding at best and hostility at worst, is difficult to describe. The backlash against civil-rights-seeking efforts of gay and lesbian groups makes it even more imperative for people of conscience to speak out.

I suppose I should be grateful (and I am) that I am still allowed to be a member of the New Hampshire Sisters of Mercy. Several attempted and successful purges of sisters have occurred in the United States during the pontificate of John Paul II when sisters have spoken out on controversial or political issues. It is to the credit of our community's leaders, some of whom did not agree with my decision to publish the article, that they did not seek to dismiss me, even though they were criticized by many people both within and outside the community. Our community allows individual sisters to take public stands in one's own name; even though this was an embarrassing public stance because of the bigotry that exists in society, respect for the freedom to take a stand prevailed.

It is a powerful experience to have membership threatened for saying who I am, for expressing in particular language the aspect of myself that is sexual, that is loving, that is spiritual. To say publicly that one is lesbian is different from taking a stand on justice issues. Not a matter of being considered right or wrong, liberal or conservative, naming one's sexual identity is connected with the right to exist. It is saying: "Here I am. You have helped me to grow in strength and confidence all these years. Now I can share this gift of my identity with you. I hope it helps you to understand your gay students, clients, parishioners, relatives, friends, and perhaps yourself."

The message, however, was received by the sisters and others in an atmosphere that is, for the most part, fearful, for our society perceives gay and lesbian persons as a danger to children and as persons whose expressions of love somehow threaten those outside the relationship. I tried to respond to as many letters, calls, and visits from persons in and out of the community as I could. Their feelings ranged from anger to bewilderment to joy. Most of the happy people did not write or call the community leadership, whereas those who were angry did not hesitate to contact them.

A very close friend refused to read the article altogether. Some friends were concerned that they would be vulnerable to accusations of being lesbian themselves not only because of their association with me, but also because of their being Sisters of Mercy. Other friends of every age and political stripe sent messages of support. Most of my friends who were my age (forty) or younger were the most supportive, encouraging, and even delighted about the article. Many had gay friends and relatives who had told them they were gay. My parents, who are intelligent, caring, faith-filled people, do not always love what I do (for example, publicizing my sexuality), but they always make their love for me very evident. My sister and only sibling has been one of my strongest supporters. During the publicity for the book she went into her workplace and announced that it was indeed *her* sister and wasn't it wonderful! My family did not bring me up to be lesbian; they brought me up to be honest about who I am.

Although individual members of the New Hampshire Sisters of Mercy are spread out all over the world, the majority live and work in New Hampshire and see one another quite often. I have been a member who has served on numerous committees, visited most of our members in their homes, and been elected to assemblies and chapter. While I have been on the "fringe" of some parts of society—having lived in low-income housing, gone to jail for civil disobedience, and demonstrated for peace issues—I have never been a "fringe" member of the Sisters of Mercy. I was not surprised that sisters would be not only some of my severest critics, but also my greatest supporters.

We women religious have struggled to be able to discuss *any* kind of sexuality, especially a type of sexuality that many in society still consider aberrant. Sexuality was often considered a problem to be solved, a subject to be joked about, something too personal to be shared in open discussion. While we broadened some expressions of prayer from "Jesus-and-me" to global consciousness and extended our ministry from "my classroom" to "the future of humankind," discussion of who we are sexually remained as discreet as Kotex in a brown paper bag. It would not matter if there were not so many persons suffering from the misunderstanding and fear of sexuality in general and homosexuality in particular. Although individuals and small groups have shared informal discussions on sex, rarely in a community setting have we discussed any aspect of sexuality. Only seventeen members attended a 1983 workshop presented by Jeannine Gramick and Bob Nugent on homosexuality, for example, and we have yet to have the community address the complex issues of abortion and birth control, though differing views on these issues are affecting the Roman Catholic church and the faith of women greatly.

North American women religious have attempted to be "one with" those who are economically, ethnically, and racially diverse from the middle-class white heterosexual majority. Gay and lesbian persons have often been in the forefront (discreetly, of course) of movements for equality and peace, often because of our own identification with the experience of those being excluded. Many lesbians and gay men are working for justice issues—for example, peace in Central America. Judith McDaniel expresses beautifully in her book *Sanctuary* (1987) the connections between her being a lesbian and being one with the people of Nicaragua, with whom she risked her life as a Witness for Peace.

The fact that I am still a Sister of Mercy of New Hampshire is due in part to my growth in feminist spirituality in general and in part to the integrity of my community in particular. My use of the word *integrity* here reflects the definition: "the avoidance of deception, expediency, artificiality, or shallowness of any kind; the quality of having spiritual wholeness, an organic unity." Although many sisters and others hailed the article I wrote as "courageous," I wrote very little that was risk taking when all is said and done. I was well aware of the level of publicity the book would receive and wrote honestly, yet cautiously, more cautiously than the women whose books and articles brought me from severe depression to more confident trust in myself, my sisters, family, friends, and God.

From the time I was in college, I was delighted to spend hours and hours in the company of other women. I thought there was something wrong with me, but thought it had something to do with receiving a vocation. How handy it was that I did not crave a man to have and hold. These feelings of certainty and satisfaction rapidly disappeared when I realized that I did want and need affection, but from a different source. Reconciling the religious life with normal sexual feelings was a ten-year process in which I read voraciously until I read myself into the women's movement. Then there was light.

And then there was the day when two thirteen-year-old girls confronted me on the sidewalk of a battered urban New Hampshire neighborhood. One of them said, "Paula's mother says you're a lezzie. Are you?"

"No," I responded aloud to them, but "Yes," I acknowledged to myself.

Since there was no one I trusted with this information, I retreated to my books. From Kate Millett's *Sexual Politics* (1970) to Judith McDaniel's *Sanctuary* (1987) to Janice Raymond's *A Passion for Friends* (1987), women have shared powerfully with us and we, women religious, have reaped the benefits.

Our own experience as women religious and the way we love are tremendous gifts to share with other women not in religious communities. Our struggles, our bonds, our spiritual heritage, and our longtime connections are precious and yearned-for by many women. May the sharing, already begun, continue and deepen.

References

Curb, R., and Manahan, N. 1985. *Lesbian Nuns: Breaking Silence.* Tallahassee: Naiad Press.

McDaniel, J. 1987. *Sanctuary.* Boston: Beacon Press.

Millett, K. 1970. *Sexual Politics.* Garden City, N.Y.: Doubleday.

Raymond, J. 1987. *A Passion for Friends.* Boston: Beacon.

9 The Mirror Child

SISTER VICKIE

I am a lesbian and I am a nun. The realization of these two identities has only coalesced in my forties. The twenties and thirties were like the terrible twos and the terrific threes. The complementarity of my religious commitment with the realization of my sexual preference took almost twenty-five years to evolve. I am now in my mid-forties and am experiencing perhaps for the first time a healthy realization of who I am.

I grew up in what I considered to be a very normal family. I never felt that there was any dysfunctional component to my upbringing. Today when everyone is looking to their early life for the dysfunctional areas that have caused adult addiction or emotional immaturity, I can only reflect back and find nothing but what I consider a rather ordinary and healthy early life.

I entered my religious community when I was nineteen, one year after graduating from a high school taught by the sisters. I had dated in high school and the year after. I enjoyed male company but never really felt fulfilled in relational experiences with men. I always wanted to have children; I loved little ones and I knew that I would be a teacher. When the extended family would get together for holidays or celebrations, I was always happiest in the midst of the younger kids, entertaining them and enjoying myself thoroughly. I decided to enter my religious community after experiencing little satisfaction or sense of belonging in a relationship with a young man who was seriously considering a permanent commitment with me. I was positive that I did not wish such a permanent commitment with this man, although I felt unsure about a religious commitment. At age nineteen I was impressionable and idealistic and wanted desperately to do something different with my life, to be special and unique. As a result, I entered religious life and learned about living in an apostolic community dedicated to teaching. I studied the theology of commitment, and after the normal period of preparation took first vows and began my studies. I was twenty-one, the presumed age of making mature decisions, the legal age for voting and drinking. But I was far from being an autonomous person.

My years in religious formation did very little to enhance my self-image and may have left it a little tainted. Those years of introspective navel gazing focused on developing the self as a religious person with little depth or quality in the area of personal maturity. Maturity was subtly defined as the ability to remain within the confines of the hallowed walls; it was fostered by learning the expectations of authority figures and conformity to the rules, either written or unwritten. There were benefits to such an arrangement: I learned how to expect and provide for the finer things in life, how to be a perfect lady, how to cultivate the right kinds of relationships with the most influential people, and how to survive and survive well. That learning facilitated my growth and maturity in a unique way.

The Terrible Twenties

I liken my twenties to the terrible twos. Children in this developmental stage exhibit some of the earmark tendencies of my twenties. At age two, children are ready to leave the maternal nest, strike out on their own, test the waters, investigate the possibilities, and ultimately learn that there are limitations and restrictions to life for everyone. My twenties were no different from those terrible twos, except, of course, that I was twenty years older.

My first apostolic assignment was in a region of the country more than a thousand miles from anything I considered familiar.

For all practical purposes, it could have been the Wild West. I dutifully accepted my first assignment, packed my bags, and flew to my new home. I felt confident about my ability to teach since I had been told that I was a good teacher. I knew I could adjust to a new living arrangement since I had successfully accomplished that feat a number of times before. I could get along with the people in the school and parish community since I was endowed with a pleasant and pleasing personality. What I did not bargain for and was not prepared to experience was the feeling of loneliness and insignificance that accompanied my first assignment.

I invested myself heavily in my work; it was good therapy since it could occupy hours of my time. I invested in making my community a pleasant living situation, planned parties, made people laugh, and was generally accepted as a good religious within the local community. I should have felt great, but I did not. There was a certain emptiness, a longing for more that kept gnawing away at me. I tried running away from my feelings at first. I learned that alcohol can afford one of the quickest but least complete escapes from reality. I never considered myself an alcoholic, and I rarely drink alcohol today, but I was desperately looking for something or someone to relieve the pain I was feeling deep inside.

My first sexual relationship with another woman happened at that time. Feeling vulnerable, unhappy, unfulfilled, confused, and lonely, I had a huge supply of kindling wood for a fire that was about to rage in my life. Another sister in the local community whom I did not know well took a liking to me. She was very solicitous, a good listener, older, and, I thought, wiser; her presence brought a certain lightness to my heart. I thought of her as a very good friend. One night all my terrible-two tendencies were plunged into overdrive. It happened so naturally: a simple embrace, a kind word, a feeling of caring. I love how I felt with her. For the first time I felt like a real person; a certain surge of energy and life filled my body. I wanted to explore, to experiment, to live life to the fullest; and for a number of years I did just that. My relationship with her grew and flourished; I was in love in a way that I never knew was possible. I cared deeply, passionately, and longingly for this one person who was fulfilling my need to be loved.

Meanwhile, my relationship with the other members of the local community began to deteriorate. Although I tried to rationalize their sentiments and gestures of disapproval, I knew that I was falling farther away from everyone else and was becoming closed in my overall ability to care for other people. Even my relationship with my own family was becoming strained. My guilt drive was working overtime. What began as such a wonderful and inspiring experience was slowly disintegrating into a love-hate relationship. My terrible twos were evolving and I was slowly moving into another stage of maturity.

I reflect back on these years with thanksgiving. I learned how to love; I experienced a deep and abiding feeling for one other human being, which I had never felt in my life. If the time and circumstances were different, perhaps I would never have learned to love. I consider this experience a gift. I wonder what I would be like if the chance to love so profoundly had not happened. My spiritual directors and counselors tried to convince me that as a religious the feeling of need I was experiencing could be fulfilled through prayer and through a deep and abiding relationship with Jesus. Locating that Jesus in prayer was an awesome expenditure of my energy at age twenty, and I was frustrated and uncertain of his personhood and existence in my life.

I did not consider my relationship with this woman abnormal; I did, however, have some grave questions about how the relationship could be maintained along with our religious commitments. For many, the obvious concern is chastity, but my major concern was community. Living a life dedicated to others in community for the sake of the ministry seemed to me incongruous with living a life in seclusion with one other sister. I could not justify my activity and my need for fulfillment within my community commitment to my sisters. Eventually I agreed to move to another mission a thousand miles away; the geographical change facilitated the gradual breaking of the relationship. As time passed and distance prevailed, I began to grieve for what had happened to me and to hate the sister for what I considered a deprivation of my freedom to participate fully in community. Only after much prayer and many years of anger and hurt could I be reconciled with the fact that I needed someone and she fulfilled that need for me.

Some writing today focuses on the immature longings of young women who entered religious life in the 1960s. Much can be said about those not yet matured feelings of love that I began to feel only before I entered my community, those feelings that were relegated to the back burner for many years but could not be totally extinguished. Many women who entered religious life in the late 1960s were just beginning to experience their sexuality. The early years of training attempted to contain those feelings in a structure that was being questioned and changed. As a result, there are many women religious whose need to love sexually, passionately, and longingly has been sublimated and who may never know what it means to love and be loved. I believe that my own sublimation and my eventual awakening combined to make me a warm, loving, and concerned woman, eager to help others find love and fulfillment in the life-style they have chosen.

The Terrific Thirties

At thirty, I was alive in a new way, energized by some undefined drive to achieve, and eager to invest in a special apostolic ministry. I liken this period to the threes because the child at three is more secure, ready for adventure, and unafraid of any obstacles in the path. I felt like a woman ready to give birth with all the anxiety and fears birth entails, but also with all the joy and energy birth requires.

I asked for and received an assignment at a small inner city school that was constantly struggling to stay alive. I spent almost a decade of my life immersed in this difficult ministry. I worked very diligently, was tired and frustrated at times, but was so exhilarated by the success of my efforts that I was willing to invest anything to keep this dream alive. As a result, my defenses were weakened; my needs, which I had dutifully sublimated to my work, were beginning to cry out for attention; and I was burnt out to a degree that threatened personal destruction.

This was a time of dependence; everyone and everything seemed dependent on me for its very existence. My co-workers looked to me for help, the children and their parents turned to me for assistance, my family was calling on me for support, my community was relying on my talents and gifts and vision; I was needed by all, or so I thought. It seemed as though I shared in those divine attributes of omnipresence and omniscience. I felt needed and in control but never really loved. Instead, I began to feel used. That hated feeling made me vulnerable and able to be easily hurt.

I was seeking someone who confirmed my sense of worth. In my vulnerability I succumbed to the advances of a sister from another community. We had worked together for a number of years; she knew me well and was also solicitous of my needs. After two days of a sexual relationship I decided that to repeat any sexual behavior would be deadening for both of us. My desire to fulfill everyone's needs was carried too far, and I was deeply angry with myself for losing control, the very thing I had prided myself on possessing. The realization of the loss of control in my life as a whole led me to consult a psychiatrist, a nondirective woman who helped me isolate my fears about myself and look at myself in a healthy way.

For the first time ever, I admitted that I was a lesbian, although I did not use the word at the time. I could acknowledge only that my sexual preference was for individuals of my own gender, and that men did not pose a sexual attraction for me. Although I loved to be with men and found them exciting and interesting, I never felt sexually attracted to them. A friend once told me that I could get men to do anything, that they were like putty in my hands, that my manner and small size made them feel virile, and that I could manipulate them for my own purposes. She was right. I thought of all men as my big brothers; I loved them deeply but not sexually. Women, on the other hand, were attractive to me sexually. Many times I had wondered about some strong feelings for different women I worked with but never realized that there was an unacknowledged and unaccepted dynamic within me. Working with the psychiatrist, I became aware of my inner strength to love and my need to be loved. I realized that my protective barrier could be dropped and that I could learn to love as a sexual being because I understood what sexuality meant. Although somewhat concerned about being hurt again, I was willing to reach out to others in a less restrictive manner and to try to really love again. So ended my terrific thirties.

The Fantastic Forties

A wise woman once told me that the decade of the forties was a fantastic period of one's life. I was fearfully approaching thirty at the time and thought that getting old was one of the worst things we were asked to accept. Now in the decade of my forties, I believe the woman was right.

I started this decade thinking about a career change preceded by a year or two of professional enrichment. My community suggested that I take a sabbatical. Instead of a mid-life renewal program in which one returns home looking and acting new because of an apparent biological and psychological makeover, I opted to start a masters program at a state university. I could live in one of our community houses close to campus and commute daily for classes. That arrangement afforded me the use of a car and a great deal of freedom at this juncture in my life.

I encountered a situation with one of the female professors that nearly left me devastated. In an independent study course, I met with this professor privately on a weekly basis. At first I did not mind the arrangement at all; I received much individual attention, a great deal of affirmation, and I felt good about myself. After about six sessions I began to feel something deep inside that I could hardly believe; I was falling in love with this woman. I do not know if she had any sexual feelings for me, although I definitely think that the emotional attraction was not one-sided. I adored her; she was bright, articulate, challenging, alive—in fact all the things I wanted to recapture at that moment in my own life. She thought I was intellectually stimulating, committed, hungry for knowledge, and she was in awe of my religious background. The combination of these mutually admiring sentiments left me weak and I began to dread our weekly meetings. I thought God was playing a very ugly trick on me; just when I finally felt that my life was beginning to take on some semblance of normalcy, I found myself in love with this woman.

This time I did something different; I thought and prayed before I acted. This time I waited patiently for my heart to catch up to my head; this time I put things in perspective. I did not do this alone; luckily I found some friends who were willing to struggle with me through these difficult times. I discovered a new part of me that can discern and decide on actual fact and not just on feeling. I was in a new and better space.

In the final analysis, I learned more about myself. I discovered the self that can love passionately, sexually, and even intimately, but not genitally. I found the self that can reach out to other women in warmth, concern, and anticipation without needing to feel genitally fulfilled in the process. I learned that I have a potential for loving other persons that is eager to be tapped and even willing to be hurt. I came to realize that, as a lesbian and as a nun, I have two powerful energies for loving that can make a difference not only in my life, but in the lives of the many and varied people I touch daily. I have been gifted with a potential for loving that hungers for fulfillment not in an isolated relationship with one other human being, but in the relational expression of caring that has become part of the very core of my being.

My reflections on the experiences of my twenties, thirties, and forties are personal stepping stones that mark my journey to find fulfillment. Fulfillment is a difficult thing to describe to another; but one feels when it is there and when it is missing. I have found deep fulfillment in my religious commitment and my sexual preference. I have come to the realization that genital expressions of caring are not part of my personal understanding of what it means to live a lifelong commitment in a religious community. Sexual needs and feelings of love must be tempered by my desire to live out my commitment within community. I do not believe that I, as a religious celibate living in community, have the option for genital sexual expression. We are called to live out a sexually loving life that exposes us to many challenges in expressing that love. The challenge is not to live austerely, but rather to live fully, to embrace our humanness as giftedness, and to accept our limitations as invitations for growth.

I look forward to the fabulous fifties with eager anticipation of new revelations of who am I and how I can accept the graces that my God has waiting along the path.

10 Patient Weavers

MARY LOUISE ST. JOHN, OSB

Fragile as a spider's web
Hanging in space
Between tall grasses,
It is torn again and again.
A passing dog
Or simply the wind can do it.
Several times a day
I gather myself together
And spin it again.

Spiders are patient weavers.
They never give up.
And who knows
What keeps them at it?
Hunger, no doubt,
And hope.

May Sarton, "Love"

One must be a patient weaver if one is to spin that delicate, intricate web of wonder called "women loving women." And if one is a woman religious in a homophobic church, my perception of today's institutional church, one must be even more determined in the pursuit of weaving a pattern of integrity and truth. I know only too well how weary one can become with the weaving, but I am convinced that the energy expended is well spent in view of the beauty of the creation.

From the time that I was a very young child, I knew I loved differently and that my most nourishing bonds were with women. I had no name for what I was experiencing, but I was certain that such feelings were deep and real, and that they were growing only stronger as I grew older. Through the years, I struggled with the guilt that made me think I was less than God wanted me to be because of the way I loved. When I entered religious life at the age of twenty-six, I knew I wanted my life to be centered in the Godness who had created me, but I felt there was a hidden, secret part of me that could never become one with the offering I sought to make. And so it was, until I reached my thirties.

At that time, the supportive, reflective, prayerful environment of my community life led me to an inner openness that allowed me, finally, to embrace the fullness of my personhood as it had been fashioned by God. I thought that this self-acceptance would be enough to sustain me and that I would now live quietly with my newfound peacefulness. At the age of forty-one, however, I fell deeply in love and was wonderfully loved in return. This gift of a vibrant, passionate, life-giving love drew me to deeper levels of my being as well as to a more profound experience of the Godness within. With this gift have come moments of gentle joy and purifying pain, both of which have led me to new insights. The delights and decisions that have been an outgrowth of this particularly precious love relationship have brought me home to my true self and deepened my sense of responsibility toward those who, like myself, are searching for the truth that links their God-life and their life of loving, which, I propose, cannot be separated. It is the heart of these insights that I wish to share in this chapter.

The first insight is that, for the woman religious, the tearing of this delicate web of love between women can be caused by a multitude of circumstances. One of these is a community vision that sees the celibate as being asexual, a sorry state that would eliminate the need for a vow of chastity altogether. The sadness of this situation is that the woman religious never feels safe enough in this environment to explore the meaning of her sexuality, whether heterosexual or homosexual. Without such freedom, she may become locked into a false understanding of her personhood, experiencing interior and exterior conflict that drains her of energy and prevents her from reaching out to others in a healthy manner. One hopes that religious communities are growing in their ability to enable their members to become who they are in the safety of an open, loving environment. The following passages from *Call to Life*, the norms of life and governance for a number of Benedictine monasteries in North America, propose a style of search that is honest and relatively open-ended. They leave room for the reality that the living out of celibacy, like the living out of poverty and obedience, is a lifetime process that one learns in a loving atmosphere:

> Through fidelity to her vow of *conversion* through the monastic way of life, the Benedictine woman acquires that sensitivity to God's presence in herself, in others, and in the created world which helps her to *grow in openness.* . . . This *conversion becomes a reality* in the life of a monastic through her *dedication to rebirth, growth, and final maturity* in union with Christ. In such a life, the primary aim of the Benedictine vocation "to seek God" . . . is realized.

> The monastic way presupposes commitment to consecrated celibacy and poverty. By sharing deeply on human and spiritual levels, the members of the cenobitic community sustain one another in celibate love. The Benedictine way provides a form of community life in which members can *maintain supportive* and *loving relationships over a long period of time* in an atmosphere of *faith, affirmation and healing.* ("The Vowed Life," p. 12; emphasis mine)

> *The newcomer must discover her need for intimacy* and *determine* whether it is compatible with the celibate life. She must have *realistic expectations of celibate community life* and be able to face the fact that chaste love and faithful attention to God in prayer will sometimes seem to demand more of her than they immediately give back in satisfaction and assurance. At the same time, she must *consider* if she is *capable of expressing the degree of love and friendship that is essential to both personal growth and community life.* ("Formation," p. 26; emphasis mine)

As I repeat these words from *Call to Life*, I am deeply aware of their "size" and implications. I know only too well that to relate to them honestly involves a certain struggle, but I believe we need people who say to us, "It's all right to struggle." Perhaps the struggle will empower us to lay down guilt, whether self-imposed or imposed by others, and take up responsibility for who we are and how we behave. Too often, guilt is the great manipulator in our lives, even to the point of paralyzing us. When we learn to dance without demons, we strip them of their power to be a death force in our lives. For the lesbian woman religious living in a community that sees all religious as asexual, guilt can play havoc with her humanity; it can tear asunder that fine web of love she seeks to spin. In such an atmosphere, how will she ever learn that the core of celibacy has to do with loving freely and nonpossessively, loving with open hands and expanding heart?

A second insight discloses a danger to the delicate web of love for lesbian women religious: the often disproportionate emphasis given to the genital expression of love in general can be a trap. This is not to negate the value of the physical/genital aspect of loving, but rather to place it in perspective. If a person becomes fixated on this aspect of lesbian loving, there is the danger that she will never discover the deep riches of what I term "lesbian spirituality." To be confined to a closed physical/genital understanding of lesbian love is to be in touch with only the tip of this vast iceberg, which reaches to mighty depths. In my view, we lesbian religious have treasured gifts to bring to one another, to the church, and to the world, once we tap into the spiritual and emotional wealth of our woman-love. Among these gifts are a sensitivity and a tenderness that gather in the groaning world to be held, healed, and hallowed. Such tenderness ventures forth in vulnerability to be one with all who are born of the blessed womb of God. Could it be that our love for other women, our "affectional preference" (Lewis 1979, 11),[1] is capable of empowering us to be great lovers in community? Could it be that this love, lived well and honestly, in the context of community, could energize us to be movers and shakers in relation to community concerns involving justice, nonviolence, and peace? Having had a taste of oppression ourselves, we can readily relate to such issues with strong conviction and personal commitment. Let us at least allow ourselves to pursue this possibility.

I am not naive enough to say that such gifts are always present or always lived out. I would venture to say that often they are not. This is because fear and lack of freedom, both personal and communal, have foreclosed the development of these creative forces. I am also aware that one's own personal development, interpersonal relations, and prayer life require tremendous amounts of energy and openness and that all of these evolve interdependently over long periods of time. These areas of growth are the soil from which the gifts of compassion and constant love spring.

I maintain that love is the greatest offering that we lesbian religious have to bring to the church. There is no doubt that we attempt to make this offering through a humanity that struggles to become free under adverse social and ecclesial circumstances. It is my hope that more and more of us may gather the courage and be given the support to bring forth our gifts in joy.

Daily I ask myself how I am being a patient weaver as I attempt to create this beautiful web called woman-love. How am I reaching out and networking with others who share this common bond of being women who love women? Over the past several years, my involvement with other lesbians who are seeking to discover and deepen their selfhood has expanded greatly. Initially, I shared with my prioress the path that my journey home to my true self had taken. We dialoged about where the future journey might take me and how I could continue to grow in my unfolding recognition of the gift God has bestowed on me by creating me as I am. She sent me forth with her blessing to grow in wisdom and the wonder of loving. Now, I realize that this is not, and will not be, the experience of many women religious who go to their superiors with the "good news" that they are lesbian. From that time to this, I have shared with a number of my sisters in community what my "affectional preference" is and how this influences my search for God, as well as my search for true and tender human relationships. To this point they, too, have been exceptionally open and loving.

Having had such affirming experiences within my community circle, I have felt strong enough to push the boundaries a little farther. I became a member of an organization called Conference for Catholic Lesbians (CCL); wrote an article about my own adventure of "coming out" that appeared in their quarterly publication, *Images;* offered to be a contact person for my locale; and began thinking with CCL about ways to reach out to other lesbian women religious who might be interested in networking. On a local level, I have met with the vicar for religious, who happens to be a woman, to discuss possible channels for spreading the word that there is interest in initiating a local support group for lesbian religious. She and I also discussed possibilities for education on this topic for religious communities in the area. The vicar meets regularly with the superiors of the four major communities in my locale and has agreed to "plant the seed" of expanded understanding by telling them of our conversation. I am also contacting administrators of various spirituality centers in the area hoping that they may be a channel of information for the religious whom they serve, as well as a source for education for those in spiritual direction concerning the topic of homosexuality and the spiritual life. It is my hope that such contacts will open up pathways for those who are trying to bring integrity to their lives as lesbian women religious, expanding the possibilities for exploring the issues of identity, self-esteem, and intimacy.

In these ways, I am attempting to weave a "web" that can withstand the winds of adversity. You may ask what keeps me spinning. I can only reply from the deepest source of my own integrity, which is the Godness within. I believe that living a vowed, celibate life does not exempt me from becoming as fully human as possible. This endeavor necessarily involves searching out the processes of my sexuality, which happens to be lesbian in orientation. My search for longlasting, God-centered relationships may be a little more challenging than the average, but I am convinced that these are possible in my life. Because the living out of my sexuality has been under more social and personal stress than that of heterosexuals, perhaps I have had to be more conscious of my choices and their consequences. Perhaps my awareness of what loving means and involves has had to be more highly developed in order for me to remain a healthy individual. Over the years, I have been encouraged to continue my spinning when I would come upon the works of such boundary-stretching thinkers as Adrienne Rich and Isabel Carter Heyward who, themselves, claim and celebrate their lesbianism. Through their writings, I have been enriched and more fully freed for loving.

At this time in my life, it is Heyward (1984) who articulates best what it means to truly take the responsibility of relationship seriously. The following are powerful statements on this subject:

Sexual lovers and good friends know that the most compelling relationships demand hard work, patience, and a willingness to endure tensions and anxiety in creating mutually empowering bonds. For this reason loving involves *commitment*. We are not automatic lovers of self, others, world or God. Love does not just happen. We are not love machines, puppets on the strings of a deity called "love." Love is a choice—not simply, or necessarily, a rational choice, but rather a willingness to be present to others without pretense or guile. Love is a conversion to humanity—a willingness to participate with others in the healing of a broken world and broken lives. Love is the choice to experience life as a member of the human family, a partner in the dance of life, rather than as an alien in the world or as a deity above the world, aloof and apart from human flesh. (pp. 186–87)

To say I love you is to say that you are not mine, but rather your own.
To love you is to advocate your rights, your space, your self, and to struggle with you, rather than against you, in your learning to claim your power in the world.
To love you is to make love to you, with you, whether in an exchange of glances heavy with existence, in the passing of a peace we mean, in our common work or play, in our struggle for social justice, or in the ecstasy and tenderness of intimate embrace that we believe is just and right for us—and for others in the world.
To love you is to be pushed by a power/God both terrifying and comforting, to touch and be touched by you. To love you is to sing with you, cry with you, pray with you, and act with you to re-create the world.
To say "I love you" means—let the revolution begin!
God bless the revolution! Amen. (p. 93)

To my mind, these wise words have much to say about lesbian loving as it can be lived out in the context of celibate commitment.

It is my contention that when a woman feels she must conceal her true sexual/affective identity in religious community, it is even more difficult for her to live her vowed commitment to celibacy. Under the stress of such "secrecy," the love energy that flows through her cannot easily be channeled to healthy, creative outlets that can serve to transform her as well as society. When the lesbian religious gives responsible expression to the truth of who she is, I believe her vow of celibacy can be revitalized, contrary to common belief that such expression will undermine her celibate commitment.

This chapter is not a work that determines definitions. Rather, it is more a "perhaps" paper: *perhaps* this is the meaning of such and such an experience; *perhaps* we could think about such and such an issue in these terms; *perhaps* our vision can be stretched to search new horizons. Ultimately, I hope that the thoughts I have shared will be a challenge to continue the conversation, a call to consider on a personal and communal level such questions as: Is there such a thing as lesbian spirituality? What are the gifts that lesbian religious have to bring to community life and to the church? How can we create an environment in which lesbian religious can be open and affirmed in the totality of their personhood?

As we lesbian religious address these questions, we ask for patience to continue weaving the fine and fragile web of women loving women, for empowerment to transform unjust situations, and for constancy of prayer to sustain us in our search for integrity and truth.

Note

1. The author uses the term "affectional preference" rather than "sexual orientation" in reference to lesbian relationships in an attempt to broaden understanding of such relationships beyond the sexual/genital aspect.

References

Heyward, Isabel Carter. 1984. *Our Passion for Justice: Images of Power, Sexuality and Liberation.* New York: Pilgrim Press.

Lewis, Sasha Gregory. 1979. *Sunday's Women: Lesbian Life Today.* Boston: Beacon Press.

Sarton, May. 1980. "Love." In *Halfway to Silence.* New York: Norton, p. 43.

11 A Priest Forever

WILLIAM HART McNICHOLS, SJ

No one takes this honor on himself, but each one is called by God.

Hebrews 5:4

The Letter to the Hebrews has always attracted me. It is a contemplative school of the priesthood anchored solidly in Jesus, which both cautioned and soothed me during the time of preparation for ordination. There is a rhythm and eloquence in the writing of this exhortation that is almost liturgical in its sonorous tone. Throughout the letter we are taken on a meditative tour of the faith of our biblical ancestors, yet the author pleads with us insistently to see that Christ's priesthood transcends the Levitical priesthood. One prays readily with this elegant, poignant letter as it paints a graphic and humbling portrait of the true priesthood. I have chosen some especially vivid words from the Letter to the Hebrews, to discover a possible meaning for the vocation of a gay priest.

I knew I was a priest around the age of five, not too much earlier than the time I began to experience a glimmer of my given sexual orientation. Perhaps one is born a priest. This seems true to me, in the same way one is born with healing gifts, athletic gifts, artistic gifts, leadership, or the blossoming of the inner staff of the shepherd. Certainly there is a discipline and training that must follow, but I don't believe one can apprehend a gift or nature. I could sense the priesthood within me as one senses one's own peculiar spirit, family, ethnic culture, or environmental surroundings. It was as though I had an internal portrait sketched within as an outline, which over the years would evolve and appear more clearly drawn. I never had the sense of choosing the priesthood, or choosing my family, or my sexuality, or "artistic" spirit. These were all placed within me, given to me, and I am to continue to consent, in a kind of Marian spirit, to follow the appearance of this multidimensional vocation. I said yes long before I understood the actual forms of the priesthood.

I was continually surprised by some of the priests I encountered in my elementary and high school years because many seemed so rigid, angry, and ashamed—broken in a devastating sense. Something of their humanity had been maimed or destroyed. I saw this not critically, but as an abuse and as a warning for myself. How did this destruction happen? How did one avoid the dangerous pitfalls? How could one love and serve a church structure that reduced so many of its priests to service in fear, to a kind of macabre cloning, to life moving under the heavy yoke of the lockstep? These men spoke of those in positions of power with a humiliated kind of subservient fear. The men who became priests for the title, the prestige, and the power obtained exactly that and nothing more. The real power, which is spiritual, was missing. It was as though these people had a kind of life, but little spiritual life. The ones who retained some semblance of humanity and spirit paid dearly by being broken, either through their own weaknesses or through some institutional humiliation, or something worst of all, through the mauling of the "people of God."

I grew to love priests very much. Their suffering was transparent to me. I saw little real love or gentleness coming into their lives, and very little contemplative time alone or inner support. I felt a secret brotherhood with them, even as a child, and mused darkly on what appeared to be the cost of the priesthood of Jesus: one must be like the broken and battered priests in order to have credibility. One must have some kind of visible wound or imposed status as an outcast to slip through the narrow door as a shepherd. And yet one must not trumpet even this weakness as a key to the reign of God but remain with the publican in the vestibule, conscious of the free gift of grace, beating one's breast for the many ways we are wont to judge. But what of prophetic action and voice? What of the priest who overturned the temple tables? All of these questions and images were swirling around within me as I followed the lives of priests, from afar, hidden in the garment of childhood.

> He too lives in the limitations of weakness. That is why he has to make sin offerings for himself as well as for the people.
>
> Hebrews 5:3

There is a sacred and unique nature to each individual's priesthood, which I believe takes years of ascension and descension into the world of Scripture, prayer, and tradition of the living and "triumphant" or transcendent community of the church to uncover. Priesthood has not been a separate role or job to me, as much as some try to make it so. In no way is it a profession or position I can shed at the end of a day. In no way is it an outfit or persona or bearing I can put on or take off physically. For me it corresponds more to the ancient image of the interior sacramental seal on the soul. For me it is more like motherhood or fatherhood, which one cannot shed.

Knowing I am also gay is a component of the priesthood formed for me by Jesus, which continues to reveal its character and meaning. For me personally, it would be no more difficult to balance or to integrate being gay and priest than being a priest and artist, or priest and teacher, or priest and retreat director. Most of the difficulty comes from without, in the relentless violence and persecution of religions and societies. None of this, I believe, is from Jesus himself. From him comes the wounding of the call and the continued wounding of humility to keep the call alive. From him comes an accountability of his way of love and strength, and the mission to dress and heal the wounds of all those broken like myself. I am simply stating a kind of vision of the priesthood that may also be found in other Eastern religious traditions; if one does not find suffering in oneself, then one must seek it out to be an authentic spiritual being. To be a recognized homosexual in this and many cultures is to bear a stigma and a weakness. Just by telling the truth of who I am gives me a chance to bear the outcast status required for the knowledge of the secrets of God's reign. My duty is not to sit in ceremonial pride with that status, but to share my real weaknesses with people in a communion of those also stigmatized.

Although he was a son, he learned to obey through suffering.

Hebrews 5:8

Over and over it is apparent to me, through years of immersion in the lives of the saints, that God is a God of vibrant and shocking variety. When one is touched by God, one does not become a clone or a martinet, but painfully unique. These saints, it seems to me, were molded and fired in a crucible by the very church they were inspired to revive. The church is often in the position of testing the authenticity of individuals by their witness and mirror image of the Gospels. I often wonder just how difficult this is for those who are in positions of power. I wonder what they feel and think and suffer, especially if they move against their knowledge of Christ and the Gospels.

Priesthood today is sadly a most explosive and painful subject. More and more the consciences of observant Christians are awakening to see the discriminatory policy of a strictly male priesthood. This policy seeks to keep women, who are already carrying on the work of the priesthood of Jesus, from being officially ordained in the institutional church. And no one has to be reminded of the treatment of gays and lesbians in the Catholic church since we are still bleeding from the bludgeoning pastoral letter issued, ironically, on All Hallow's Eve.

At this particular period in history I grieve for the loss of joy and trust felt during the time following the spring of the Second Vatican Council. What has been poured into Catholicism again, and had been largely and mercifully absent for almost twenty years, is a palpable sense of fear. People fear the hierarchy again. They fear the vigilante terrorist groups who sell souls to authorities in the name of orthodoxy. They fear again even the word *church*.

They are backing away again, unable to expose their struggles and real need of healing for fear of violence. The fear is real. Once again to be gay or lesbian, or a host of other unwanted categories, is to fear attack or molestation from within and without the church. One longs to feel safe inside the flock, guarded by the shepherds; but suddenly, as in some commercial horror film, the roles are perversely turned and the shepherds and the flock may be the very agents of one's betrayal and murder. This calls up Ezekiel's nightmare vision of the scattering shepherds in the prophecy of chapter thirty-four.

Suffering comes at times from feeling alienated in "both worlds." I am often saddened and discouraged by seeing the blatantly reductive elements in the gay male culture and the male church; they are sadly similar. Both seem equally obsessed with sexuality. Both degrade and exclude women with strange and unimaginative rationales. Perhaps gay priests could begin from within to heal the male church and the male culture of its broken sexuality. It is my experience that men, straight and gay, are programmed from early childhood to be object-oriented toward sex. There is great pressure to conform to the male view of sex, which separates sexuality from love and relationship and focuses on body types and parts. The male church focuses on sexuality in ways that are clearly foreign to the gospel. When one studies the Gospels, one could never come up with an emphasis on sexuality. The "alter-Christus," Francis of Assisi, symbolically married Lady Poverty in imitation of Christ. What might happen if the men in power were to descend on the people and servants of the church with searing letters on gospel poverty? How many clerics would lose their homes, possessions, and priesthoods for this failure to follow the Gospels? Yet vengeance or a turn of the frightening hand of power is not what the Gospels are about. The whole use of power must be borne and transfigured by the shepherds.

> He offered up prayers and petitions with loud cries and tears to the one who could save him from death.
>
> Hebrews 5:7

Dark days have descended as the accusers now point to a disease that is supposed to have been sent by God to infect gay people. The accusation is that God finds gay men so repulsive that God seeks to eliminate them. Only a mad, Hitler-like, exterminating god would choose one particular people, and their sins, to afflict. With this kind of logic, apparently God also hates the people of countries afflicted by other disasters and disease epidemics. God has chosen to afflict the Vietnamese, without mercy for years; recently God struck Mexico with an earthquake, Brazil with rain and floods. The Biafrans have been sent floods and famine, and the Ethiopians are methodically starved, while the Africans have been suffering with AIDS for over twenty-five years. The corollary is that God harbors other peoples of society and chooses not to afflict them. Following this line of reasoning, we see that God has a special love and care for lesbian women, who have escaped punishment altogether, and who have the greatest rate of success in faithful relationships, over and above heterosexual and male homosexual couples.

In September 1983 I was called to preside over the first liturgy of the anointing of the sick for persons with AIDS at Dignity, Manhattan. I admit I was afraid. At that time people were still very uncertain about how the disease was transmitted; I knew this meant publicity within the city as well as in religious publications around the country. I had just closed John Farrow's moving biography of Damien de Veuster of Molokai, *Damien the Leper*. I decided that, if Damien could live his life constantly misunderstood and exposed to a highly contagious disease, then I could celebrate one mass. Since that first mass of anointing, I have been catapulted into what is now called "AIDS ministry." I began by taking the excellent training at Gay Men's Health Crisis, and then began part-time work at the St. Vincent's Hospital Supportive Care Hospice Program, run by Sister Patrice Murphy. I also started getting referrals and calls from hospitals and people in and around New York City.

I sought to be converted by the suffering Christ; some of that prayer has been mercifully answered. I found that not in a condescending "charitable" ministry does classical conversion take place. For example, Francis of Assisi was converted when he conquered his fear of leprosy by diving down from his horse, as an impetuous twenty-five-year-old, and embracing and kissing a man with leprosy who was passing by. Francis was converted. The leper was not in need of conversion; he was Christ.

I do not pretend for a moment that I have been able to walk stoically in and out of the world of this disease. For the first six months, at least, I left hospitals and apartments in a kind of numbing fog. Sister Patrice once commented that, in all her years of hospice work, she has never seen such suffering. And the one who draws near also tastes the suffering. Yet what I have also seen is the people with AIDS teaching and causing a slow but steady and irreversible conversion in those who minister to them. Doctors, nurses, social workers, sisters, priests, bishops, ministers, rabbis, and volunteers of every stripe are confronted, often for the first time, with gay people as human beings. The illusions of separation, the caricatures, judgments, generalizations, and superstitions vanish as the reality that "these people" too have families, friends, spouses, and lovers, as most people do, and they are suffering monstrous deaths. The grief and suffering is taking its toll. The coldhearted prejudice, either intellectual or visceral, is being shattered by the truth people witness. One could also cite innumerable examples of the horrors that continue to go on, but in some cases there is conversion; the cross seems to be the only way to elicit a change of heart.

> The Lord has sworn an oath which he will never retract: you are a priest, and forever.
>
> Hebrews 7:21

All of what has gone before in my life and training seems to me now to have been a preparation for this priesthood. Along with the obvious tragedy and heaviness, there is joy and fulfillment as God continues to fashion and make "all things new." Once a month, I offer a mass of healing and anointing for persons with AIDS, their families, and friends at Our Lady of Guadalupe Church in New York City. At the end of the mass two laywomen, two laymen, and myself lay hands on people and pray for spiritual, physical, and emotional healing. In this specific way and in many others, I feel urged to give away the exquisite treasury of the church with the extravagance of a Saint Lawrence. The sacraments, images, writings, prayers, and the awareness of the Mystical Body of Christ—all of these are given to people who hunger and thirst for them.

I feel the presence of some special souls who have gone before us, the saints called into the work of AIDS, and I try to celebrate their presence in art cards, books, and posters. Perhaps to some they appear naive in the face of the earthly conflicts, but for me one must image the truth to be seen, and the truth is the union of heaven and earth in compassion for persons with AIDS. One large painting I did for the hospice office, called *The Epiphany: Wisemen Bring Gifts to the Child*, portrays the church as Our Lady of Guadalupe, who is the mother and revered icon of the poor and the outcast. She holds out her child to two wise men, Saints Francis of Assisi and Aloysius Gonzaga, who bring their gifts of two persons with AIDS to the child Jesus. Both of these saints had great physical suffering in their own lives, and both were wise to find Christ in those who suffer most. Neither the poor man Francis nor the boy Aloysius was an ordained priest, yet both enflesh the kind of humble service Jesus called for at the Last Supper.

This brief life is still a mystery to me. I search for truth and hunger for simplicity. I stumble under my own wounding flaws and contradictions, which at times threaten to stop me. But I get up, I beg not to be incapacitated by my own accusing voices or those of others. Let me *do* something, I pray. Let me visit the sick, speak the truth with a friend, or illustrate and create. Let me pray for and with the church, let me pray for and with my gay brothers and sisters, and let them all, someday, be one.

Postscript

Although this chapter refers at times specifically to the institutional priesthood, I very much want to include those many people who are unable to exercise their priesthood for reasons of gender or sexual orientation. I also wish to include those who are simply unable to function with holiness and integrity within the institutional church at this time. I dedicate this chapter to my father, Stephen L. R. McNichols, who has always taught, and continues to teach, me to love to tell the truth.

12 Inheritance for the Disinherited

BROTHER AMOS

Lately I have been noticing a shift in the style of vocation-recruitment posters. These days the allure of advertisements that fill the rear pages of pious magazines is distinctively ersatz medieval: crudely conceived pen-and-ink drawings of overdressed men and women in silhouette, looking longingly skyward for some hint of the Parousia.

Not so in my day, in the post–Korean War days of my youth when the long, gray-flanneled arm of Madison Avenue reached everywhere. In the 1950s vocation advertisements were slick and immediate; no crude drawings for us, no overdressing, no postponed bliss, but rather in a series of glossy photographs, which might have passed for Margaret Bourke-White's, we were lured to God with the promise of adolescent dreams fulfilled: gym shorts for all, basketball hoops, and acres of approving smiles.

Neither image, old or new, reflects recognizable experience. Although I might admire more the consummate craft of the posters of my youth, both styles project an image bordering on the fantastic. Moreover, the posters of my youth were, in my case, counterproductive and deterred me from attempting religious life at all. It struck me that their appeal was to all those people I surely was not. In fact, their appeal was to all those kids who were like the kids in the posters: the Irish girl, long-lashed and zitless, forever crowning the Virgin in May and appearing nightly in the Christmas pageant; the eternally bemused altar boy who looked just like Chuck White in the *Catholic Messenger* and for whom the curate had developed an encouraging fondness. On balmy days these and their like were sped off in borrowed station wagons and tempted to sample the goods at remote motherhouses and seminaries; and although I overachieved like mad and fetched and carried for every nun and priest who noticed me, I was never asked. Predictably, when some years later I summoned the courage to contact a vocation director on my own, he, too, looked like the vocation poster child: all teeth and hair and manicure.

To my surprise, when I arrived at the novitiate, there were no poster children at all. After several weeks, when the initial irresponsibility of novitiate life had lapsed into a meditative fatigue, I concluded that this oddly assorted group was actually it, and there was nary a poster child among us. Of course, there was a suspicious-looking zitless smile here and there and a familiar dimple or two was to be seen buffing the superior's bedroom, but even these, one by one, disappeared, usually by night, and never, never to be spoken of again, outside of a charitable prayer, of course.

I found myself, perhaps for the first time and quite unaccountably so, home. I no longer pressed my nose to a brittle glass or watched others glide through happy lives while I lumbered through my own. I was, simply, no longer alone, no longer an alien. Nothing could explain why except, of course, the strange and obvious presence of these unexpectedly disparate, mismatched others. I could not easily account for who these others were or who they had ever been. I would not have chosen most of them for my friends. There seemed no real theological bond among us. All our discussions of the deity devolved into a practical polytheism. Debates on moral values led only to bitter dispute; cultural prejudice abounded. Some of us loved the novice master; others thought he was as mad as James Cagney in *Mister Roberts*. Some couldn't wait to get into the "real" work of the community; others wanted only to "pray."

My search for the nature of that puzzling bond goes on, but I have, at least for the present, settled on one explanation. It is clear to me now that our common bond was not the shared and pious hymns, but rather a shared discomfort in the worlds from which we came. In those worlds all of us, I suspect, were strangers, displaced persons for whom the world held neither comfort nor release from pain. From beneath the prayer-card rhetoric we so earnestly shared in those days, a less sure but more authentic voice sometimes broke through: the clear, forlorn cry of those who are alone. That is the voice I recognized as my own and that was the harmony I found. The poster children did not come or stay because they, of course, did not need to. All of us, more hungry than they, did.

That cry, however, was more felt than heard, a presence sensed as absence, like some half-friendly ghost, not spoken of but, nonetheless, traceable in the petty insistences, the sometimes desperate fun, the strange alliances, the unfocused fears. Perhaps it was the claustrophobic space we shared; perhaps the analogic world view that fueled our prayers and made the east and sunrise more charged with meaning than any paranoid could wish. More likely, it was simply the freedom from the hostility of our separate worlds; but the cry was unavoidable, and I knew it was my own.

Time eventually laid bare the separate wounds of each of us. I had, to some extent, already identified mine with my sexual orientation. I suppose it is more accurate to say that before I identified it I had had it identified for me at school. A thousand innuendos I could not first comprehend had been hurled at me like rocks, and when unkindness finally broke me down and exposed me to myself, I withdrew into a solid cloak of shame. My life became airless, defensive, and self-regarding. The terror in my parents' eyes and their eternal silence, the arrogance of unforgiving priests, the violence of boys in Catholic schools whose camaraderie hardened into smugness because God and the religion teacher had sanctioned my exclusion—all had helped convince me that isolation was, if not my only course, at least my safest. Moreover, my few tentative forays into the gay community confirmed this. There I saw only what was obvious and nothing that I knew: a noisy circus waiting for a crowd to please, an outlandish masquerade that frightened me into accepting the most grotesque of the epithets that had been hurled at me.

When relief came, briefly but significantly, it came again as music, not as metaphor but sound. Banished from study hall one afternoon to prepare a piece on the piano I played at school assemblies (a more subtle exclusion in the name of art), I heard a violin out of nowhere begin to play behind me. When I turned to look, I saw one of the brothers, my English teacher. He put his bow up to his lips to silence me, then pointed to the music and nodded for me to continue. And so we did, without a word, throughout the afternoon. I did not turn again because I did not want him to see me cry, but when the music ended, he touched my shoulder and left as quietly as he had come. I know without that kindness that I would not have thought religious life a possibility at all.

It took four years for me to respond to that touch, but once I had surmounted the obstacle of the discouragingly wholesome vocation pitch and finally arrived at the novitiate, I found a peace there akin to that afternoon of music. My English teacher/violinist was not gay (he is old now and far away but still my friend), nor were the majority of brothers in the novitiate, but he and they understood, for whatever reason, what it means to be uncomfortable in the world. Somewhere "inner than the bone," they understood insult and oppression and that kind of hostility that indelibly sticks to the bodies of the poor and often gathers them into those quiet revolutions that break down the barriers among us.

Needless to say, we lived in no Garden but somewhere after the Fall. Because we were who we were, because we had come together, gay and straight but all broken, we at least identified our lapses from poverty as genuine lapses and not as positive career moves. It was more difficult to profess the oppressor's creed there, and almost instinctively, we recognized the difference between human needs and those created by the culture. Only when we forgot the discomfort with the world that had brought us together and split our private wounds from our public speech did we lapse into the arrogance that sometimes made us brittle and cruel. We mercifully had few heroes.

I suppose because the novitiate was Arcadia, so full of significances and meanings, I was able to identify myself with something broader than those opprobrious innuendos that had been hung about my neck at school. What my fleeting tours of the gay community had suggested, the novitiate helped to dispel. Friendship, uncomplicated by expectation and performance, was possible. It was possible for me to love without terror, to share my life with other men without fear of cosmic reprisal, to see something more than what was obvious, and on that foundation to grow to love the enemy world and finally to forgive it.

While hindsight necessarily deceives, the shuttlings back and forth between the shelter of my own self-loathing and the courage to stand as a religious in the world seem less important to me now than the outcome: the presence of loving friends, the satisfaction of my work, and a comfort before God and the world. This is not to deny, however, that our choice to live as brothers in the world is a form of protest against ecclesial hierarchies. Locke says that "brother is the name of friendship and equality and not of jurisdiction and authority" (p. 92) and that therefore revolutions are made by brothers against oppressive fathers. Perhaps more importantly, living as a brother defies the one-dimensional culture that once silenced us, filled us with self-doubt, and crushed our courage.

As Marcuse (1964) describes it, the culture that dominates our century and has its roots somewhere in the thirteenth century feeds off repression. It convinces us that to oppose it is to risk the loss of the quality of life that the culture itself has brainwashed us into accepting as normative and good and that it alone can guarantee. By convincing us that only majority and rationalist values are substantial and that personal impulse is whimsy, modern institutions of all kinds tend to deify reason and succeed in flattening out the spectrum of possible values. They force us to accept only a model of reason whose limitations encourage suspicion of personal depth, shatter integrity, and make us desire a style of life that is, no doubt, efficient, but that is had only at the high price of repression and intolerance.

Certainly the rationalist, one-dimensional culture had no idea what to do with me (nor did the unforgiving priests who had succumbed to its rationalist models) and was quite frank about it. It beat me, and I, naive, trusting, and isolated, thought at first that it was absolutely correct. I know now that the discomfort I felt as a gay man and the discomfort my other brothers felt in such a culture was sheer good common sense. Some would call it grace. Our decision to enter religious life was not only a form of self-defense, but also a reflexive form of social protest. Our decision to remain is a refusal to play the victim of that rationalist model, a refusal to allow ourselves to be hacked off from some deep and mystical root. When we do not forget who we are, we create a second dimension, an alternative to what Pynchon (1966) calls the "exitlessness, the absence of surprise to life that harrows the head of everybody American" (p. 128).

An indication of our corporate strength is the rabid fight we put up whenever our leadership launches into one of its frequent campaigns for making the brothers bourgeois. The inevitable failure of these turns to "normalcy" is our inheritance and a great sign of hope and glory. As brothers we are least creative when we are most forgetful of the wound and when we fail to deny the rationalist values that inflicted the wound. Such lapses from the alternative second dimension give added strength to Marcuse's analysis and raise again Wilhelm Reich's question: how could the masses be made to desire their own repression? We are most despairing when we begin to measure our own lives against the rationalist model of the dominating culture, when we forget what Auden (1966) calls "the baffle of being" (p. 29) and assume that we are no more than the neat sum of our analyzable parts. When we do become as unforgiving of ourselves as was the world from which we came, we have lost sight of the mystery that lies at the center of our lives and is deep enough to absorb us all and welcome us home.

I am forever trying to connect the beast and the monk in me. By now I should be wise enough to know that these opposites conflict only under the scrutiny of unaided reason, only in the great binary sorting machine that is our modern habit of thought. At either end of the connection I am positively hateful not only to myself, but to those who have to put up with me. To accept that both beast and monk are in fact already reconciled and form one continuum that defines who I am, just as male and female define who I am, is to accept a messy paradox that our binary culture cannot abide and in which Easter, celebrated with water and fire, rejoices. That baffling mystery is especially close to the heart of this gay and often lustful religious.

The forgetfulness of wound also supports another pernicious habit of modern thought—nostalgia. It would be comforting to believe that, awakened from the nightmare of Nazi Germany, our culture would have responded with a collective retch to the least sniff of nostalgia that propelled Hitler's infernal machine. Nostalgia, however, has become all the rage again, driving the nouveau chic, dominating the economy, and inspiring those artless vocation posters and their promise of perfect bliss. Evidently, we have not learned that the past is often a lie, and that to reproduce it is always easy, always destructive, and a certain sign of the exhaustion of the imagination. Because nostalgia conceives of the past only selectively, it is easily idealized. Institutions find nostalgia a handy, perhaps necessary, grease for their corporate machines. It certainly keeps the nuts from squawking. When we allow nostalgia into our religious lives, we again lapse into the one-dimensional model of the prevailing culture and deny a great inheritance. Too much damage continues to be done "in the name of the founder."

The impulse behind nostalgia is the antithesis of the impulse behind prophecy. Those of us who have been born gay are perhaps more intuitively aware of the "baffle of being" than are our straight brothers and sisters. With them in religious life, however, we search together for speech to express our common experience of marginalization. When we respond from that uncomfortable experience and not from the comfort of the central culture, we transcend the isolation within which that culture needs to keep us. By finding a voice in common with the silenced and oppressed of our time and with the poor, both in and out of our communities, we find a speech for our silence that is necessarily a prophetic speech. It is the speech of human survivors, "the unofficial story told by voices of despair in dialogue with faith" (Gilman 1986, 48), the speech not of memory, but of the unaccommodated imagination.

I do not know how my life would have evolved without my violinist friend or without the brothers among whom I found a voice for my speech, a human voice that echoed my own. I have remained a religious for twenty-five more or less productive years because I found in those first few years in religious life an ease and sense of well-being that my first twenty years in what we used to call "the world" failed to give me. Perhaps all would have been well; perhaps not. Nonetheless, "what I dared not hope or fight for" (Auden 1966, 15) is now, in my middle years, mine.

References

Auden, W. H. 1966. *Around the House.* New York: Random House.
Gilman, Richard. 1986. *Faith, Sex, Mystery.* New York: Simon and Schuster.
Locke, John. N.d. *Two Treatises of Civil Government.* New York: Everyman.
Marcuse, Herbert. 1964. *One-dimensional Man.* Boston: Beacon.
Pynchon, Thomas. 1966. *The Crying of Lot 49.* New York: Bantam.

13 We Shall Not Cease from Exploration

FATHER PAUL

Every person's story is "the same but different," as someone once said. I am a gay priest whose story is very similar to many others, but is also unique. I shall tell that story as briefly as I can and try to delineate some of the issues that I see flowing from it.

I knew from a very early age that I was attracted to other males. I lived in a small Maryland town, where a lot of sexual experimenting went on. I assumed that all boys grew up this way and was shocked in later life to meet people who had had no adolescent sexual experience. One man, aged sixty-three, who recently came for counseling to me just after his mother died, had never had sex with another human being. It was a revelation to me that this could happen.

During puberty and adolescence, I had sexual contacts with a few girls, but mostly with boys, by choice. Two of them emerged as especially important. The first was a friend about my own age who also experienced homosexual urges strongly. We discussed our feelings and had sex together at times, but he was most important as a confidant. My principal erotic feelings were directed toward a boy several years my senior who was handsome and athletic and very open to sexual experiences, both homosexual and heterosexual. He was my first major love—a "crush" I realize now—but the affair was tremendously important to my growth.

134

Isolating my sexual experiences this way makes my growing years sound like an unbroken orgy, but actually the sex was integrated into a busy, happy, normal life. My family was warm and loving, with both parents very strict disciplinarians. I was brought up in a Catholic home, although my dad was Protestant. I went to public schools because no parochial school was nearby. This exposed me to a variety of viewpoints and kept me from being overwhelmed by the church's antisex teaching, which is still harsh but was especially so in the 1940s and 1950s, when I grew up. My father, one of the finest men I have ever known, had a very earthy attitude toward the flesh, and my own attitudes have been strongly influenced by him. Mom was Irish and a wee bit Jansenistic in her attitude toward sex. One of my most delightful memories of growing up was my father's ribaldry played off against mom's tendency to be repressed on sexual matters. I always suspected that she was pretty earthy too, if you scratched the surface a little.

One other feature of growing up that comes to mind is the failure to satisfy gender role expectations. This is one of the most common experiences of gay persons, I have found. Most of my boyhood chums were crazy about sports, especially baseball. My own brother was good enough to consider a semiprofessional career in baseball. I played sports when I was very young, but found that my interests began diverging before too long. I found music and reading to be more interesting, certainly by the time I was into the teens. I would be glued to the radio on Saturdays listening to the Metropolitan Opera or Toscanini, while one or more of my brothers would be clamoring to hear a baseball game. I was the oldest and pretty strong willed, so the Met and NBC Symphony usually won the day.

As the high school years passed, my sexual activity continued, but I found myself becoming more introverted. Slowly the thought of becoming a priest grew in my mind, a possibility first mentioned to me by one of my Protestant aunts! The actual decision to enter the seminary came fairly late in my senior year; after graduation I left for the novitiate of a nearby religious order.

That year in a country setting was one of the most "pure" I have ever spent. I even avoided masturbation, although it was extraordinarily difficult. At the end of the fifteen months, my class was transferred to the seminary in Washington, D.C. The provincial gave us the final retreat before first vows. One of the liturgies on retreat was the feast of the beheading of John the Baptist. I remember his telling us that the moral of the feast was, "Don't lose your head over a woman." He did not discuss the possibility of losing it over a man though. He did mention, as we were about to depart for the seminary in Washington, that we would be with older men (theologians) as well as our fellow collegians. We were to "beware of the theologians," he said, which of course gave them an immediate air of mystery.

During that first year of college, my father died at forty-eight of cancer, surely the most traumatic loss of my life. I was totally unprepared for the finality of the event. My mother and three brothers had lived with his deterioration during the year I had been away at novitiate and as a result dealt with the loss far better than I. My mother's death years later was painful too, but she had lived a full, happy life well into her seventies.

When I returned to the seminary after dad's funeral, I was obviously forlorn. One of the forbidden theologians began talking to me, and a very deep friendship rapidly developed. The friendship deepened into a love affair that was reciprocal and intense. This was the 1950s, and genital sex in a seminary was practically unheard of. So that was never an issue for us; but Joe and I did everything else in words and touches to communicate our affection. It was an idyllic experience that came to an end when the superior called us in separately and gave us an obedience not to see each other again. He spoke strongly about the dangers of "particular friendships," the code phrase at that time for homosexual relationships.

One of the incidents not long before the superior's intervention that remains in my mind is of Joe suddenly asking, "Do you think we have a particular friendship?" I answered negatively, explaining that what we had was positive and good, so it couldn't possibly be a PF. "I'm glad I asked," Joe replied.

The superior was right, of course. We had a classic PF by the standards of the system. But to this day I would call the relationship positive and good and one of the most important of my life.

My friend went on to ordination, but left after severe problems with alcoholism. Later he even attempted marriage, disastrously as it turned out. I suspect that most of his problems relate to his inability to name and accept his gayness.

I was very careful after the "PF episode" to avoid another passionate entanglement. I realized that I would be bounced if I was not "careful"; so I got careful. I fell in love again, but found ways to sublimate the feelings and especially the sexual urges. This is what we were told to do incessantly, and I did it. I avoided sex with anyone, but also avoided involvement and became a very nontactile, distant person. In other words, I became what the system wanted. This careful nonnaming of who I was continued throughout the seminary years and into the first few years of my priesthood. Reflection, especially on sexual matters, was buried in a maelstrom of activities.

The issues kept on the back burner erupted with force about the fifth year after ordination (a classic time for such turbulence, as I found out from many other priests). I took a leave of absence for two and a half years from the priesthood, first moving to San Francisco and later to a small midwestern town. I began slowly dealing with some of the issues, but did not come up with any satisfactory answers. This is not surprising, since I was trying to figure out how to hold on to being a priest without denying my gayness. Under pressure from the provincial to finalize my decision on whether I would leave the priesthood, I eventually returned with reluctance and even anger. I look back now and see that the provincial was right. I would have waited forever for perfect answers, of which there is a very short supply in an imperfect world. I have grown to love Rainer Maria Rilke's (1954) lines: "Be patient toward all that is unresolved in your heart and try to love the *questions* themselves. . . . Do not seek the answers, which cannot be given to you because you would not be able to live with them. . . . *Live* the questions now" (pp. 34–35).

I returned to my order and began teaching again, a beloved ministry that I have practiced both as priest and layperson and at all levels from elementary and high school to college and adult education classes. The sexual question continued to burn, and one of the features added to my life was an occasional visit to gay movie theaters on visits to a large city. There would be sexual contacts in the theaters, but most important was that the visits made me feel connected to a larger gay community. I knew that I was running into gay people where I taught and in my order, but even in the early seventies that was not something talked about a great deal. So I felt isolated, and the theaters told me I was really not.

After several years I was transferred to a school in a larger city, where a Dignity chapter was being formed. They needed a chaplain, and I realized I needed them and an experience of gay community. So I took the chance and attended the first mass. A very symbiotic relationship has continued for the last ten years, surely the most productive and happiest in all my years as a priest.

The celibacy issue has been resolved for the most part. I am attempting to be celibate at this time. Contact with the Dignity people, who needed and wanted a minister, not someone seeking sexual contacts, as well as the support of my religious community and several dialog groups, have guided me toward this choice. I am not sure it is a rock-solid, eternal commitment, but it is the best I can manage after years of struggle. I have observed how very consuming relationships are through the years. They need and deserve a tremendous amount of time and energy. Inevitably this has to be traded off from other relationships, and you get pulled in many directions as a minister. I do not wish to pontificate and say what all people should do. Many rabbis, ministers, and doctors seem to combine good marriages and demanding vocations, so I am sure it can be done. It just does not appear to be what God calls me to at this time.

What I have now, instead of a single intimate relationship, a "significant other" who enriches my life, is a host of people who love me in different ways. I have had periods of self-pity, some of them pretty strong, about not having a beloved friend. But I can see clearly that the totality of love coming from many people and from God is sufficient to make me a very happy person.

One of the issues that leaps out at me, as I reflect a little on my life, is the importance of dialog. If you cannot articulate who you are to yourself and others, you live in a foggy, unhealthy world. It is always tough to put things into words, but it is absolutely necessary. I remember a student who became annoyed at a low grade I had given him and exclaimed, "I have very deep thoughts. I just can't put them into words!" I tried to explain to him (gently I hope) that without the words, you do not have thoughts, least of all profound ones. You have feelings, possibly very strong ones, but feelings that have to be clarified and balanced with the rational side of one's personality.

I have been lucky enough to have many groups and people who have forced me to put my feelings and thoughts into words and by this process to hear what I have been thinking. My own religious community for many years provided such a forum. This is worth mentioning first, since it has happened so rarely in my experience. Some of my "communities" have been closer to hotels, where you know the other people by name but do not know them in any deep way. I think a dialog community has to be relatively small. You are not likely to bare much of your soul in a massive group. Six or seven people seems ideal to me. One year our community had exactly six people, with two heterosexuals, two bisexuals, and two gays! That was a year of great dialog. I have learned as much, or more, from sensitive heterosexuals as I have from my fellow gays. The most basic thing that has emerged for me is the similarity of our problems and challenges. Achieving intimacy is as difficult for a heterosexual as for a gay person, and the obstacles are much the same.

In addition to my religious community, I have had the opportunity to dialog with Dignity members on many occasions in small sessions. These occur on days of recollection, retreats, and sometimes just informally among friends. The gay people I have encountered have been among the most spiritual and admirable people I have ever known. You do not have to be gay to be deeply spiritual, but it surely does not hurt. When I read the putdowns of gay people by church leaders and think of the real gay people I have known, the disparity is mind-boggling. If the officials in the Catholic church and their equivalents in other churches and in secular society actually listened to the lived experience of the gay community, they would not write some of the worthless documents they produce with such regularity.

Besides my religious community and Dignity, I have been in

several support groups. One of them was composed of three priests, a brother, and a layperson—all gay. It dealt powerfully with some specific gay issues. The other groups were mostly made up of priests, although a deep bonding with a woman religious in one of them has occurred. She has been tremendously helpful with her insights and love. As a teacher, I have also enjoyed extensive dialog with students, and we have probed some very deep questions. I would not, however, go into my sexuality in any depth in one of these classes. Adolescents have enough problems without burdening them with my burning issues as well.

The spirituality that I have worked out in these various groups has focused strongly on the person of Jesus. As the years have gone by, I have come to see him as the beloved friend that I mentioned earlier. I realized this in a discussion group on "change" in which I participated. I remarked that I had gone through a tremendous number of changes, many of them turbulent, but that I always had a remarkable feeling of continuity and stability. The discussion leader challenged me to explain this more specifically, and as I groped for words, I heard myself quoting a line from T. S. Eliot's (1943) *Four Quartets* about "the still point of the turning world" (p. 5). If I understand Eliot correctly, there is a still point that gives meaning to the turbulent dance of life. That still point is the Word made Flesh, Jesus. I explained that Jesus was certainly the still point for me in the rush of events and experiences that I dealt with daily. Jesus is the great organizing principle, the source of cohesion and unity, the anchor, so much needed in a fractured, chaotic world. To put it in a more personal way, Jesus is my lover, the one who holds me and helps me in tough times and who multiplies my joys.

Jesus as lover or bridegroom was an image once popular among nuns in describing their vocation. A film I saw recently on the Little Flower, called simply *Thérèse*, presented this bridal spirituality powerfully. I think gay men can relate to Jesus in an analogous way, thinking of him as the great lover, the spouse, to whom you pledge your life. Biblical images such as John resting on the chest of the Lord certainly bolster this approach. A lot of reflection and work remain to be done in formulating a uniquely gay spirituality.

Related to this central place of Jesus, one can mention also the more general search for God. I have always liked the Hindu idea of *atman*, that is, finding God within yourself. When you arrive at the deepest level of your identity, you find God (Brahma) residing there, and also find out most truly who you are. The search for God and for identity become one. Saint Teresa of Avila (1979) presents a similar idea in *The Interior Castle*. She describes the soul as having seven rooms. The first six represent the different stages of spiritual growth. When you arrive in the seventh, the inner sanctum, you encounter the living God. This is also where you come to know the deepest and truest part of yourself. And if part of that deepest identity is the fact that you are gay, then inevitably your search for God has to be in a gay context. I can only know God as the unique person I am, and part of that uniqueness is my sexual orientation.

Far from being a curse or bane, then, my gayness is a blessing from God. I have come to realize personally, as the years have passed, that my best traits and gifts are connected with being gay. They are the ones that enhance my ministry the most. The great challenge, then, for gay religious and priests is to integrate sexuality and spirituality and to realize that our journey has to be as sexual, as homosexual, persons. We have no other choice. God calls us to love and celebrate who we are. He made us the way we are, and it is good.

I certainly do not want to imply by my comments that sexuality is our total being. But it is one very important part of it. I can never achieve true spiritual growth and maturity without coming to know that part of me, accepting it, and celebrating it. A retreat leader on an all-gay retreat once advised us to go into the chapel and say, "Dear God, I'm pretty sure you know this. But I just wanted to tell you that I'm gay and to thank you for the gift." I have repeated that prayer daily for the last few years and feel pretty great about myself and about God.

The name for the process I have just been describing is "coming out." It is a lifelong process and begins with yourself. I have to come to know who I am, name it, and accept it. The process then continues with others. Do I come out to my friends, my co-workers, my superiors, my family? Families always present a special challenge. I have told only one of my brothers the full story, although I have dropped massive hints to the other two and will no doubt complete the process with them one day. The one brother has been a tremendous blessing. To have someone in my own family who knows me fully and who loves me as I am is great.

Every new acquaintance brings the question of "coming out" to the fore once again. Sooner or later in every relationship I have to ask, Do I reveal this part of me or not? Inevitably there will be mistakes made. One of my worst was with a fellow priest. The revelation was so traumatic that our friendship cooled down considerably and was almost destroyed. I was positive he had some gay feelings and I was puzzled by the strength of his rejection. It became clear later when I heard that he had gotten into legal problems for molesting minors in another assignment. He was unable to handle his own turbulent sexuality, let alone try to assimilate mine. His inability to dialog and share himself is the major reason, I would guess, for his failure to deal with his compulsive behavior.

Another level of coming out is the public declaration of being gay. In a homophobic society and church, this is a sure invitation to bigotry and discrimination. One simple way to do this, in my case, would have been to use my real name on this essay. I have chosen a pseudonym because I am not ready to deal with the emotional and economic pressures that would result. Yet another part of me is angry at society, at the church, but also at myself for not taking the risk. I suppose this is another of Rilke's unanswered questions that I have to try to live with. In any case my masochistic bent has always been underdeveloped. I do not like to give others the weapons with which to maim me. One of the principal motivations for making a public declaration would be the many people who think they have never met a gay person (including many who have met and known me). Blacks and other minorities have a real advantage in not being able to hide their minority status since this forces them to deal with the issue of racism out in the open. The world would be astonished indeed if all gay and lesbian people suddenly turned lavender! But we will not, of course, and the coming out process has to continue being a matter of individual choice.

A problem that arises for all gay religious, and particularly for gay priests, is the disparity between public perception and private reality. The result is that we live in a schizophrenic world that can be very frustrating. More than once I have looked out at a large church congregation and thought, "What if you really knew?" For some, it would not matter, of course. For others, it would destroy any feelings of respect I have earned. One priest in our "Communication" newsletter described the dichotomy as that between a shaman (God, spirit, priest) and a vampire (flesh, sex, man). That is a little more dramatic than I would put it, but I know what he means. There is no satisfactory answer to this riddle in a gay-hating church and society, so it becomes one more question to be lived with. This is an area where dialog and strong support groups are particularly necessary.

One of the questions that inevitably arises is: why stay Catholic, and especially why remain a priest? Church leaders and members vent their homophobia in myriad ways. Many in the gay community are utterly puzzled by the allegiance of gay Catholics and other Christians to their churches. I fully understand the feelings of the many gay persons, women, and others who have left the Catholic church in disgust. But I am more akin to one Dignity member who said she plans to leave the church "a week after the pope does." The Catholic church is mine as much as it is Pope John Paul's or Cardinal Ratziner's or anyone else's. My Catholicism is a deep part of my identity, as is my sexuality. I do not plan to give up either. In any case, I would not know where to go in order to avoid human imperfection, mine or that of others. If I joined any other church, I would find the same reminders of human weakness and stubbornness, I am sure. In the final analysis, my hope is in the Lord Jesus, not in mere human leaders. I have resolved to seek Jesus in the Catholic church, because that is where my roots are and what I have given my life to.

Eliot's *Four Quartets*, which I mentioned earlier, is one of my favorite poems and has been the source of much inspiration. Toward the end of the work, Eliot (1943) offers these lines:

> We shall not cease from exploration
> And the end of all our exploring
> Will be to arrive where we started
> And know the place for the first time. (p. 39)

It is better to be a little humble in Eliot's presence and not pretend you know fully what he means. There are nearly always many levels of meaning in his rich, powerful writing. But what I get from these lines is that our journey, our exploring, always aims at getting back to our roots, to the deepest part of our being, to the place where God is most fully. And when I reach this psychological and spiritual place, and it takes a lifetime of searching, I will find my beginnings. I will know my gayness and the other deepest parts of my identity that God gave me.

I have already been privileged to make much of this journey. I recently celebrated my fiftieth birthday, always a special milestone, and spent some time looking into the "dark backward and abysm of time," as Shakespeare puts it. The thought occurred to me that I would like to live a lot of my life over—not to make any major changes, but just to enjoy it again. I also used the day to say to God what I am sure he knows: "I'm gay and thank you for the gift."

References

Avila, T. 1979. *The Interior Castle*. Translated by K. Kavanaugh and R. Otilio. New York: Paulist Press.

Eliot, T. S. 1943. *Four Quartets*. New York: Harcourt, Brace and World.

Rilke, R. M. 1954. *Letters to a Young Poet*. New York: Norton.

14 The Land I Love In

MATTHEW KELTY, OCSO

I wanted to be a priest and a monk since the time I knew what the words meant. And I have known that I was gay just as long, though it was a long time before I knew what that was all about. I was fifteen years a priest when I became a monk and it was another ten years before I became fully reconciled to what kind of man I am. Probably, of the three, coming to terms with being a gay person was the most difficult, and that mostly because it meant dealing with ignorance, fear, anxiety, and public attitudes of contempt.

A child seems to have considerable resilience and adaptability or perhaps not too much self-awareness, but by the time I was ten I was tasting the shame of total ineptitude in sports, particularly competitive sports. This remained with me another ten years, for if there was anything preparatory seminaries encouraged, it was sports, competitive sports. That tapered off though, and I could adjust to community by way of dramatics, music, writing, and this made up for other lacks in an acceptable way.

Life in a religious community much appealed to me and I enjoyed the intensity and tension; it forced this introvert to acquire some feeling for the extrovert world and it forestalled one-sidedness. I did not know in any conscious way that I was gay; the matter was never mentioned, nor was I aware of any gay interest or activity, or even a hint of it, in the world around me. For all practical purposes it was not something that concerned us. What we learned about this subject we learned from the morals texts. I recall only two incidents in thirteen years of seminary. Once a major seminarian touched another in a vulgar way; he was dismissed. On another occasion when someone left the community I was told only one word: *homosexuality*. I knew better than to pursue the matter.

This suppression, this ignorance, this unwholesome falseness began to cause problems some years into the priesthood. I had been editing a magazine for about ten years, helping in parishes, preaching an occasional retreat; apparently I was an adequately successful priest. I had known the taste of mission life in a primitive country before I got into the editing, but something was eating my heart out and I did not know what it was.

A sudden change in publishing policy left me without assignment at an odd time of the year and I seized the chance to make a retreat at Gethsemani, a contemplative monastery in Kentucky. The idea of attending the retreat had been at the back of my mind for a long time, but I knew when I took the train that there was more to it than a retreat. One look at the place and the people in it and I knew that was where I wanted to be. I asked to be admitted and the Trappist superior said, if without much enthusiasm, that I could be. When I returned to my religious house, I asked the superiors, received a lackluster permission ("You'll be back"), wrote to Rome for final permission, and put the letter on the altar of the Blessed Virgin under the linens on December 8, 1959. The answer came: You may.

I do not know precisely what fascinated me so; architecturally the place was not much. (It still isn't!) The services were complex, yet nobly beautiful. There was a certain softness, tenderness, a vulnerability about the men; yet their life was hard, demanding. It was perhaps a tone, perhaps a superb combination of male and female. They seemed to me very much men, yet men of a very special kind.

The most dramatic, specific grace in the first ten years at the abbey was when I came upon a complete set of Carl Jung's work in the library. It was a gift of God and the Bollingen Foundation.

By way of Jung I came nearer to understanding myself; his notions of the conscious and the unconscious, the persona, the shadow, the anima, the process of individuation, the role of the archetype—all this was food for my mind and heart, body and soul. It changed my perspective wholly.

I liked the life when I first arrived at Gethsemani and have ever since, even if my initial adjustment was very difficult. The place rings for me. It always has and still does. I fit in. They like me, love me. I like them, love them. I have been able to take part in community affairs and use whatever God gave me. I do not feel I have gone beyond my competence, nor do I feel a sense of being unfulfilled.

God has treated me gently. I grew into an interest in solitude and though I got no permission to pursue it, I was asked to head a small experimental community for three years. It was a wonderful experience and a perfect preparation for what was coming, for the next abbot gave me leave to live as a solitary in a primitive country for nine years.

Living in that small community made it possible for me to acquire material on homosexuality, since there had been nothing in the abbey and no one there to talk to about it. Now, for once, I was able to get adequate information. By the time I arrived in New Guinea I was at peace with myself, knew I was gay, accepted it, rejoiced in it as gift and grace from God. I was a long time getting that far. The church was no help at all; by "church" I mean church in general and seminary and monastery in particular. At that time the issue of homosexuality was not publicly acknowledged and therefore it did not exist. If it does not exist, then why talk about it or think about it? That was, objectively, very cruel. The responsible leadership did not know any better at the time. Thus, my understanding of what it is to be gay is basically Jungian and personal. I worked it out myself and I like what I worked out. It is good enough for me; more than good enough, it is very good.

To wit: all men (and this is regrettably only half a story) are bipolar; that is, they are feminine as well as masculine. Most men do not consciously know this, are unaware of it, and through marriage and in loving union with a woman come to terms with their own feminine aspect, integrate it, and become whole persons. Some men already know at a young age that they have a feminine dimension; they need no woman to discover it and come to terms with it. They already have the feminine within and know it, if they do not love it, in as many ways as there are men. There is really no such thing as a heterosexual or homosexual man; there are, rather, men who experience their bipolarity in an infinite variety of ways and degrees, early or late in life. Since most men have a woman to love, whom is the gay man to love? God, surely, in the context of community and a noble, celibate service. This is the pattern of history, for then the sexual is absorbed in the loving communion with God and community.

It is my conviction that gays make superb celibates, the best celibates, the more so in community. I do not think the heterosexually oriented man should try to live celibacy. It is too risky, for there seems small hope that the feminine of such a male will emerge in a culture such as ours, in which, until lately to a degree, men do not know how to relate to one another warmly and affectionately. They build poor communities, poor brotherhoods, cold and lacking in love. How will the feminine emerge in such a context? More integrated men can relate to one another warmly, heartily, without affection or fear. They can build beautiful communities and over the centuries have done so.

The whole gay syndrome involves the inner dynamism of masculine-feminine forces within and is very creative in every sense. From this tension is born art of every kind: poetry, drama, dance, liturgy. From what sort of men do priests, prophets, dreamers, seers emerge if not from this?

When this all came together for me, and it did so suddenly, I wrote it down in a journal during Holy Week, 1974, and later published it as a small book. But that week was a long time coming—fifty years. I have no intention of nullifying my sexuality by calling it a disordered orientation. I do not easily dismiss the gifts of God. When such gifts are crudely rejected, who can wonder that celibacy attracts few in our culture? The wells that are the source of life for the church are loathed.

My father was not professionally trained, but he was nonetheless a successful mechanical engineer. He superintended the manufacture of sluice gates, large valves for irrigation projects, dams, and the like. As a hobby he had his home and his garden.

He loved flowers and I remember as a child going through stages with him: first, a time of dahlias, then some years of peonies, finally some years of gladiolus. We always had a large and lovely garden. This exposure no doubt had a profound impact on me, for I associate flowers and sex, sex and flowers. Flowers, after all, are sexual organs. It has always intrigued me that God should have lavished so much unnecessary love on flowers. Does a bee need the loveliness of the rose to entice it to enter for nectar and so pollinate? Why, then? To tell us, presumably, that sex is more than fertilization. It is also beauty. Nor do I see the growing, gathering, or wearing of flowers as disordered because, clearly, they are basically sex organs for creativity. That, I believe, is why God made flowers.

I find it odd that God should have been so munificent in nature and should make all so fruitful. The grain we eat is seed, is fruit, is part of the germination and dissemination process of apple and pear and peach. Is it disorder to eat a peach designed to foster fertility? Is it wrong to eat an egg, an ovary, an embryo? In other words, it is possible to see sex as more than sexuality.

When the New Guinea highlands were first "opened," the outsiders from the white world were greeted enthusiastically by a people hidden for centuries. The men showed the white man welcome by grasping their sexual organs in the manner of the biblical Hebrews. They thought that natural and normal. To touch another in a most vital area was both to show love and to receive it. In that land, too, a man did not go near his wife once she had conceived nor until she had weaned the child years later. The men were accustomed to sleeping together in the men's house, body to body, skin to skin. Thus they were tender and affectionate with one another, sometimes sexually. To them this was not sex, for that is woman and child, but simple regard for one another. At puberty rites in some tribes the initiate would drink the seed of an uncle or other male in order to acquire manly qualities, a practice not wholly lacking in logic.

This is not to suggest that we are to derive sexual mores from flowers, grain, or from primitives, but that our approach to sex may be a bit tight, rather narrow and rigid, if not distraught, disordered, and fearful. Men can presumably live without sex but not very happily without love. A celibate community is a commu-

nity of love in which sexual expression, far from being called for, is
actually detrimental to communal love. But when one is not called
to community life how then does one love? And whom? And in
what way? Since there are men whom a loving God made who do
not relate sexually to women, but to other men, companions in
the inner marriage, how is it that a pair's showing faithful love for
each other is unacceptable? Faithful love is difficult, involves
sacrifice, knows failure, as one raising roses finds beauty along
with thorns.

Our society punishes, repudiates, persecutes gay men because it
hates the feminine. The gay man's whole gift is precisely in making
evident the feminine dimension in every male, the call to integration and wholeness. Because our masculinized society is so
addicted to war, violence, aggression, and contempt for the
maternal earth of land, sea, and air, society has contempt for any
male who integrates the feminine. One of the purposes of religious
celibacy has been to serve as an integrating force in oneself;
celibacy in religion has also been a model for integration in
marriage. But there is no disgrace for those not graced with the gift
of celibacy; a gay man in love with another man can be a witness
to something we all need. Being gay is a gift from God, a grace.
That a secular society should not recognize this gift need not
surprise us. What is surprising is that the church so often seems
not to acknowledge it.

I firmly hold to the utter holiness of marital union. One of the
most significant actions of which the human is capable is creating
eternal life with God. To make gay love the equivalent of the
creative union of man and woman seems to me a confusion and
misunderstanding. God makes gay persons even though marriage
is not the usual route for them. Their use of sex as a means for
expressing love in a responsible way is to use the gifts of God in a
way that is appropriate. If their use of sexuality is not creative in a
biological way, it is just as obviously creative in other ways.

I do not flaunt these views, nor do I insist that one or all of them
are correct. They are simply the fruit of over seventy years of living
with my own reality. I carry on no gay apostolate. I am just one of
the monks. My life as priest, as monk, as gay, is not in what I say
or even in what I do, but in what I am. And I think that is really all
that matters. That, then, is the land I love in, the country I live in.

15 Lord, Make Me an Instrument of Your Peace

RICHARD JOHN CARDARELLI, OFM CAP.

On October 13, 1987, I held hands with members of my affinity group as we rushed forward to the steps of the Supreme Court. Before us scores of police stood behind blue-and-white barricades, blocking our access to the halls of justice. Several lesbian activists crossed the police line first; my group decided to sit with hundreds of others, singing, chanting, and scattering thousands of paper pink triangles on the steps. After about an hour, there was an opening in the police line, and we moved closer to the judicial sanctuary. As I crossed the barriers, my habit rosary caught one of the barricades and knocked it over. Our Blessed Mother is acting with us, I thought, tearing down the blockades of prejudice and fear.

Within seconds, I knelt down in that holy place, clinging to my close friends: another religious priest, a religious brother, and two Catholic laywomen. Our two support friends were joining us in prayer from the so-called legal side of the police line. "Our Mother and Father, Who art in heaven . . . Hail Mary, full of grace . . . Glory be . . ." As we began to sing, the first of our friends was

151

handcuffed and taken away. "We shall overcome, someday . . ." In our attempt to pray for civil rights for lesbian and gay people, we were placed under arrest. As part of our active resistance to a system that oppresses and enslaves our own people, we tried to tell the truth, the whole truth, and nothing but the truth, and we were fingerprinted and photographed. On account of our noncooperation with institutional violence and hatred toward our sisters and brothers, we were stripped of personal belongings and thrown into holding cells. "Out of the closets and into the jails!" "You may lock us up, but we choose to remain *free!*"

Sitting in the cell, I reflected on my life's journey and how I was able to reach this point along the way. The arrest procedure was familiar to me; I'd committed civil disobedience for peace six times before. My first action to protest the arms race took place at the end of a course on nonviolence taught by Father Dan Berrigan at Maryknoll School of Theology. Before enrolling in Maryknoll's Institute for Justice and Peace, I had worked and marched for peace for sixteen years, employing all sorts of legal means. Father Berrigan and other teachers challenged me to take further steps in the peacemaking process. With fear and trembling, I prayed for peace at the Riverside Research Institute in New York City and was arrested. Again and again I ventured to pray for disarmament at Electric Boat in Groton, Connecticut, and at the Naval Underwater Systems Center in New London, Connecticut, and was led from police station to courtroom to give witness to peace. That well-known fear and trembling accompanied me each time. I knew that peace has its costs, however, and empowered by the Spirit of God and the friends with whom I acted, I was ready and willing to sacrifice my life.

And now in Washington, D.C., sitting in a cell, I realized that justice, too, has its costs. But God was still with me, and my friends remained at my side. It became clear to me that I was now at a crossroads in my life's journey, and that I may, indeed, be called to offer sacrifices for the sake of my gay brothers and lesbian sisters. My priesthood was about to take on new dimensions as Christ's command to lay down my life for my friends became concretized in my Holy Communion with the lesbian/gay community.

Where there is hatred, let me sow love. Where there is injury, pardon.

I knew from a young age that I wanted to be a priest. As a child, I was in love with God and was eager to learn more about my Catholic faith. I recited my prayers, memorized the questions and answers in the Baltimore Catechism and delighted in the Bible stories. My Sunday missal was my most prized possession, rivaled only by the Bible given to me by my Protestant grandfather. My rosary beads accompanied me everywhere, tucked deep in my pants pocket. Receiving Jesus in Holy Communion at mass filled me with peace; kneeling in prayer before a statue of Mary filled me with warmth; and lighting a candle in church filled me with hope. O God, I want to give you my life, I would pray. Let me be a holy priest.

I also knew from an early age that I was somehow different from other boys. While other kindergarten boys built castles and forts in the sandbox, I preferred to play house, color pictures, and tell stories. As classmates shared knowledge of athletes and ball players, I told them all about movie stars I'd watched on television. And when my friends bragged about their love for Annette on "The Mickey Mouse Club," I remained silent about my crushes on Spin and Marty and the Hardy boys.

Not only did I feel different from my friends, but this "difference" I later labeled "bad." My closest friends soon became interested in girls, yet I did not want to share them with the girls. At high school dances I danced with the girls but lusted after the boys. The locker room was both heaven and hell; I saw what I liked but was forbidden to touch. Falling in love was even more painful than finding myself sexually attracted to male classmates; keeping secrets of the heart led me into the depths of loneliness, alienation, and self-hatred.

For adolescents, the questions "Who am I?" and "What shall I do with my life?" are difficult to answer. For me, the question *"What* am I?" was even more agonizing. An answer came late one night as I watched the film *A Children's Hour* on television. In a final scene, the character played by Shirley MacLaine confessed her love to a character portrayed by Audrey Hepburn. As she tearfully berated herself as dirty and hateful, I identified with her feelings and began to sob uncontrollably. And when she hangs herself out of despair and shame, I panicked. Is that *my* future, cursed with the same sinful disease? I am a homosexual, I admitted to myself. I've let God down, I've let my family and school down. I can never be a priest. I hate myself, and if anyone ever finds out, they will hate me, too. *O God, forgive me!*

Where there is doubt, faith . . . Where there is despair, hope.

After graduating from high school with my secret intact, I began studies at an all-male Catholic college. My self-hatred intensified, as did my fear of being "found out." The movie *Boys in the Band* was released during my freshman year. Having read the play and memorized every line, I identified with Michael, the Catholic homosexual and alcoholic. I myself began to drink and found what I thought to be an escape. But my commitment to studies kept the drinking to a minimum.

I remained active within the church while in college. I taught C.C.D., worked on teams for college retreats, and attended mass daily. The religious lessons, the retreat talks, and mass homilies all focused on God's love and God's command to *be who we are*, lovable sons and daughters of God. Of course, I knew that I was the exception. No one, not even God, loves the homosexual.

This belief brought me to the brink of despair. While I began to protest against the war in Vietnam, I became a victim of the war going on inside of me. As I marched for peace in the world, I prayed for peace in my soul. And still the Vietnam conflict raged across the waters; and still the conflict between being Catholic and homosexual stormed within.

During my junior year, I studied French literature in Paris at the University of Nice. I met another homosexual student and finally shared my gayness with him; together we toured the gay subculture. My first visit to a gay bar was traumatic; it was raided by the police, who roughed us up a bit before leaving. I learned quickly that being "out of the closet" has its risks. I also discovered that it was time to decide between being gay and being Catholic. I chose to be gay and stopped going to mass. It was an easy choice, I thought. My increased intake of alcohol helped me remain faithful to that choice. My heart ached more than ever for my beloved God, however, and I could not handle the pain anymore. One night, I knelt beside my bed and prayed that if God wanted to take me to heaven, now was the time. If not, God would somehow save my life. I swallowed a fistful of pills and waited for God's decision. I woke up the next morning to a crowd of friends hovering over me. I wept in their arms, both ashamed at what I had done and overjoyed that God had saved me. I later took my rescue from death as a sign that God wanted me to live and to give my life fully to my Creator and the church as a priest.

I returned to the United States and to the church and searched for a religious community. I eventually chose the Capuchin Franciscans without knowing much about them. I wanted a conservative community in which I could hide my real identity and learn how to be someone else.

Where there is darkness, light . . . And where there is sadness, joy.

The day I received the Capuchin habit marked a new beginning for my life. By putting aside my secular clothing, I believed I was casting aside my gay identity; by donning the religious habit, I was putting on "the new man," freed from worldly concerns. I was going to be a friar and a priest, and if it meant denying my homosexuality, then that was a small price to pay.

The walls of the monastery, however, were unable to protect me from those sexual feelings and emotional attractions to others. Furthermore, I fear that homophobia was rampant not only within my own fraternity, but also throughout the whole province. I tried desperately to hide farther and farther in the closet, but I began to suffocate in the darkness, and while I tried to cry out for help, I felt that there was no one I could trust within the community. By spring, I found it difficult to walk. My legs were becoming paralyzed, and doctors were baffled by my condition. Some thought the problem was due to kneeling on the hard chapel floor, but I knew it had nothing to do with my prayer posture.

It was by chance that I read an advertisement for Dignity, an organization of gay/lesbian Catholics and their friends. Actually, it was more than mere chance; it was an answer to a prayer. I wrote a letter to the group, asking for a priest who would give me guidance. Within a week, I was visited by a Franciscan friar who listened compassionately and assured me that it *was* possible to be a priest and be gay. He suggested that I attend a Dignity mass in Boston to meet other gay and lesbian Catholics, but I told him that, since I was cloistered during my novitiate year, I could not leave the property.

Long after this friar left, I continued to fantasize about attending mass with other gay Catholics. Finally, I decided to sneak into Boston and make my dream come true. On Palm Sunday 1974 I stood on the sidewalk in front of St. Clement's Church, processing with scores of others waving palms, carrying banners, and singing exultantly. Tears ran down my face as I limped along into the church. I knew that I had found my own people, a family that shared my particular crosses and that promised me a taste of resurrection joys.

My life was transformed that day. Within a few weeks, I left novitiate and returned to school to obtain my teaching certificate. Meanwhile, I joined the Boston chapter of Dignity and tried to start a chapter in Connecticut. In April 1975 I heard about a priest in the Springfield, Massachusetts, area who wanted to start a Dignity chapter. I attended an organizational meeting held in Amherst, where, in addition to the diocesan priest, I met a former Passionist, a former Pauline, and a former Franciscan. I committed myself to the birth of this new chapter, a family in which I felt reborn. My legs were healed as I learned to walk proudly as a gay man. My emotional scars disappeared as I dared to love without fear. Thanks be to God, Dignity cured me of my self-hatred and taught me how to serve God and the church as the person I was created to be. Because of Dignity's ministry to me, I eventually returned to the Capuchin order, ready to minister as a friar and priest. After so many years of sadness, I was at long last filled with joy!

O master, grant that I may not so much seek to be consoled as to console, to be understood as to understand, to be loved as to love.

I was blessed with very dear friends in my novitiate class, and their friendship has sustained me over more than a dozen years in religious life. Although I continued to hide my gayness from superiors, I was able to share this important part of my life with several of my classmates. I still lived in morbid fear of being "found out" and thus "kicked out," so I took refuge in alcohol once again. Eventually I got into therapy, telling my secret to someone outside the community. It wasn't until after I was ordained that I dared tell my spiritual director. To my surprise, he'd known for years. He was a great support to me and helped me to believe that God was calling me to minister to the lesbian/gay community.

My first assignment as a priest was to serve as chaplain to the girls' Catholic high school that was the sister school to my alma mater. This placement also enabled me to serve my own Dignity chapter as chaplain. I was returning to the very place where I first agonized over my sexuality and to a family of people who enabled me to claim this sexuality as a holy gift from God. For more than six years, I have faithfully served the young people of the Norwich diocese, affirming their specialness, lovableness, and holiness. This fidelity is due to my rootedness in the Dignity community, which has supported me through the deaths of my brother and father, which has helped me to understand God's will for me, and which has helped me to really believe that *I* am loved.

Dignity has been my most immediate experience of church. As a safe, nurturing community of friends, we worship our God with heartfelt devotion and steadfast commitment. Just as Dignity once saved my life, so we continue to save others' lives. We have led some people back to church; we are the reason many stay in the church; we have helped others to join our church. In the midst of continued persecution and oppression, we are growing even stronger. Like the early Christians, we will not be intimidated by

violence and rejection. Animated by the Spirit of God, we share
with the world the good news of who we are, and as a valuable
part of the Body of Christ, we remain faithful to the call to be
Catholic, lesbian, and gay.

For it is in giving that we receive, pardoning that we are pardoned, and in dying that we are born to eternal life.

I model my priestly life on Christ, the One who sacrificed his life
out of love for the sake of the world. I model my religious life on
Saint Francis of Assisi, the little one whose embrace of the
crucified Christ in the flesh of the leper enabled him to rebuild a
church falling into ruin. Both Christ and Francis have helped me
to celebrate my gayness as an instrument of grace for myself and
for others. I am convinced that my sensitivity to the suffering of
others and my compassionate commitment to justice and peace
concerns are due to my homosexuality and the long process of
accepting it. As I have struggled to integrate my faith, ministry,
and personhood in the face of rejection, hatred, and fear, so, too,
am I particularly in tune with those persons who are battling
alienation, self-doubt, and despair. I am at one with those who
question the meaning of life and who have been crippled with
alcohol abuse. Having overcome the deadly effects of homophobia
in my own life, I am free to affirm the innate goodness of all
persons, young and old. At long last liberated from the slavery of
heterosexism, I am at liberty to rescue those burdened with
prejudices and bigotry.

Whenever I celebrate mass, baptize a child, witness a marriage,
pray the words of absolution with a penitent, or anoint someone
who is sick, I am reminded of the sanctity of life and the dignity of
the human person. My preaching and teaching always underscore
these foundational moral themes. By my religious vows of
poverty, chastity, obedience, and nonviolence I have publicly
committed myself to upholding these values for all of humanity.
Thus, as a priest and as a religious, my sacramental and prophetic
ministries are intertwined. To heal, reconcile, and share Holy
Communion, I must denounce whatever wounds, divides, and

dismembers. In order to bless and make holy, I ought to promote unity and justice.

Amen!

I return, then, to the steps of the Supreme Court. I celebrate a liturgy for liberation, praying within the confines of Communion rails marked "Police Line—Do Not Cross." I preach a "Sermon on the Steps." "Blessed are you who are persecuted by Supreme Court justices; your reward is great in heaven." I offer up my body; I sacrifice my blood. I am consumed by a political system that refuses to liberate my sisters and brothers. I look out over the crowds singing, "We are a gay and lesbian people. And we are singing, singing for our lives." As I am led away, I think of Jesus. "Are you a king?" they asked him. "Are you a queen?" they ask me. I remember my story, my journey, my pilgrimage. I look at my friends. "Yes!" I exclaim. "I am a priest. I am gay. I am proud. And I'll be back!"

16 You Are My People

BROTHER JONATHAN

I am a gay man and a religious brother. I start this from the beginning because both these parts of my identity have extraordinary influence on my perception of the world and religious life. I put gay man before religious brother because I was aware of my sexual identity long before I entered a religious order.

I am certain that I knew I was attracted to men as early as five years of age. I have a recollection of this, as well as an equally strong awareness that this was not something I could share. It was my secret.

As I reached puberty I knew my attractions were not what the other boys in the class experienced. I was different. I was frightened by this difference, and since I had no one to talk to about it, I had to secretly look up the word *homosexual* in the dictionary. It was just the beginning of my journey into my sexuality and what this powerful force meant in my life. Of course, I remained "in the closet" during those years although there was some sexual experimentation with other boys during that time.

Religion and spirituality were also powerful forces in my life. I was, by any standard, a pious child. Being an altar boy, frequent attendance at mass, and the nuns' hope that I was "the one" who would have a vocation to be a priest—all these marked my early life. I cannot recall how often I was given a prayer book, holy card, or vocation talk by some well-meaning nun. It all had its effect. Again, I had a sense of being different from my peers. I felt, in some deep level of being, "the call." A growing desire to pray and serve the people of God did emerge; yet it was not a desire to the priesthood that they had all hoped for. I wanted to live in a community with other men. Although I was never taught by brothers, their vocation attracted me. As I look back, I am sure it was the community life of the nuns that was a decisive influence. They lived together and seemed to have fun doing it. The parish priest by comparison seemed lonely and isolated. I already knew, by the experience of my sexuality, what isolation and loneliness were all about. And I knew I could not live that way by choice.

Before being accepted by the congregation to which I had applied, I met some of the young brothers. I was a little alarmed when one of them told me that two of the brothers in his community were being "chaptered." To be chaptered is to be kicked out of the community. While he would not say why they were being sent away, I knew it was because of their homosexuality. What I did not know at the time was how many of the brothers in formation were gay and quite active in the bar scene of the city we lived in. Again, in my isolation, my fears convinced me that I had to be very careful lest any one have reason to believe I was homosexual.

I was not reassured when I took the psychological tests. I was convinced that such tests were really meant to discover who were the hidden homosexuals. I agonized over it, not wanting to appear too macho or too feminine. The questions themselves seemed loaded with meaning. For example, "Would you rather be a truck driver or an interior decorator?" That seemed just too obvious. As these types of questions continued to appear I became more convinced that they were meant to uncover my big secret. I never knew how they read the results of those tests, but I was accepted.

Contrary to what many may think, I never found being homosexual in a same-sex community to be a great problem. The day-to-day reality of living together usually killed any infatuations quickly, and there were many obvious benefits. Moments of "high camp" provided a way for us to communicate and act out one's unique identity in a safe and acceptable way. Although it allowed us to form a loose network of bonding at a time when there were few alternatives, I see it today as an unhealthy way to live. One

never really had to deal with one's sexuality. I must, however, give
the congregation credit for exposing us to homosexuality in a
nonthreatening and nonjudgmental way through various guest
speakers. But I have learned that nothing can make homosexuals
deal with their sexuality until they are ready to do so.

I was one of the reluctant ones. I lived "in the closet" in
religious life for many years. I never talked about my sexuality or
homosexuality in general. I simply did not want to deal with it.
Some readers may be confused at this point. How could I know
from the age of five that I was attracted to men and yet remain so
closeted? I learned my lessons well and was conditioned by my
environment. Very simply, to be homosexual was bad. And, I
thought, what difference did it make? I was celibate. I was not in
love with anyone. As I look back on that period of my life, I realize
how emotionally shut down I was. Blocking my sexuality also
blocked my affective life. Only after five years in religious life was I
even able to write the word *homosexual* in my journal. Even that
little bit of self-disclosure was frightening to me not because
another might read it but because, once I wrote the word, I was
committed and there was no turning back.

Two events occurred that forced me to deal with my sexuality in
a more honest way. The first involved a friend of mine in the
community who "came out" to me on a walk we were taking
during our annual eight-day retreat. It was no great surprise to me,
and yet I could see how concerned he was that I accept him.
Besides being a friend, I was also his superior and received this
information as his superior. I responded with compassion. Because he was celibate, I did not see why his being homosexual
would make any difference. I affirmed him and encouraged him in
his sexuality, but I did not share my secret as you would expect of
a friend. The doors remained shut even to those close to me. I
think my friend understood what was happening. I felt a growing
pressure from him to reveal myself to him in a similar way. We
both knew I was homosexual, but admitting it out loud to another
was just as traumatic as the first time I wrote the word *homosexual*
in my journal.

At the same time I began to realize that a young woman my age
had fallen in love with me. I loved her also but knew that she had

hope that this love would be fulfilled in a way that I knew was impossible for me. By refusing to tell her about this part of my person I knew that I was deceiving her. The integrity of both these relationships demanded that I disclose my secret. I could no longer pretend. To do so would doom both relationships to being superficial and limited.

I came out to both of them. Until the very moment I did so, I still feared their rejection. But I have never regretted that decision. To my brother in community it was a moment that was to bind us deeply in the years ahead, even when he chose to depart religious life. And it only deepened the love and respect this woman and I had for each other. This is not to deny it was painful for her, but I could not, in truth, spare her the pain. There was a period of grieving together for what could never be, whether I was in religious life or not: a sexual expression of our love.

Coming out to these two people was the first step, and for me there was no turning back. Slowly I began to share this with other significant people in my life. I have felt only affirmation and a real deepening of our bonds of friendship. In time I also had to share it with my parents, although I knew it would cause much pain in our relationship. To deny them this vital part of me was to doom our relationship to shallowness. They chose, while accepting me completely, not to talk about it after the initial disclosure. Although this disappoints me, I realize I cannot rush them any more than I was rushed. It remains an unspoken topic between us. My being in religious life makes it easier for them since they do not have to wonder who I am dating or if I will bring someone home to meet them. By my not having a boyfriend or lover they never really have to confront my sexuality.

One other incident, another moment of truth, stands out in my journey into integrating my sexual identity and religious life. I was the vocation director of our community in the United States. The superior general was visiting this province and came into my office one day to "chat." Almost in passing he mentioned that we really had to be "careful not to accept those kinds of people." The implication was obvious, though never mentioned specifically; "those people" were homosexuals. One novice had just been arrested for soliciting an undercover cop in a park. In my superior's mind this was what one could expect for allowing such people into the community. I was stunned because this ban had sweeping implications for all the gay members of our community.

I was devastated and turned to friends in the community, both gay and straight, to learn how to respond to such ignorance. I wondered if the superior knew I was gay. Did he have any idea how many gay men there were in the priesthood and religious life? Gay men had lived celibate lives and had worked for the church from the early days of the first apostles until the present.

I realized I could ignore or waffle on my superior's words. He would leave soon and we could just go on as before. But it seemed to me a moment of truth. I respected him enough to want to enlighten him a little, and I did not want to live in a community with such a policy toward gay men since to do so would be to live a lie.

My own integrity demanded that I reveal that I was gay. For my superior's growth it was necessary that I put my future in this community on the line. Before talking to him I prepared myself for the worst. I surrendered it all to God. Maybe this was an answer to prayer, and I was to leave religious life. Maybe this was the resolution to the tension I felt living as a gay religious in an atmosphere that did not affirm my own sexuality.

My superior was shocked and told me that he had never suspected I was gay. Since he really did not know what to say, the whole matter of accepting gay candidates was dropped. Clearly nervous and frightened over the issue of homosexuality, he has never again mentioned it. I am sad for him because I believe that to the extent that he refuses to face the issue of sexuality, he has stunted his emotional and spiritual growth. The spiritual life cannot be compartmentalized; refusal to grow in one area arrests growth in all the areas of human development.

During all these years of fear and pain, growth and deep wonder over my sexuality, the passages of Scripture that always spoke loudest to my heart were those from Psalm 139 and Isaiah: "It was you who created my inmost self, and put me together in my mother's womb; for all these mysteries I thank you: for the wonder of myself, for the wonder of your works" (Ps 139:13–14). "The Lord called me from birth, from my mother's womb He gave me my name" (Isa. 49:1); "Can a mother forget her infant, be without tenderness for the child of her womb? Even should she forget, I will never forget you" (Isa. 49:15). And then the challenge: "Saying to the prisoners: Come out! To those in darkness: Show yourselves" (Isa. 49:9).

I felt that immense love for me as a child, teenager, and adult. I knew in the depths of my heart that God loved me, even as a homosexual. In a special way I understood Jesus' passion and the passion of the poor through my own experience of being oppressed as a gay man. In my denial of my sexuality I agonized with Jesus on the way to his death. To be laughed at and called names such as "queer" and "faggot" felt like a whip across my back, as did the lash of the centurion. To be misjudged and condemned for something over which I had no control pierced my heart as the lance did Jesus' heart. I understood what it was like to be an invisible person; I knew that internalized self-hatred prevented me from truly loving God or other people fully.

In coming out I also realized that what had caused me such pain, and what everyone else considered such a cross, was a real gift to me because I saw things with "new eyes" and heard with "new ears." Looking at the wild diversity with which God had fashioned the world, I could not imagine how such a loving God could create something that everyone else called unnatural. Who decided what was natural and what was unnatural? I have a sense that my sexuality was formed by all the events of my life from the time of my conception. Just as a potter carefully molds a vase, so too God formed me as a spiritual, sexual being. I was not just an accident. The creation begun in my mother's womb continues today in my sexual and spiritual personhood.

A God who would give creatures such a beautiful thing as sexuality and then insist that they deny and never express it seemed cruel. This would clearly imply you were never to become the fully loving person you had been created to become. Slowly I began to realize that the pain of accepting and learning to love my uniqueness as a gay man was the instrument God used to form me and to make me sensitive to the cries of all minorities: the poor, blacks, Chicanos, women. Christ's anguish, his passion, his rejection, his death, and his eventual transformation were expressed in the reality of my own journey. In my sexuality I came to know a personal Jesus. I had followed his steps to Golgotha. Just as sexuality had been my death, so it had been my resurrection and transformation.

Owning my gay sexuality changed my whole life. When I told another person I was gay, I chose to affirm my sexuality. This new consciousness was an answer to prayer. The more I affirmed my gay sexuality, the more my life became whole. It affected my prayer life, my work, and my relationships within and outside the community.

I need to be open about my sexuality because I need to associate with and be affirmed as good and loving by other gay men and by lesbians. With them I have a sense of completeness, and of total and unconditional acceptance. Although I value all my friends, I know I need my gay friends in a special way. They remind me that self-hatred had been taught to me from childhood and that I will easily fall back into that self-hatred unless I continue to affirm and be affirmed as good. As a religious who has worked with the poor and persecuted in the United States and in Latin America, I see how the forces of oppression are subtle and ultimately destructive unless we bond together in community. What we cannot do alone, we can do together. Ironically, it is my sexuality that has brought me and bonded me to both God and the poor in a way I could never have imagined. It is a major part of my person, not because I want it to be that way, but as a result of the oppression and hatred directed at gay people by our church and society.

Sexuality enhanced my religious life, my personal spiritual journey, and also my work for the poor and oppressed. It made me sensitive to others' suffering in my community, to women's issues in church and society, and to the cry of all oppressed and marginalized people. I was not black, or Chicano, or poor, or of the wrong social group—but I was gay. And that one factor gave me a choice. I could "pass," as the light-skinned blacks used to say, or I could confront the blatant homophobia in my community, church, and society. I have chosen the latter.

I look back now with more insight than I had when I first joined religious life. I suspect God used motives that were less than pure to bring me to religious life. Although I felt a call to follow Jesus and serve the people of God, I suspect I also came here for a certain safety and dignity that being a gay man in the world would not provide. Perhaps my own homophobia and fear were part of the reason I became a religious. After exploring my sexuality, however, I believe my reasons for staying are a little purer.

Being open about my sexuality has never seemed the real problem to me. But church officials wish we gays were back in our closets and once again invisible because our presence calls them to reexamine all their assumptions. In my experience as a superior in my community, the real problems are always with those who are repressing their sexuality, for they are like time bombs waiting to explode. Massive denial and silence prevent the church from fully integrating sexuality and spirituality, but until this integration is accomplished any moral pronouncements will continue to fall on deaf ears.

While church officials preach celibacy to gay men and women as the only acceptable and moral way of life open to them, I know of efforts being made to ensure that gay men and women will be screened out of religious orders and seminaries. Yet I wonder how anyone can be celibate without a loving and supportive community. For me, the community provided the loving environment that allowed me to begin to explore the gift of my sexuality. By being loved, accepted, and affirmed as precious by my community, I was able to accept and affirm that part of me that I had denied and hated.

Today I live in the San Francisco area and work with AIDS patients. As a gay man ministering to the gay and lesbian community, as well as those dying of AIDS, I have had to examine sexuality once again. I am "out" here in a way I have never been before. I can make no real efforts to hide my sexuality from those to whom I minister. To hide my sexuality requires an energy I no longer have and a violence to self I can no longer endure; so I have come to the "new Jerusalem" with its wide open Golden Gate to complete the healing journey I embarked on many years ago. San Francisco, a world model of tolerance of minorities and care of those dying of AIDS, has opened its gates to a people who wandered in the trackless desert too long looking for a home, and it welcomes all those with AIDS to come here to die with dignity. Their own will never reject them. I see here a community of gay men and lesbians struggling to live with the devastation of AIDS in their lives. I see a responsible, caring, and loving people who have formed a deep, bonded community and have rediscovered family.

Trying to integrate sexuality and spirituality in a church deadly afraid of sexuality is very difficult and, in the present climate, even dangerous. But this integration is my call from the Lord and my answer is, "Yes, Lord." If I can do anything as a gay religious, I hope it will be to help gay men and lesbians love themselves as I know God loves them. Although they have not often felt this love from our church, I hope gay men and lesbians will rejoice with me in our homosexuality, for indeed my sexuality has been God's loving gift to me. Through sexuality God entered my being and spoke to my heart with a passion that has turned my whole world upside down. Through sexuality God has transformed my life profoundly by vitally connecting me to the very core of who I am in the depths of my physical, emotional, and spiritual being as well as to the God of my youth.

Harvey Milk, the first openly gay supervisor of San Francisco, said it was the duty of all gay men and women to come out as we no longer have the luxury of our closets. Coming out was not a political statement for me, as Harvey Milk might have perceived it, but was one stage of my journey toward wholeness. Since each person follows his or her own rhythm in dealing with and accepting sexuality, no one can tell others to come out. Everyone must follow her or his own heart concerning the right time to share this information. Attitudes will not change until the oppressors see that the oppressed are those they love: a father or mother, sister or brother, beloved child, favorite uncle or aunt, nephew or neighbor or best friend. Frederick Douglass (1950) reminds us that "the limits of tyrants are prescribed by the endurance of those whom they oppress" (p. 437). We have found our limits.

Although I do not know the future, I know that my life will never be the same. I have begun to experience the joy and exhilaration of a community of men and women who have in the past twenty years known the victory of Harvey Milk and also the anguish of his assassination. A community's basic human rights have been under attack from religious, political, and social leaders. When a people, devastated by AIDS, are faced with losing all, there is nothing left but the freedom to be who we are and to be proud of it. We need each other lest we despair in isolation and give up the struggle. To return to our closets is to admit defeat, for in our closets self-hatred, fear, and disintegration will again become the norm for our lives. To "come out" today is to choose the values Jesus preached—love, both of self and others; freedom from fear through bonding into community; and wholeness of being.

All of this is imprinted on my heart and soul. I have been marked and will never be the same. When I see the life-and-death issues we face, I realize how trivial are the concerns of so many church people. Issues such as religious dress, Catholic schools, conformity, liturgy, and even power fade into irrelevance.

My role, so unclear, may be only a modest one of offering a home, a place of safety, and a warm welcome to my gay brothers and lesbian sisters. I must do my part and cannot wait for the extended church family to do its share. As a bumper sticker puts it: "When the people lead, the leaders will follow." T. S. Eliot (1943) states: "The end of all our exploring will be to arrive where we started and know the place for the first time" (p. 58). Owning one's sexuality is coming home for perhaps the first time in one's life.

Although I now experience a certain ease in my journey toward sexual and spiritual integration, the past was not always easy and I suspect the future will hold new hurdles. Again the words of Isaiah give me hope: "The oppressed shall soon be released; they shall not die and go down into the pit, nor shall they want for bread. . . . I have put my words into your mouth and shielded you in the shadow of my hand, I who stretched out the heavens, who laid the foundations of the earth, who say to Zion: You are My people" (Isa. 52:14, 16).

References

Douglass, F. 1950. The West Indian Emancipation Speech. In *The Life and Writings of Frederick Douglass*, edited by P. Foner. New York: International Publications.

Eliot, T. S. 1943. *Four Quartets*. New York: Harcourt, Brace and World.

17 Without Shame

FATHER AELRED

It is a great consolation in this life to have someone to whom you
can be united in the intimate embrace of the most sacred love . . .
with whom you can rest, just the two of you, in the sleep of peace,
away from the noise of the world, in the kiss of unity, with the
sweetness of the Holy Spirit flowing over you.

Saint Aelred of Rievaulx

Recently I attended a seminarian/priest get-together sponsored by
our diocesan vocation office. At the end of the evening many of
the younger men hugged one another rather intimately. Two of
the newly ordained deacons even kissed each other on the lips
unselfconsciously, but with genuine affection. No one, including
the bishops, seemed shocked. Most of these fellows are probably
just close friends, while some, like myself, certainly must be
homosexual.

What a difference from my student days and early priesthood!
No hugs, no kisses, no anything. Physical contact was almost
completely forbidden. A few persons became afraid of touching
their own bodies, even modestly, let alone the flesh of anyone else.
As a result, it took me a long time to grow comfortable with
intimate feelings or interpersonal relationships, and a much longer
period to understand, acknowledge, and accept my love for other
men without a sense of shame.

Because of the church's repressive silence, it has also taken me years to learn that, however chaste their vows, numerous saintly priests of the past were noted for passionate male friendships. Although perhaps not gay, these clerics nevertheless experienced the same deep emotions usually associated with homosexual people of my own generation. Such holy individuals, as I now realize, have existed throughout every major cycle in Christian history, from earlier epochs (Saint Basil the Great, Saint Gregory Nazianzen, Saint Paulinus of Nola), to medieval times (Saint Anselm of Canterbury, Saint Bernard of Clairvaux, Saint Thomas à Becket), and in the twentieth century (possibly Saint Maximilian Kolbe). What a marvelous revelation this is for me!

Indeed, as I now know from extensive study, the church has always had some undoubtedly gay priests since the time of Christ himself. We truly were, and still are, everywhere. This discovery gives me immense confidence and reassurance. Prominent clerics who had a homosexual dimension in their lives include popes (John XXII, Julius II, Leo X), cardinals (John Henry Newman), bishops (Saint Louis d'Anjou of Toulouse), abbots (Saint Aelred of Rievaulx), priest-poets (Gerard Manley Hopkins), and many more whose sexual orientation has been long suppressed by our ecclesiastical historians. No longer! Together with other excited lesbian and gay researchers, I am uncovering the past to chart a better future.

Seminary: Naive Background

Unfortunately, while I was growing up, I knew of absolutely no gay role models, priestly or otherwise. Moreover, after I entered the seminary, I heard literally nothing even about celebrated male friendships, regardless of our sainted clerical forebears.

On the contrary, I remember lectures and regulations and reprimands about the dangers of intimate relationships with fellow classmates. We were forbidden to seek out special companions during our recreation breaks. We were called into the rector's office if some faculty member noticed too close an association with another student, especially of a different grade.

In fact, although the rules were derived from sexual concerns, I understood very little about human sexuality, let alone about same-sex orientation as a given reality. And I certainly did not then perceive that I was gay, despite some genital involvements with male friends during the previous years of parochial school.

After joining the seminary ranks, I recall hearing words such as *queer, fag, pansy,* and *bugger.* But upon approaching my spiritual director, I received only very basic information about the "facts of life." I learned nothing about healthy celibate sexuality or the meaning of homosexual preferences. Throughout my seminary training, I developed crushes on a number of priests and always managed to choose an "idol" for spiritual direction. I still remember the joy of telling my innermost secrets to one particular confessor who always laid his hand on the penitent's shoulder as a source of amazing comfort and encouragement.

Fortunately, despite restrictions, I also had several very dear friends, although we never became genitally involved with one another. I remember discussing our personal "problems" of masturbation in an effort to understand what I now believe normal in one's development. I likewise recall conversing with some classmates about the beauty of a man's body and sharing with others my delight over statues of naked or near-nude male figures. Sometimes surreptitiously, at my own leisure, I sought out books about Greek and Roman mythologies to view the pictures of partially clad gods and men. Naturally, I also relished our communal showers.

I never regarded myself as one of those degenerate "fruits" or perverted "fairies" we sometimes heard and read about. I was a clean, devout, well-behaved, above-average student, who happily studied in all-male seminaries and prepared for the all-male priesthood of a sexless Jesus. Yet I was living in darkness about my innermost makeup, while presumably walking in the light.

Priesthood: Evolving Awareness

After ordination to the priesthood I continued, rather unconsciously, to develop and clarify my healthy homoerotic interests. For example, I loved to admire the grace of male dancers in their performances of classical and modern ballet. Perhaps only vaguely aware of being somewhat different, I held many unembarrassed discussions with my fellow priests on the subject of sexual variations.

Eventually I had my first homogenital experience since the time of those harmless sexplorations during grade school. It happened with another priest, who was my closest friend. An intense guilt inhibited the full pleasure of the adventure for both of us, and we availed ourselves of the sacrament of reconciliation as soon as possible the next morning.

Shortly thereafter I started upon a period of anonymous and promiscuous sex, of which I am hardly proud today. I was in my thirties but going on nineteen. Fearful of discovery, guilty yet weak, I prowled the usual homosexual haunts for affection, tenderness, and warmth. But I still considered myself a heterosexual person who was deliberately perverting his natural instincts with the wrong gender. The awareness and especially the acceptance of a gay identity would be a long time in coming. I doubt whether I would have needed such noncelibate experiments if the church had taught me the real truth about the goodness of homosexual love.

One evening at a nearby gay bar, I spied another, younger, very handsome priest with whom I had long been secretly "in love," though unaware of his sexual preferences. During our hesitant conversation, eventually overheard by other friendly patrons, more Catholic priests came forth and introduced themselves; the first was from a neighboring diocese, the next from a well-known house of studies. I will never forget my joyous, heartfelt excitement upon realizing I was not the only homosexual clergyman in the world. I will always treasure that initial wondrous experience of sharing mutual concerns and affirming similar interests amid self-defined gay priests.

With a growing consciousness of my true sexual identity I began exploring the many-faceted areas of gay and lesbian life. In search of self-understanding, I participated in discussion groups about affectional orientation, attended liturgies for homosexual people and their friends, enjoyed plays and movies with gay themes, and bought gay papers, pamphlets, and nonpornographic periodicals. Having lived so long in a "straight" world and an "uptight" church, I now desired and found the needed role models to help me comprehend the meaning of my sexual self.

Most importantly, I discovered Dignity, the organization of lesbian and gay Catholics and their supporters. More than any other group, Dignity enabled me to perceive and share the truth about my sexuality without fear of ridicule or violence. Dignity members reached out with acceptance, encouragement, and affirmation and thus aided me to grow in self-respect and Christian maturity. With Dignity friends I found it possible to express myself freely in a physical, nongenital manner. I gave and received affection with both sexes through handholding, touching, hugging, kissing, even dancing. Such natural responses drained off energies previously directed toward indiscriminate outlets and assisted me in reasserting my moral commitment to Christ. Because I felt increasingly good about myself as a homosexual person, erotic urges could be controlled and morality once more assumed its proper place in my life.

Although I was again reconciled to clerical promises, I began falling in love one day with someone from another town and another religion. I needed to decide between celibate priesthood and sexual fulfillment.

After much consultation, personal reflection, and ardent prayer, I opted to remain a priest and to stay with my lover, provided that we gave no scandal to others and avoided schizophrenic fallout in ourselves. I did not regard my behavior as in any way reprehensible, unlike the earlier promiscuous period of mostly anonymous sex. In fact, throughout the years of our committed and faithful relationship, I became a more effective minister, deepened my spiritual perceptions, and drew closer to Christ than I had ever been before.

Today I no longer have a lover and on occasion still experience his loss very deeply. I treasure our precious years together and thank God for the gift of another person who taught me more than an asexual church ever could. Although I am now living as the Roman hierarchy would wish, I do not feel graced with the charism of celibacy, and yet I definitely know that I am called to service. We need a priesthood with options; we need a Catholic community that accepts and blesses multiple types of ministry and relationships.

I feel especially angry and frustrated with those bishops who strenuously oppose legislative efforts to guarantee the rights of lesbian/gay people against unjust discrimination. Even when proposed bills clearly make sexual orientation (*not* genital behavior) a protected category and specifically exempt religious organizations from any compliance contrary to their beliefs, some major prelates still issue statements grounded in ignorance and conducive to violence. It pains me to see my homosexual sisters and brothers treated with such insensitivity. How difficult it becomes to reassure them of God's love when they are thereby denied reasonable laws for fair housing and equal employment opportunities!

Nowadays I move very freely in gay and lesbian circles, sometimes with other diocesan or religious priests, although most remain cautiously closeted outside our own gatherings. I myself belong, for example, both to a gay classical music club and to the gay community center, which wholesomely affirms homosexual identity through its many programs. Periodically I attend meetings of a gay priests' support group in the local area and have gone to retreats for gay clergy elsewhere around the country. I especially cherish several national organizations of gay priests and lesbian religious, such as Communication Ministry and Christian Community Association, which publish insightful newsletters and sponsor liberating reunions for their membership. I deem myself healthily adjusted to my sexual orientation and yearn for the time when both church and society can accept me as an openly gay individual.

Reflections

I say it "without shame" (Gen. 2:25): I am homosexual. I now know it without any doubt, despite the years of church-induced repression. Indeed, I have matured to the point where I can shout it with pride and joy. If I still hide behind a pseudonym, I must do so not because of guilt, remorse, or fear of stigma but to protect myself from the ignorant reactions of others and the very real possibility of ecclesiastical vindictiveness.

I am gay and happy. I am not neurotic, morbid, or maladjusted. I feel it perfectly natural to love a man instead of a woman. Yet, contrary to popular opinion, I am not repelled by the other sex and relate with ease to both genders in social and religious circumstances.

Like most gay men, I am not effeminate, although I have learned to move beyond the traditional sexist notions of masculinity and femininity. Like other gay persons, I am not oversexed, although for purposes of this article I have mainly described sexual matters rather than my many different accomplishments; in fact, I have come to regard sexuality as one of God's greatest gifts to us and as a beautiful component of all human relationships. I am not attracted to young boys any more than most heterosexual males are interested in young girls; however, I do take notice quite naturally when some fellow is shaping into a handsome man, just as most men admire the girl who is becoming a beautiful woman. There are absolutely no apologies necessary for anything about my same-sex fantasies and feelings.

Because I have tasted the gall of homosexual oppression, I have grown more responsive to the needs of those who suffer in any way. Since I experience the meaning of differentness within myself, I instinctively reach out in support of other minorities who are rejected due to their innate characteristics or given situation.

By appreciating my own distinctive affectional preference, I have also discovered within myself certain singular qualities that were either developed or sharpened through the painful years of hard-won adjustment. I now believe that gay and lesbian persons, as Richard Woods states in his book *Another Kind of Love* (1978), often acquire "the ability to see with different eyes, that is, to disengage themselves from the value-systems uncritically accepted in society at large . . . [and] the power to risk decisions which straight men and women, because of their greater stake in the dominant social system, cannot even consider" (p. 112). Due to the negative sanctions of an unsympathetic public, I myself have learned to examine motives and analyze behavior, to tolerate ambiguity and sharpen critical skills, and thus to forge ahead in imaginatively new directions. I feel that the resultant questioning of conventional attitudes and concomitant skepticism about time-honored practices have become a constructive force in my life and service. Rather than see the world through the eyes of the majority, I hold a view and a vision that not only set me apart but also influence my readiness to deal with the contingencies of human existence in a more creative manner.

Some phobic people fanatically judge homosexuality a cross to be borne or a curse to be escaped rather than a life to be lived and a gift to be blessed. I have come to view my own sexual orientation as the source of many important vital traits that are making my ministry more sensitive and increasingly effective. Though indeed only one facet of total personal makeup, gayness has nevertheless enriched my priestly vocation with special positive characteristics that stimulate dynamic outreach and provide gratifying fulfillment.

Reference

Woods, R. 1978. *Another Kind of Love: Homosexuality and Spirituality.* Garden City, N.Y.: Image.

MINISTERIAL
PERSPECTIVES

18 The Sycamore Is Not the Only Kind of Tree Outside My Window

JOHN P. HILGEMAN

As I write this, I can look out my window and see evidence of the most beautiful St. Louis spring I have ever seen. Outside there is a stately old sycamore tree that only a week ago was bare, but now is covered with small green leaves that will be as big as my hand in another week or so. The grass is growing in clumps; flowers are all over the neighborhood. The sun is marvelous. The cat who lives with me is lying on the floor by my feet. I have seen her grow from a tiny kitten into a large, intelligent white cat.

Lesbians and gay males are like trees and cats. They begin as specks of matter. They thrive on food, light, water, air, and nurturing; they have their seasons of life. Like trees and cats, they must overcome storms and disease. They can be mutilated and killed.

Last night a woman wept while pleading with me for advice on how to get her mid-twenties daughter to leave a forty-year-old lesbian who was "trapping" her into lesbianism. Calling homosexuality a disease of the devil that would send her daughter to hell, the mother said she felt like vomiting every time she thought of her daughter having sex with a woman. I tried to express to the mother that, if her daughter is truly a lesbian, she may have been

181

aware of her orientation for some time. I tried to let her know that homosexuality is not a satanic disease that can corrupt people, but is as natural an element in some people's personality as race and gender and is as impossible to change.

God has made a truly remarkable world. The sycamore tree is not the only kind of tree outside my window; there are oak and maple trees outside as well. There were several other cats in the same litter as the one that lives with me. One was a black Siamese; another was a small semi-Siamese white cat. One was a male cat colored like the sunrise.

When *Voyager II* flew past the planet Uranus and its moons, it saw things that had not been seen on any of the other planets or moons of the solar system. Who knows what things will yet be discovered in the vast universe in which we are only a tiny speck, what geologic wonders, and what forms of life? Is Uranus unnatural because its magnetic axis is tipped 60 degrees from its axis of rotation? Or is the moon Miranda unnatural because it has a combination of terrains not seen on any planet or moon to date?

Are gay people unnatural because they are sexually attracted primarily to members of their own gender? Are our eyes so open and our minds so intelligent that we can know with surety the plans and will of God? We need to approach our gay and lesbian fellow human beings with open eyes to learn, with open hearts to love and be loved, and with open arms to encourage and nurture, to be encouraged and nurtured.

Lesbian and gay people have similarities to each other but are also unique individuals. In the seasons of a human's life there is a time for awareness of one's sexual identity and orientation to develop. That awareness comes in stages at different times to different individuals. Some gay men are first aware of an attraction for males as early as four or five, whereas most lesbians speak of an awareness coming much later in life. Many people become aware of their sexual orientation and identity in their teens, but some people never become aware. The big problem of sexuality in the ministry is asexuality; many priests and brothers remain unaware of their sexuality.

Seminaries and houses of formation have often made it difficult and sometimes impossible for men to deal with their sexuality, whether they are heterosexual, bisexual, or homosexual. Open discussion of sexuality has been discouraged, and any kind of sexual experimentation is a cause for dismissal. Gay males in the ministry experience a problem in integrating their sexuality into their lives for two other reasons. The first is that society as a whole discourages the integration of homosexuality into a person's life. The social ideals are heterosexual marriage and family, or some other kind of heterosexual relationship or behavior. Movies, television programs, textbooks, marriage laws, comments of relatives, laws against homosexual behavior, legal discrimination against gay people, remarks of peers, lack of positive gay role models—all reinforce heterosexual identity and militate against developing a homosexual identity.

The second reason for the integration problems encountered by gay males in the ministry is the opposition of church leaders not only to an open discussion of the morality of homosexual activity, but also to ministry to lesbian and gay people, to the homosexual orientation itself, and to the basic human rights of homosexuals. Four examples come to mind immediately: (1) the Vatican's silencing of John McNeill and his eventual ousting from the Jesuits, (2) the opposition of Archbishop Hickey to New Ways Ministry and the order from the Congregation for Religious and Secular Institutes to Jeannine Gramick and Robert Nugent to leave New Ways Ministry, (3) Cardinal Ratzinger's removal of Charles Curran's canonical mission to teach as a Catholic theologian, and (4) the loss of Archbishop Raymond Hunthausen's authority in pastoral ministry to the homosexual community.

Church leaders and Vatican documents still speak of homosexuality as a disease that can be cured, despite overwhelming psychological evidence to the contrary. The document *Educational Guidance in Human Love* (Baum 1983) says: "Homosexuality, which impedes the person's acquisition of sexual maturity . . . is a problem. . . . Pastorally, these homosexuals must be received with understanding and supported in the hope of overcoming their personal difficulties and their social maladaptation" (p. 36). The Vatican letter to the Catholic bishops of the world on the pastoral care of homosexual persons calls the orientation "a disordered sexual inclination which is essentially self-indulgent" (Ratzinger 1986, 380).

In recent years, there have been many instances of church

leaders actively opposing the rights of lesbian and gay persons. John Cardinal O'Connor in New York fought not only an executive order in court, but also a bill in the City Council that even exempts religious institutions. He also joined bishops around the country in expelling Dignity chapters from church facilities. Imagine the problems for gay priests who are expected to follow the lead of such bishops! In his letter to the Catholic bishops Cardinal Ratzinger (1986) stated that "there is an effort in some countries to manipulate the church by gaining the often well-intentioned support of her pastors with a view to changing civil statutes and laws" (p. 380). In one extraordinarily violent sentence, the letter expresses both opposition to the legalization of gay lovemaking and a perverse understanding of gay bashing: "When civil legislation is introduced to protect behavior to which no one has any conceivable right, neither the church nor society at large should be surprised when . . . irrational and violent reactions increase" (p. 381).

The message given by periodic purges of gay seminarians is that one had best be silent about one's orientation and not work for gay civil rights. Being discreetly sexually active and feeling bad about it is subtly acceptable, whereas being out of the closet as a gay celibate and feeling good about it is not tolerated. Together these factors present major obstacles for gay religious, seminarians, and priests to overcome on the road to sexual integration. The pastor of a Metropolitan Community Church congregation said that the Catholic priests with whom he talked over the years were burdened with the enormous oppression of these social and ecclesiastical pressures and the fear of being found out.

Homophobia

Underlying all these social and religious reactions to homosexuals and homosexual activity is homophobia. Homophobia, a term coined by George Weinberg, means prejudice against homosexuals. The woman who said she felt sick when she thought of her daughter having sex with a woman did not feel sick when I asked her to imagine her daughter stealing a million dollars or using artificial means of birth control. Cardinal O'Connor has not led a campaign to prevent divorced and remarried men from holding the office of president.

Believing or feeling that homosexuality is sick, sinful, or bad, homophobic individuals view gay people as flawed in some basic way or as even subhuman. They may believe that gay people molest children, recruit people to homosexuality, or are a danger to weak or even healthy people. Perhaps one of the reasons AIDS has triggered such a violent and irrational reaction toward gay people is that it is felt to be somehow expressive of what homosexuality itself is.

Many people feel that male homosexuality is a flaw in masculinity and that it makes men "feminine." In a society that places great emphasis on being male and that holds women in an inferior position, homosexuality is felt as a special threat. Often the most homophobic males are those who are least sure of their own masculinity. A friend of mine used to be called "fag" by some vociferous schoolmates whom he later encountered in gay bars.

Perhaps the whole image of masculinity, femininity, and homosexuality is part of hierarchical homophobia as well. In the church structure, the hierarchy dress in robes, lace, and ornate, multicolored vesture and perform roles that are commonly performed by women in our society: counseling, teaching, and feeding people. It is generally believed that a large proportion of clergy and religious are gay.

A line from a song in the musical *South Pacific* goes: "You've got to be taught before it's too late, before you are six or seven or eight, to hate all the people your relatives hate." Because society and church teach children that homosexuality is bad, sick, sinful, or all three, gay children learn the message well. Unless they grow up in an accepting family or a neutral environment, the fear and hatred of homosexuality taught by society and church turns into fear and hatred of themselves. Unless they have access to knowledge, acceptance, and positive role models, they will continue to hate and fear their sexuality and will be unable to assist other people in loving and accepting theirs.

When people love themselves, they are free to love other people. That is implicit in Jesus' statement "Love your neighbor as yourself." When gay seminarians, brothers, and priests hate or fear themselves, they act out in destructive ways and sometimes turn to food, drugs, or alcohol to stifle the pain. They may suffer severe depression, lose themselves in work, or become cynical and bitter. They sometimes become trapped in the pursuit or power or wealth or may experience a split between their sexuality and the rest of their lives. They sometimes become involved in cycles of dangerous and even compulsive sexual activity in public places or with minors. Guilt, remorse, and self-hatred can follow the behavior and in turn lead to further destructive behavior. Sometimes they project their self-hatred onto other people, "inform" on other gay people, or join in campaigns against gay rights ordinances. The reader may remember the tragic story about ten years ago of the priest who was outspoken in his opposition to gay rights until he was arrested soliciting an undercover policeman in an adult bookstore.

Coming Out of the Closet

One of the most helpful methods of survival for gay people over the years has been the closet. Not everyone can fit into the closet and so some boys suffer the abuse of being called "sissy," "fruit," "faggot," or "wimp" or of being beaten up by their peers. Not all boys who suffer this abuse are gay; but they often are thought, in some way, to be gay. Able to fit into the closet at least part of the time, most gay people manage to avoid being harassed, beaten, fired, and thrown out of public places and apartments.

Extracting its price, the closet becomes like a pair of outgrown shoes or a pair of tight pants that cut off one's circulation. The closet also becomes a chamber that imprisons gay people in their own homophobia, their own fear and self-hatred, and keeps them from being the people God created them to be. The reader has probably heard people say, "If people are gay, that's okay. But they should keep it to themselves." The underlying message here is that being gay is bad, so people should hide it. The closet is then no longer a protective defense, but a cell that hides a shameful secret, a personal skeleton.

Coming out of the closet means many things, including one's first awareness of being gay and one's first sexual experience. It involves sharing for the first time with someone else that one is gay, telling the secret to family members, friends, and maybe even a television audience, or participating in a parade.

Coming out is a basically healthy process of opening the windows of a musty house or of lancing an infested wound. People with internalized self-hatred need to share themselves with other humans in order to see themselves in a more realistic light and let themselves be loved. Coming out is a growth process—a flag unfurling or a bud opening. Keeping one's sexuality totally hidden is like never learning to speak or burying a talent in the ground because sexuality, so central to one's existence, is a gift from God. People who do not come out to some extent never get beyond self-hatred, fear, and destructive behavior; they never fully mature.

Coming out, even for heterosexuals, is the messy process of reaching sexual awareness and integration. With the help of many social supports heterosexual people usually learn how to express their sexuality in appropriate ways during their teens. But because of societal pressures, gay men and lesbians often go through this adolescent process in their twenties, thirties, forties, or even later.

In the early stages of coming out, people are sometimes indiscriminate and come out when they should not or in ways that are self-defeating or angry. Superiors and bishops need to know the mechanisms that are operating and be able to offer guidance and patience. Mature gay people are in the best position to help someone who is coming out.

The process of coming out inevitably involves hostility and anger. Oppressed people, whether they are gay, black, female, or belong to some other oppressed group, grow up with internalized hatred. As they begin to realize that their negative self-image is wrong, their self-hatred turns to anger and even fury toward their oppressors. This is the healthy anger of people aware of their own worth, unwilling to be mistreated. As energy that can eventually be channeled in an enormously creative way, this kind of anger has powered the civil rights movement, the women's movement, the revolution in the Philippines, and the gay liberation movement.

The coming out process also involves forgiveness and reconciliation. Gay people can achieve a state of peace and an ability to forgive and accept the shortcomings of others when they forgive and accept themselves. It is truly remarkable that there are many healthy gay people in the priesthood and religious life who have overcome enormous obstacles and have accepted and integrated their sexuality into their personalities.

Assisting Our Gay Seminarians, Priests, and Religious

Bishops, provincials, and others in authority must first face their own sexuality if they are to help gay seminarians, religious, and priests, or they risk projecting negative feelings about their own sexuality onto others. They need to give positive messages about homosexuality from the earliest stages of formation, to encourage discussion about sexuality, and to provide an atmosphere in which people can question and learn. People will not talk about their sexuality if they expect criticism, reprisals, or other negative consequences for doing so.

Verbal and other attacks on gay people must be seen as unacceptable. One of the senior Tertian masters of U.S. Jesuits told his charges that there were two things he would not tolerate: homophobia and racism. That must have been very reassuring to those who were gay. Here was a safe haven.

On the other hand, at one seminary several gay students continually found pornographic material in their mailboxes. After several months, one of the students wrote a letter to the student body addressing the issue. The rector removed the letter from the bulletin board where it had been placed, saying it was better to ignore the situation and let things blow over. His refusal to deal with the situation openly encouraged the homophobic behavior that needed to be addressed and condemned; he ignored the sickness of the person who had placed the pornography in the mailboxes. What a tragedy if that person is ordained.

I once heard a priest say in a sermon that the alleged increase in homosexuality was causing our civilization to decline; I heard another priest preach that gay men and lesbians are like rats. That kind of bigotry must stop.

Fear and uncomfortableness surrounding the topic of gay priests and religious stem from the church's lack of understanding about sex. Many people, including church officials, believe the myth that gay equals scx. Although the Catholic episcopacy teaches that all lesbian and gay people are called by God to sexual abstinence, church officials often project a belief that gay and lesbian people cannot be sexually abstinent. The fact is that there are many gay people both in and out of priesthood and religious life who are truly celibate.

The second misunderstanding on the part of the bishops involves the *sensus fidelium*. Catholic bishops are unmarried males who present their teaching as the teaching of Jesus. God, in a sense the most sexual of all beings, creates sexuality and spawns creatures in unimaginable numbers; God is the most spiritual being and yet more at home in our bodies than we are. Many people, female and male, married and unmarried, homosexual and heterosexual, lay, cleric, and religious, question episcopal teaching on sexuality because their own experience gives them different answers. If the *sensus fidelium* means anything, it ought to be taken seriously by the bishops in this area in which they apparently have no direct experience.

A third issue of disagreement, more than misunderstanding, involves sexuality and ministry. Episcopal discipline requires that all priests, seminarians, and religious be unmarried and sexually abstinent. However one may interpret the teaching of Jesus on sex outside of marriage, Jesus himself did not require that religious and priests be celibate and unmarried. Many priests and religious differ with this church discipline.

The fourth area lacking understanding on the part of church officials is intimacy that involves sharing one's feelings and hopes, struggles and dreams, with another human being. Accepting another and being accepted by that other person, the ability to disagree, to express negative as well as positive emotions, and to work through problems are all part of intimacy. True intimacy requires a basic equality with another person; it is a creative and energizing force in a person's life that enables that person to be more loving and generous. There are many examples of nongenital intimacy in Christian history: Jesus and John, Clare and Francis, John of the Cross and Teresa of Avila, John Henry Newman and Ambrose St. John.

Although intimacy need not involve genital activity, it is clear from the marriage model that it often does. Since genital involvement is a common outgrowth of intimacy, sometimes religious and priests, in their search for some kind of intimacy, become genitally involved with people. Even one-night stands may be a pursuit of some form of intimacy.

During my first year in the seminary the superior warned us about "particular friendships" and of the danger that such relationships could lead to sexual behavior. I was only thirteen and wanted to be friends with a certain student, not to have sex with him, but the superior's warning scared and confused me. I can now see that I wanted an intimate relationship, a friendship, based on equality and mutuality. Destructive relationships based on need, jealousy, exclusivity, control, and submission are the kind of relationships that cause dissension in communities. People involved in these kinds of relationships may need help in learning how to be intimate. But avoiding intimate relationships because they may lead to sex is avoiding growth in becoming a full human being.

The fifth issue needing greater understanding is psychosexual maturity (Cavanagh 1983). As people mature psychosexually, they go through various stages such as awakening, fantasy, superficial sexual relationships, mutuality, and integration. People need to grow through these and other stages and through various forms of sexual behavior if they are to arrive at sexual integration. If they stop growing along the way, or regress to earlier stages, they are more likely to act out in compulsive masturbation, promiscuity, infidelity, or other sorts of problematic behavior.

Sometimes priests and religious make a commitment to celibacy and chastity before they have even become aware of their sexuality or while they are in an early stage of growth. They later are faced with at least three moral choices: (1) remaining at one level of growth in order to stay true to their commitment, (2) working through the stages of behavior and thus moving toward a renewed and integrated commitment to celibacy, or (3) relinquishing their commitment altogether at some point if that is the direction in which their inner self is leading them. Bishops and superiors can be especially helpful if they encourage people to risk the journey of growth. Since celibacy and chastity are like other virtues into which people grow, the path along the way is sometimes rocky and uncertain.

We can assist gay religious, seminarians, and priests by encouraging positive and healthy role models for them. One of the reasons gay priests talk to a Metropolitan Community Church pastor is that he, as a gay minister who likes being gay, provides a positive role model. Without role models, people have the tendency to think "I'm the only one." If it is important to have black religious, priests, and bishops as models for the black community, it is equally important to have openly gay priests, religious, bishops, and popes for the gay community. The heterosexual community also needs to experience the variety, creativity, and humanness of self-acknowledged gay people.

When I was in the seminary, the dean of students in his talk on celibacy spoke of the relationship of priests and women. Since several of the students were gay, his talk was irrelevant to them. French teachers must know French, and theologians must know theology. Similarly, people in formation work must be well enough informed about homosexuality and gay people to be able to deal knowledgeably with their gay charges.

Some time ago a gay student who was depressed confided in his rector. Cautioning him not to tell anyone, the rector sent him to a well-meaning but ignorant therapist who told him he was not gay. (A therapist cannot tell but can only assist people in clarifying their sexual orientation.) Happily that young man eventually found someone who could help, but he could have been helped much sooner if the rector had known what he was doing. People in formation work must be able to refer gay people to professionals and others who are well informed.

In the early stages of coming out, gay priests or religious need time to be comfortable with themselves and should not be pushed into ministry to other gay people before they are ready. If they are not at peace with their own homosexuality, they become ludicrous authority figures and run the risk of laying their own guilt trips on other gay people or of becoming sexually involved with the people to whom they minister.

Support groups, one of the most helpful aids to gay priests, brothers, and seminarians, can shorten the coming-out process by years. Although support groups exist in most major cities throughout the country, the group itself is often in the closet in order to protect the members from clerical and religious harassment. Superiors and bishops could render their people a great service by encouraging the formation of such groups. In a sense, support groups are a gay person's family. Most other oppressed people can find identification, support, and knowledge from their biological families. Black children are raised by black adults, girls by women, and so on. But most gay children are raised by heterosexual people who do not understand the first thing about being gay. Gay people need a gay family that can help them with knowledge, support, and identification.

The struggle for gay liberation is also the struggle of gay religious, seminarians, and priests to be free. Superiors and bishops should encourage gay religious, seminarians, and priests who become involved in the struggle for gay rights. At the very least, they should not stand in their way. Bishops and superiors should also know what gay liberation is really about. It is not about sex, although one of its goals is the elimination of laws that make same-gender sexual activity illegal. These very laws are often used as a basis for denying gay people rights to jobs, housing, and access to public accommodations. Gay liberation is really about the respect that gay and lesbian people deserve as humans, about the equal value that lesbian and gay people share with heterosexual people in God's eyes, and about equal protection that should exist under the law.

It does not take very long for people who work with religious, seminarians, and priests to realize that a high percentage of those in the ministry are gay. Perhaps the celibate life-style of the Roman Catholic ministry has a special appeal to some gay people. Since present Catholic teaching maintains that gay sex is sinful, the celibate life-style is a way of following that teaching while living in loving and supportive relationships with other people of the same gender who share similar ideals. Celibate ministry is a viable alternative for people who are not suited for heterosexual marriage. Furthermore, for people who have to deal with social rejection on many levels, the life of a religious, priest, or brother offers social respect and the opportunity for creative work.

In the ministry of other Christian and non-Christian religious bodies there also seems to be a larger percentage of gay people than in the population as a whole. This may imply something about the gift of spirituality that many gay people bring to the human family. Perhaps God is sending a message about the value and purpose of a sexual orientation that is so often thought to be less than ideal at best or an abomination in God's eyes at worst.

When we learn about the spirituality of gay men and lesbians, which leads so many of them into the religious life and priesthood; when we open our hearts and arms by allowing and encouraging them to grow; when we provide the patience, information, and role models that will help break the cycle of homophobia in our church—then we pave the way for ourselves to receive love, nurturing, and encouragement from a new generation of gay men and lesbians. Thus what we have reaped, we sow and reap again.

There is so much wasted energy in fearing and hating, in teaching fear and hate to people, and in keeping people in self-hate. Finding ways to release that energy is not easy, but the rewards are immense. And the future of our world may rest in the balance.

References

Baum, W. 1983. *Educational Guidance in Human Love.* Boston: Daughters of St. Paul.

Cavanagh, M. E. 1983. The Impact of Psychosexual Growth in Marriage and Religious Life. *Human Development* 4, no. 3:16–24.

Ratzinger, J. 1986. Letter to the Bishops of the Catholic Church on the Pastoral Care of Homosexual Persons. *Origins* 16, no. 22:379–80.

19 Supporting Our Lesbian Sisters

JO LOUISE PECORARO

As I sat down to write this article in a green and azalea-blossoming patio in New Orleans, a flood of memories returned to me. One among them was my first contact with a group of gay people, eight years ago.

The neighborhood center where I was a caseworker was used as a meeting place by Alcoholics Anonymous, groups concerned about Central America, a women's coffeehouse, and a number of gay and lesbian social, political, and religious groups. After a few months, a Dignity member invited me to Dignity's next Sunday Eucharist in our center's dining room. An Italian woman who had just come out to her mother was going to be there with her "Italian mama," who was very upset. Talking to me, a nun whose name was not exactly Irish, would be good for this Italian mama!

With a little apprehension I showed up, but the Italian mama and daughter did not. I found myself the only woman among twenty-seven gay men, most of whom I did not know. After liturgy, I was invited to supper at a black soul-food restaurant with twenty gay men, some dressed in tuxedos because they were going to a gay Mardi Gras ball later that night. What an evening! I experienced so much warmth, affection, and humor and felt totally welcomed. As we parted that night one of the men

194

commented, "You know, I think gay people feel a certain kind of bond with sisters. We're both a part of oppressed minorities in the church." Thus began my involvement with the Catholic gay community.

Scarcity of Known Lesbian Sisters

How can we in our religious communities support our lesbian sisters? The question reminds me of my first SIGMA (Sisters in Gay Ministry, Associated) meeting of seven sisters in Detroit in 1982. I felt anxious that I would discover that most of the sisters would be lesbians and veterans in gay ministry, and I would feel isolated. Much to my surprise, this was not the case. In fact, most of us had "backed into" gay ministry. When the topic of support for lesbian sisters was discussed, we unanimously agreed that we knew very few sisters who were self-defining lesbians and none who was out in her religious community. The few lesbian sisters we knew were, in most cases, one or two friends who had come out to us because they trusted us and thought we would be accepting.

Since that meeting I have not seen a significant change in the number of "out-of-the-closet" lesbian sisters. Our lesbian sisters are still in large part invisible. In 1985, when our community hosted the New Ways Ministry–sponsored workshop "Women Religious Exploring Their Sexual Orientation" in the southern region, only six sisters attended.

There are probably several reasons why self-defining lesbian sisters are so few. First, the basic issue of human sexuality has not been dealt with among our sisters as a whole. Second, there is much homophobia among us. Our communities are not yet places where people are comfortable with, accepting of, and unprejudiced toward gay and lesbian people. Ignorance, and sometimes hostility, are certainly not conducive to lesbian sisters disclosing this aspect of their personal identity. Perhaps when we are more affirming of homosexuality as being good, healthy, and natural, our sisters will feel less intimidated and more self-accepting.

I suggest that we support our lesbian sisters in three basic ways: education of ourselves and of the church and society of which we are a part, networking and support groups, and political action.

Education

In an article written for the National Sisters Vocation Conference newsletter, Jeannine Gramick (1982) gave some pertinent
suggestions regarding sexuality education for women religious:
"Myths and stereotypes can be slowly eradicated by an ongoing
educational program in sexuality. Even today, some religious do
not know that same-sex attractions are experienced by most
people, but those attractions do not necessarily indicate that a
woman is lesbian. One's true sexual identity is discovered in a
heterosexual atmosphere" (p. 6). She goes on to say, "Adequate
education about sexuality should include historical, cross-cultural,
legal and moral perspectives as well as discussion of such topics as
femininity/masculinity, roles and stereotypes, comfortability with
one's own body and sexual history, intimacy and friendship"
(p. 6). In this context, the question of sexual orientation can be
explored.

There are numerous ways of educating ourselves on homosexuality. My religious community began with a presentation at a
congregational gathering in 1980; the myths and stereotypes, as
well as the realities, of gay and lesbian people were presented. This
one workshop among twenty related to ministry and social justice
provoked so much interest that an evening "replay" had to be
scheduled to accommodate everyone. On another occasion our
province joined other religious communities in the area to sponsor
a panel on which lesbian and gay persons shared their personal
stories and dealt with topics such as the historical perspectives of
homosexuality, the paradox of coming out, responses of family,
involvement with church, and legal and political aspects of being
gay. Some participants mentioned the significance for them of
meeting "flesh-and-blood" gay people and hearing them share on
such a personal and moving level. About one hundred area people
in positions of influence listened intently to the words of the
panelists. Priests, religious women and men, community leaders,
social workers, principals, campus ministers, formation personnel,
school counselors, seminary professors, and youth ministry directors—all received education about homosexuality that day.

This initial education was followed by excellent New Ways
Ministry workshops in our area conducted by Bob Nugent and

Jeannine Gramick and dealing with the sociological, theological, and pastoral dimensions of homosexuality. The possibilities are endless and New Ways Ministry is a tremendous resource.

There are other more subtle ways to educate. We can make references in retreats, workshops, and liturgies that show an awareness of the struggles and gifts of lesbian and gay people and that ratify the reality that not everyone is heterosexual. Good books and the latest information on the topic of homosexuality should be available in our libraries, communities, and ministry places; for example, *A Challenge to Love* (Nugent 1983), *Is the Homosexual My Neighbor?* (Scanzoni and Mollenkott 1978), *Homosexuality and the Catholic Church* (Gramick 1983), and *Bondings*, the New Ways Ministry newsletter that excerpts material from current sources. There is also available a wealth of videos, filmstrips, and helpful bibliographies for different interest groups.

Our various newsletters and in-house communiqués can matter-of-factly include consciousness-raising items regarding workshops and gay civil rights developments in our own locale. We can make an effort to round out our boards, staffs, and parish councils by inviting or helping to get elected lesbians and gay men. We can involve ourselves in feminist groups in which we will surely meet lesbians with values and goals similar to our own. I discovered that a number of the organizers and participants in marches and rallies for Equal Rights Amendment ratification, the antinuclear movement, Women Against Violence Against Women, the Latin-American struggle, and Women-Church were committed, inspiring lesbians. Coalition building is essential in these days in which we seek change that is life-giving to the human family.

Any small step toward educating ourselves and others is significant because education is so central to changing attitudes, behavior, and structures. I firmly believe that "prejudice is the child of ignorance." Wherever we are, we can be about this educational process.

Networks and Support Groups

Support groups and networking are a second way of empowering our lesbian sisters. Some lesbian sisters have expressed the need for groups in which they can know and talk with one another for mutual growth, for combating loneliness and isolation, for sharing experiences and insights. As a result of the 1984–85 workshops by New Ways Ministry for lesbian nuns, a small support group for nuns has formed. This support group is in the infancy stage compared to the many groups that exist for gay priests and brothers in most major, and some not so major, cities across the country. The editors of the book *Lesbian Nuns: Breaking Silence* (Curb and Manahan 1985) have noted that support groups for current and former lesbian nuns are forming in many places around the country.

One network that has been in existence since 1977 is Communication Ministry, Inc. (CMI). CMI publishes a monthly newsletter in which subscribers express views and share information on homosexuality and religious life. CMI also sponsors retreats, generates support groups in various places, and has a contact system "for confidential referrals to sympathetic spiritual directors, counselors, or just a friendly ear to listen to common struggle."

Two other networking groups are the Conference for Catholic Lesbians (CCL) and SIGMA. CCL publishes a quarterly newsletter, *Images,* sponsors local and national conferences, and helps connect lesbians on various levels. Through its regional coordinators, SIGMA can be very helpful in the networking of lesbian sisters. Religious community leaders can be supportive simply by being open and understanding when lesbian sisters declare their sexual orientation. They can offer networking information when appropriate.

Political Action

The possibilities for political action to support our lesbian sisters and gay brothers and priests should be undertaken under the banner of social justice. For example, we can encourage groups and individuals to endorse the Catholic Coalition for Gay Civil Rights statement that calls upon Catholics to "support sound civil rights legislation and not to oppose such ordinances on the basis of unfounded fears, irrational myths and inflammatory statements about homosexuality." The statement has been endorsed by approximately thirty-five hundred national Catholic organizations, theologians, religious communities, diocesan organizations, and individuals around the country.

We can become involved in the passage of local, state, and federal gay civil rights ordinances by letter writing, lobbying, testifying before city councils, or speaking on radio or TV talk shows to educate the public. We must not undermine our power of influence as church people.

A coalition of gay organizations and churches lost passage of a gay civil rights ordinance in New Orleans in April 1984 by only one vote. The two most influential groups responsible for its failure were the fundamentalist churches and the archdiocesan chancery. I can vividly recall the tears of disappointment and hurt in the council chambers following the bill's defeat. Once again lesbian and gay people had been "done in" by the institutional church on something as basic as civil rights!

These are a few ways in which we can be supportive of our lesbian sisters. We must learn from them how we can walk with them in their journeys of integrating their lesbianism with the many facets of their lives. Gifts to our religious communities, the church, and society, our lesbian sisters call us to ever more deeply celebrate our oneness and cherish our diversity.

References

Curb, R., and Manahan, N., eds. 1985. *Lesbian Nuns: Breaking Silence.* Tallahassee: Naiad Press.

Gramick, J. 1982. Cracks in the Convent Closets. *News/Views* (November-December): 1–7.

Gramick, J., ed. 1983. *Homosexuality and the Catholic Church.* Chicago: Thomas More Press.

Nugent, R., ed. 1983. *A Challenge to Love: Gay and Lesbian Catholics in the Church.* New York: Crossroad.

Scanzoni, L., and Mollenkott, V. 1978. *Is the Homosexual My Neighbor? Another Christian View.* San Francisco: Harper and Row.

20 Homosexuality and Seminary Candidates

ROBERT NUGENT, SDS

In the film version of the Broadway play *Mass Appeal* there is a tense and explosive confrontation between a seminary rector and the pastor of a local parish. Charles Durning, the actor who plays the rector, challenges the pastor's (Jack Lemmon's) defense of a student serving his deacon internship at the pastor's posh suburban parish as part of his evaluation for priestly ordination. The young deacon has already run afoul of the rector for defending two other seminarians suspected of a homosexual relationship. The deacon's own sexuality had been a topic of a conversation between the deacon and the rector, who has his own suspicions. "We have too many priests out of the closet already and too many others still in," Durning yells at Lemmon. "And this one was out and now he's back in."

Growing Concern about Gay Applicants

In this case film art does imitate the reality of contemporary Catholic life, where there is a growing concern in many areas of institutional church life about homosexual candidates for priesthood and religious life. The two primary reasons for this concern are the increasing numbers of self-identified and self-affirming gay male applicants to seminaries and religious orders and the growing visibility and outspokenness of gay clergy and religious in both the secular and Catholic media. Related but distinct issues are the publicity surrounding some arrests of Catholic clerics by police for illegal sexual activity, and numerous civil lawsuits brought against dioceses and orders for sexual misconduct by some priests and brothers. There is an increased awareness that Catholic priests are not immune from contracting AIDS. There have been several widely publicized AIDS cases involving the deaths of priests. In Seattle, homosexual activity as the actual cause of the AIDS virus was acknowledged publicly by one priest's superior to the parish community.

In 1988 the Conference of Major Superiors of Men and the Catholic Health Association produced a videotape for selected audiences concerned about the presence of AIDS within the Catholic priesthood and brotherhood of the United States. In this informative and extremely well-balanced treatment of the topic from theological, pastoral, legal, and other angles, on-camera interviews with religious with AIDS and their religious leaders contained candid but sensitive and responsible reflections on homosexual religious and priests.

The question of mandatory testing of candidates for AIDS antibodies or the virus itself has already been addressed. Some dioceses have quietly begun to test all candidates. The archdiocese of Boston reportedly tests not only upon admission to the seminary, but also before deaconate. Some religious orders such as the Society of the Divine Savior have adopted policies on AIDS testing. Others have opposed testing because of questions about the reliability of tests, potential breaches of confidentiality, and a witch-hunt mentality that could use the testing to eliminate a priori all homosexual applicants.

The argument that dioceses and orders need to have complete information on the health and physical condition of the candidate so as to determine his potential for ministry seems reasonable. Although the order's or diocese's financial responsibility for health care for the person is surely one of the considerations, it would be disappointing to think that the decision to admit or not was made solely on economic grounds. There are already precedents of the church's accepting other individuals with health problems such as multiple sclerosis, indeed of ordaining a man who had only a year or more of ministry before total incapacitation or death. The photograph of a seminarian being ordained in a wheelchair is no longer a novelty.

Justice would require that: (1) if mandatory testing is inaugurated in a diocese or order, *all* candidates be tested; (2) the testing be as accurate as possible with allowances for false results; (3) that distinctions are made between those who test positive for the antibody, and those who test positive for the AIDS virus itself; (4) that the results be kept in as strict confidence as possible; (5) the decision to admit or not would not be made solely on the positive results of testing, but on a case-by-case basis; (6) that the person who tests positive not be required to reveal the manner of being exposed to the virus, but be left free to volunteer that information in the proper counseling setting; (7) that the diocese or, especially, the order give serious thought to the witness value of accepting certain candidates despite the AIDS factor as a way of being open to the mysterious workings of God's grace in a vulnerable humanity.

Previous to and apart from the concern over AIDS, vocation personnel have traditionally been more interested in the implications for the diocese or order in admitting homosexual applicants. Previously both vocation and formation personnel have tended to rely more and more on the psychological testing and evaluation of prospective candidates, especially in the areas of sexual maturity and the potential for intrapersonal conflicts relating to sexuality. Increasingly in the past several years the topic has appeared on the agenda of professional meetings of vocation and formation directors. In 1989 the National Religious Vocation Conference journal included essays on homosexuality with issues for both the candidate applying and the order or diocese receiving (National Religious Vocation Conference 1989).

At a national symposium in Washington, D.C., in 1985, the topic of homosexuality and vocations was raised in the church's public forum for the first time. One of the speakers, Yale University historian John Boswell, argued that there has always been a disproportionate number of homosexual men in the clergy at all periods of church history (Boswell 1985).

It is generally agreed that the percentage of "exclusively or predominantly" homosexually oriented males in the priesthood and religious life is somewhat higher than the commonly accepted Kinsey figure of 10 percent for the population at large. Actually, the 10 percent estimate is a combined figure from 13 percent of men and 7 percent of women who are exclusively or predominantly homosexual. Estimates for the male clerical population have ranged from the most conservative 10 percent to a more reasonable 20 percent or even 30 percent, although some have advanced estimates as high as 50 percent or more. Until recently there have been no data to substantiate any particular claim. In 1986 the National Conference of Religious Vocation Directors published a special report on a survey of religious communities that asked how many homosexual candidates they actually had accepted in a five-year period (National Conference of Religious Vocation Directors 1986). Between 1981 and 1985, 25 percent of the men's communities accepted men with an acknowledged homosexual orientation. Of all the candidates accepted into postulancy or residency programs in these same years 5 percent of the males identified themselves as homosexual. It should be noted, however, that these figures do not include candidates who did *not* reveal their homosexual orientation or those who are already ordained or in final vows. There is no comparable study for diocesan seminaries at the present time. One researcher who has not yet published the results of his study claims that 20 percent of the clergy are homosexual and half that number are sexually active.

Bishops in this country, understandably, have also indicated a particular interest in the issue, although the topic has never been discussed in one of their open yearly gatherings. Behind closed doors, however, in their executive sessions the topic has arisen in several contexts. Occasionally church leaders publicly allude to the issue with the use of certain code words. Cardinal Bernardin (1978), for example, stated that our seminaries were attracting "weaker candidates" (p. 4). At another meeting on vocations, Los Angeles's Assistant Bishop John Ward suggested that if physical education were restored as a crucial ingredient of the seminary curriculum, it might help reduce the problem of effeminacy

(Bourgoin 1979). In 1985 Notre Dame's theologian in residence, James Burtchell (1985), told a convention of Catholic journalists that there is a dominant culture in many seminaries today that is given to indulgences and effeminacy.

In July 1988 a Convocation of Admissions Personnel of Seminaries, sponsored jointly by the Bishops' Committees on Vocations and Priestly Formation, was held. A continuing major concern of both bishops and president-rectors of theologates has been the selection process of potential candidates for the priesthood. One of the purposes of this meeting was to determine if greater "quality control" could be exercised in this area.

In 1980 a Committee of the New England Bishops (1980) issued a pastoral letter on vocations that included a section addressing the question of homosexual applicants. Their conclusions apparently anticipated, or perhaps even provoked, a current shift in attitudes following a generally more tolerant era of the sixties and early seventies when theological preparation was undergoing major change. During that period a commitment to fostering justice, coupled with a growing awareness of and sensitivity to many minority groups in the church, prompted some seminary authorities to take a more benign approach to gay applicants regardless of the presence of some strong counterindications to acceptance in the cases of particular individuals.

Lay voices have also been raised to express a growing concern about the impact of gay clergy on church morale and ministry. This is especially so when the concerns are linked to hearsay reports of the presence of "widespread" homosexuality in U.S. seminaries, rumors of sexual activity among the clergy, and widespread documented cases of clerical pedophilia often erroneously identified with adult homosexual orientation. Jason Berry (1987a, 1987b) has tracked and analyzed the phenomenon of clerical pedophilia in extensively researched articles in both the Catholic and secular media. Other lay voices have spoken on behalf of homosexual clergy, urging acceptance and affirmation (Commission on Social Justice 1982). Efforts to address many of these sensitive issues in the public forum have been met with varying degrees of openness from concerned church authorities.

In the fall of 1985, for example, a national Catholic organization located in Washington, D.C., New Ways Ministry, sponsored a three-day symposium called "Homosexuality, Priesthood and Religious Life: Concerns and Challenges." The event was endorsed by some Catholic orders and national organizations, including many involved in vocation and formation ministry. It was designed to explore areas such as support for gay clergy, policies for accepting gay or lesbian candidates, promoting dialog and education for the larger church community, and assessing the impact of the public self-disclosure of a gay priest or religious on the individual, the diocese or order, and the larger Catholic community. In response to the presymposium publicity, however, Archbishop James Hickey of Washington, D.C., contacted all the endorsing groups expressing his "sadness" at their support and urged them to withdraw from the event (Hickey 1985). He also publicly forbade the celebration of the Eucharist and wrote to all U.S. bishops in the hope that they would forbid or discourage participation. Hickey described the event as an effort to secure for homosexual activity and life-style an acceptability it cannot have. Ironically, the vast majority of the participants were heterosexual church personnel working with celibate homosexual clergy and religious.

On the other hand, some bishops, such as Seattle's Coadjutor Archbishop Thomas Murphy, are willing to raise the issue. Speaking in 1988 to a conference of seminary admissions personnel, Murphy said that candidates should be accepted or turned away based on whether they are equiped to be priests in the 1990s. Even though they have given evidence of a celibate commitment to chastity, Murphy said that sexual orientation of the candidate, whether heterosexual or homosexual, becomes a far more significant issue today in the context of the lived experience of the priesthood.

Vatican Signals

There have been strong signals from some Vatican offices about the question of homosexuality and clerical life. For instance, Cardinal Silvio Oddi, who heads the Congregation for the Clergy, said, "Candidates for the priesthood must be wisely culled, with particular attention paid to character weaknesses occasioned by the unnatural tendencies common in contemporary society" (Oddi 1985, 5). Although not mentioning homosexual candidates directly, his message was clear. Oddi suggested that if we are more careful about whom we accept into seminaries, we will have fewer problems after they are ordained. Speaking in Rome to hundreds of priests from all parts of the world gathered for a retreat, Oddi cited heterosexual and homosexual behavior as violations of the celibate commitment.

In the Vatican-ordered investigation of Seattle's Archbishop Raymond Hunthausen, the then-final report of Archbishop Hickey, the Vatican-appointed investigator, suggested that the Seattle archdiocese's process of selection and formation of candidates for priesthood needed to be reviewed. The archdiocese of Seattle has developed and pioneered a candidate-screening program that is considered a model for other dioceses.

The way the Seattle screening process came about was the result of the work of the National Conference of Diocesan Vocation Directors (NCDVD). Their Screening and Selection Committee carried on five years of tested reflection and use of various methods in the archdiocese of Seattle. In 1985 the NCDVD published *Assessment of Applicants for Priesthood* based on the Seattle experience. One can only speculate whether the Vatican has serious concern about the ability of such a program to screen out homosexual candidates, although the NCDVD document is actually very cautious when discussing homosexual candidates.

Some of the concerns expressed in the NCDVD document (Magnano et al. 1985) on gay candidates are: "Is the applicant's sexual orientation public knowledge? If so, how will this affect his ministry? If not, does the applicant live with anxiety that it might become public? Does the applicant feel it should make no difference? Is this realistic in the setting of the diocese?" (p. 32).

I spoke with one candidate who definitely felt that he was rejected by the archdiocese of Seattle because of what he called the "fallout" from the Roman investigation. This individual was open about his own homosexuality and said he felt capable of living a celibate commitment. In light of his own life experience and professional counseling expertise, however, he also said that he wanted to be involved in some way in ministry with sexual minorities.

The Vatican-ordered study of U.S. seminaries and houses of formation was chaired by Bishop John Marshall of Burlington, Vermont. Although unwilling to admit it publicly at first, Marshall eventually acknowledged that the study would also be taking a look at the issue of homosexuality, both theologically and practically. One report of a visiting team of clerics on an East Coast house of formation noted the lack of written policies on both homosexuality and heterosexual dating. A newspaper story on this formation house stated that both issues were of great concern to the Vatican.

In 1988 Pope John Paul II told the Congregation for Institutes of Consecrated Life (CICL), which oversees religious orders, that religious orders should be careful to admit only qualified candidates even when they are hard to find, and that only those candidates should be admitted who possess the qualities required to take full advantage of formation programs.

Bishops' Committee on Priestly Life and Ministry

In the early eighties the Committee on Priestly Life and Ministry (CPLM) of the National Conference of Catholic Bishops (NCCB) produced a study booklet on sexuality designed to generate discussion among priests and bishops. One case study concerned a gay priest experiencing strong inner conflicts about his sexual identity, doubts about his priestly vocation, and guilt about periodic breaches of his celibate commitment (Bishops' Committee on Priestly Life and Ministry 1983).

In September 1984 the Administrative Committee of the NCCB discussed a new seminary admission policy for homosexual applicants proposed by the CPLM. Simply stated, the proposed policy said that active homosexuals or those "who have a public patterned lifestyle reflecting homosexual orientation" (D'Arcy 1984, 1) cannot be considered candidates for priestly formation. No attempt was made to define or even clarify what is meant by a "lifestyle" that reflected a homosexual orientation. In the absence of such a definition, a celibate homosexual seminarian associated with a gay political, social, religious or even academic group could be considered an unacceptable candidate. Admission of other kinds of homosexual candidates according to the same policy would depend on the prudent judgment of the appropriate authorities. The proposed policy stated that these authorities should consider such factors as acceptance by the Catholic community, notoriety, and a commitment to celibacy demonstrated by a convincing and adequate amount of time spent in celibate living. In considering the admission of such candidates, the statement said, authorities should devote adequate time, reflection, and caution. This policy statement was informally approved by the Congregation for Catholic Education, headed by Cardinal William Baum, which oversees Catholic seminaries and other Catholic educational institutions.

Although the report apparently satisfied the NCCB Executive Committee, it did not please Boston's Auxiliary Bishop John D'Arcy, who registered strong objections through Bishop James Malone, the chair of the NCCB Administrative Committee. In D'Arcy's judgment the report was "flawed" in theory and "impossible to implement in practice" (D'Arcy 1984, 2). D'Arcy's main concern was that the policy would open seminary doors to sexually active gay men who would lie about their sexual activities. It would be impossible, according to D'Arcy, to separate practicing from nonpracticing homosexuals, and those "who are active and totally without personal control will immediately begin to act out homosexually in the seminary with serious harm to sound formation, and eventually to the life of the Church" (p. 2). Even assuming that it was possible to separate practicing from nonpracticing homosexuals, D'Arcy claimed that the watchful guidance urged by the report to be focused on homosexual candidates "would require a full fledged structure which is not now present in any American seminary" (p. 3).

D'Arcy urged that the letter on priestly formation written by Archbishop John Whealon (Hartford, Connecticut), Bishop John Marshall (Burlington, Vermont), Louis Gelineau (Providence, Rhode Island), and D'Arcy himself be adopted as a model for U.S. seminaries. D'Arcy claimed that the letter from this committee had been praised by Archbishop Jean Jadot; Cardinal Garrone, Prefect of the Pontifical Commission on the Family and featured speaker at Catholics United for the Faith events; and William Cardinal Baum. The letter on priestly formation virtually eliminated all applicants who were not heterosexual and advised that true homosexual candidates should not be admitted even if they have been leading a celibate life because they are "unable to tolerate the demands of a celibate priestly ministry or of rectory living" (Committee of the New England Bishops 1980, 472).

D'Arcy noted that the chairs of both the Bishops' Committee on Priestly Life and Ministry and the Bishops' Committee on Priestly Formation had made references to the growing number of private and publicized incidents of homosexual activity by priests. He said that one of the reasons we are suffering so much pain and damage to souls is because of a failure to do proper screening in the past. He asked whether there was any inner logic in a discussion that, on the one hand, quite properly decries the growing number of homosexual incidents among priests while, on the other, proposes efforts to open up the seminary to homosexual men.

Vatican Influences

There is further confirmation of a growing trend to eliminate homosexual candidates from seminaries. On June 25, 1985, Cardinal William Baum met with Bishop James Malone in Rome. Among the topics discussed was the "problem of homosexuality." Following the June meeting, Baum suggested that the topic could best be treated by including it among the indications and counterindications of suitability in a study that was currently being conducted by the Bishops' Committee on Priestly Formation. Baum said that the study might turn out to be part of the next revision of *The Program of Priestly Formation*. Published in a revised third edition in February 1982 by the NCCB, this program contains the official guidelines for priestly training in the United States; it received approval of Baum's congregation in 1981. Baum suggested that Malone share with the U.S. bishops Baum's memorandum titled "A Memorandum to Bishops Seeking Advice in Matters Concerning Homosexuality and Candidates for Admission to Seminary." The memorandum declares as unacceptable both heterosexually and homosexually active candidates as well as anyone who leads a homosexual life-style, whether he is homosexual or not (Baum 1985, 1). Baum also eliminates as an acceptable candidate the heterosexual candidate "who is given to 'dating,' albeit chastely" (p. 1).

The crucial element in the Baum memo is the now commonly accepted distinction between homosexual *orientation* and homosexual *behavior*. Like Cardinal Ratzinger in his October 1986 letter to the bishops of the world on homosexuality, Cardinal Baum is reluctant to grant any legitimacy to the concept of sexual orientation as understood by the natural sciences and human sexuality studies. This is partly because he and Ratzinger do not want to recognize the *affective* or emotional components of homosexuality, which might be open to validation as human values apart from embodied genital expression.

Baum claims that some people have blurred the distinction between orientation and behavior. But he offers no empirical evidence for this charge, upon which he draws his conclusions and bases his advice. According to Baum, the term *orientation* can now be used to include "an unacceptable commitment to or support of homosexual practices or lifestyles" (p. 1). His own response to the blurring is practically to eliminate the concept of orientation, although he employs the word in a vague and undefined way.

Baum makes three distinctions: homosexual practice, homosexual orientation, and homosexual temptation. For Baum, seminary applicants given to homosexual practices or exhibiting a homosexual orientation are not to be admitted. The applicant who experiences homosexual "temptations" *can* be admitted. He acknowledges that the temptations might even involve or depend on the orientation. But he confuses the discussion when he says that when the "behavioral impulse, inclination or appetite" (p. 1) does not involve orientation, then we have a simple case of a Christian who faces, bears, and resists many kinds of temptation in life. It is not clear what Baum understands exactly by "orientation" as distinguished from "impulse," "inclination," or "appetite," nor how he views the precise relationship between orientation and temptations.

In 1988 the Bishops' Committee for Priestly Life and Ministry held a confidential session at the Collegeville meeting of the bishops on the psychosexual development of priests, which, according to the CPLM office, was well received by the bishops.

Bishops' Committee on Priestly Formation

A draft of a statement from the Bishops' Committee on Priestly Formation (BCPF, 1985) shows clear evidence of Baum's thinking on the subject. The draft is called simply "Concerning the Acceptability of Certain Candidates." Although the statement incorporates many of Baum's suggestions, it is not prepared to go as far as Baum in rejecting heterosexual candidates who are dating "albeit chastely." More important and, I think, more dangerous are some distinctions and recommendations that far exceed Baum's confused thinking. If accepted as official church policy, the proposed guidelines of the BCPF would result in our encouraging some of the most conflicted and self-depreciating homosexual candidates for seminary formation. If this document is accepted as it stands or is included in a revision of *The Program of Priestly Formation,* as suggested by Baum, without serious modification and clarification, I fear that our problems with clergy who are troubled because of their sexual identity will be compounded for many years to come for both the church and for the individuals involved.

Fortunately, the guidelines themselves allow that their interim statement may be revised. One can only hope that this has already occurred by the time this analysis appears or, if not, that it will happen as soon as possible. The document's claim that it is "based on the best information available" (p. 1) would date the work as from sometime in the 1940s or 1950s.

The BCPF statement distinguishes two kinds of homosexual orientation based on the now-outdated classification system of the *Diagnostic and Statistical Manual of Mental Disorders (DSM-III)* of the American Psychiatric Association. Ego dystonic homosexuality is that which is a persistent source of anxiety and distress. Homosexual orientation is a constant source of distress for persons in this category, and their distress is accompanied by an internalized conviction for change. On the other hand, ego syntonic homosexuals accept and desire a sustained pattern of overt homosexual arousal as a source of sexual gratification and expression. These individuals accept both arousal and activity; they experience neither guilt nor anxiety because of the arousal.

The BCPF draft admits that the key issue is the "preferential arousal pattern" (p. 2) and recognizes that some people, for a variety of reasons, may never actually engage in homosexual behavior. Yet the draft suggests that only the ego dystonic homosexual individual can be admitted to seminary. In other words, the homosexual candidate who rejects his homosexuality and wants to change can be accepted, whereas the individual who affirms his homosexual identity and remains celibate, but is not concerned with changing his orientation, should be rejected.

Nowhere in the BCPF draft is the word *life-style* actually defined, although, as in many other ecclesiastical documents, life-style seems to be consistently equated with homogenital behavior. If life-style is a code word for homogenital behavior, then the advocated change amounts in practice to helping people abstain from overt genital expression. It is this kind of thinking that makes it difficult to take seriously the document's claim to be based on the best scientific information. Present scientific literature does not use the term *homosexual life-style* synonomously with *homosexual behavior*. A celibate homosexual who joins Courage or is involved with a gay Republican group or socializes with friends in a gay club leads a gay life-style. Cardinal Baum and the BCPF statements equate the three terms homosexual *activity*, *practices*, and *life-style* and ban them all.

New Directions in Theology

Attempts to formulate sound policies for screening homosexual candidates have been founded on an unwillingness or an inability to concede any psychological or moral value to the homosexual orientation or identity. This has been strengthened by the letter of Cardinal Ratzinger (1986) stating that the homosexual tendency itself must be judged an "objective disorder" (par. 3). It is not clear, however, that the Vatican has really grasped the concept of sexual orientation as currently understood by the natural sciences. The author has previously examined the concept of sexual orientation in Vatican thinking (Nugent 1988).

U.S. episcopal teaching has held that the homosexual orientation is morally neutral because there is no choice in one's sexual orientation. Quinn (1987) distinguishes between a *moral* judgment of the behavior and a *philosophical* judgment of the orientation. In making a psychological judgment hierarchical statements continue to describe the homosexual orientation as nonnormative, inferior, lacking, or not fully human. This is why church administrators are uncomfortable not only with scandals involving sexually active gay clergy and religious, but also with gay celibate clergy who identify themselves publicly as such for whatever reasons. Church officials seem unable or reluctant to accept data from the natural sciences that claim to validate homosexuality as a human sexual development well within the range of normal psychosexual development. Final episcopal judgment rests on the biblical and theological natural law traditions, which are seen as affirming heterosexuality as the norm for full human development and as the Creator's plan for human sexuality.

Some theologians might be willing to assert that what is humanly nonnormative is not necessarily immoral (Cahill 1983). For many others, however, this still does not address the crucial theological question: is there "anything about Christian faith and life . . . that obliges . . . [us] to claim that heterosexuality is a timelessly unchanging structure of human nature which the Creator intends as part of human fulfillment"? (Kelsey 1984, 11). Is it essential to stress *historicity* in a Christian view of what is normative for humanity? Because until the middle of the twentieth century society stated that heterosexuality was necessary to be fully human, should Christianity accept this historical judgment?

Recently there have been some small indications that point to newer directions in the thinking of U.S. Catholics on the topic of homosexuality. Some voices are beginning to suggest that the homosexual orientation as part of human sexuality might be judged as a positive human, moral good and central to one's relationship to God and others. The pastoral plan of the archdiocese of San Francisco describes the homosexual orientation as a "building block rather than as a stumbling block" (Senate of Priests 1986, 59). The same document urges counselors to take seriously the feeling of many homosexual people that there is a certain "rightness about their sexuality" (p. 59) and that they must be helped to respect their individual "secret core" (p. 66).

Coleman (1984) says that "human sexuality, both as condition and act, is never morally neutral" (p. 15). This is so because one's sexuality is so central to our human existence that "the being of a person is involved and engaged in human sexuality" (p. 14).

Where might these new directions lead? If human sexuality as a condition is never morally neutral but can be a moral good especially as a channel to other values such as intimacy, friendship, and trust; if a homosexual orientation can be valued as a building block for one's life; and if, "for the true homosexual, no amount of will power and no amount of spirituality can alter the fact that they are erotically attracted by members of their own sex" (Coleman 1984, 13), does the BCPF statement make any real contribution to improving the quality of candidates for priestly formation?

From one perspective, the fundamental issue is the psychological or philosophical judgment of the homosexual identity and its implications for moral and ethical reflection. That which is humanly flawed cannot be morally praiseworthy, as the Ratzinger letter clearly states. Because the homosexual orientation was, until recently, accepted as psychologically inappropriate, grounds were laid for moral condemnations. But when the natural sciences and some church documents deny that the homosexual orientation is a form of "truncated sexual development" (Senate of Priests 1986, 57), the path seems clear for another judgment; namely, that at least for some individuals a homosexual identity is a variant form of human psychosexual development within the range of healthy psychological functioning. In this understanding humanity is not thought of as a once and for all unchangeable creation, but rather as a life to which we have been summoned as a future promise not as a past accomplishment.

The distinction between orientation and behavior will continue to be accepted in theory and practice despite attempts in some quarters to collapse the two realities. While the distinction will not meet the needs of all those engaged in the dialog either on the pastoral or the theological level, it can serve as a useful tool for getting a handle on the discussion. It is doubtful that the Vatican's label of "objective disorder" will be readily acceptable in all pastoral or theological circles and certainly not among the majority of biologists, sex educators, and human sexuality experts. The more benign judgment of the homosexual orientation as either "morally neutral" or "morally good" will probably continue to gain ground. At the same time strong resistance from Vatican authorities to moving in these more positive directions will continue because these positive directions are seen as leading to some reevaluation and development of the traditional prohibition of all forms of same-gender genital behavior. The groundwork for such an evaluation has already been laid by the Washington State Catholic Conference (1983), which has affirmed the possibility of some development of the classical condemnation of homosexual acts.

Conclusion

This chapter has been concerned with ecclesiastical policies and not with church doctrines per se. But it is important to appreciate the underlying judgments about homosexuality in order to challenge successfully the confusing definitions and unproven assumptions of those policies. This confusion in church policies can cause harm in the selection of otherwise qualified candidates. The individual's call to ordained ministry can be rejected unjustly and unnecessarily because of flawed criteria or misperceptions about the varieties of homosexual identities.

Given the present ecclesial climate, no one seriously expects that church authorities will propose new and daring distinctions that will shift the ground of public discourse. In the face of such documents as the ones discussed in this chapter we must continually probe every fixed term and casual assumption. As concerned individuals we have a responsibility to raise disturbing and provocative questions, especially when official church agencies issue documents, statements, and policies lacking precision, clarity, or convincing arguments. A good example of the exercise of this responsibility is found in a Communications Ministry (1988) journal that treats of gay and lesbian persons in seminary and religious formation.

Cardinal Baum is rightly concerned about the issue of homosexuality and seminary candidates, as are many bishops and others in the church community. His memorandum (discussed above) concludes with the following salutary warning: "The selection of candidates for admission to seminary and the recommendation of their progress to Holy Orders are heavy responsibilities which immediately bear on the good of the candidates individually, the reputation of the clergy, and the spiritual health of the Church" (Baum 1985, 1).

For all of these important reasons seminary rectors, vocation directors, formation personnel, bishops, and all in the faith community need to share in the responsibilities involved in the criteria for the selection and formation of candidates. The church deserves much better than what is currently being offered by the Vatican, the Bishops' Committee on Priestly Life and Ministry, and the Bishops' Committee on Priestly Formation.

References

American Psychiatric Association. 1987. *Diagnostic and Statistical Manual of Mental Disorders (DSM-III)*, 3rd ed. Washington, D.C.: American Psychiatric Association.

Baum, W. 1985. A Memorandum to Bishops Seeking Advice in Matters Concerning Homosexuality and Candidates for Admission to Seminary. Rome: Sacred Congregation for Catholic Education (July 9), Prot. N. 65/85.

Bernardin, J. 1978. Other Voices. *National Catholic Reporter* 15, no. 7 (December 1):4.

Berry J. 1987a. Homosexuality in Priesthood Said to Run High. *National Catholic Reporter* 23, no. 18 (Feb. 27): 1, 16–20.

Berry, J. 1987b. Seminarians Seem to Spawn Gay Priesthood. *National Catholic Reporter* 23, no. 19 (March 6): 20–24.

Bishops' Committee on Priestly Formation. 1985. Concerning the Acceptability of Certain Candidates. Washington, D.C.: United States Catholic Conference (July).

Bishops' Committee on Priestly Life and Ministry. 1983. A Reflection Guide on Human Sexuality and the Ordained Priesthood. Washington, D.C.: United States Catholic Conference.

Boswell, J. 1985. *Homosexuality, Religious Life and the Clergy: An Historical Overview.* Mt. Rainier, Md.: New Ways Ministry.

Bourgoin, M. F. 1979. Tuesday Afternoon with the Bishops. *National Catholic Reporter* 15, no. 7 (January 19): 5, 17.

Burtchell, J. 1985. The Catholic Journalist: A Theologian's View. *Origins* 15, no. 5 (June 20): 74–78.

Cahill, L. S. 1983. Moral Methodology: A Case Study. In *A Challenge to Love: Gay and Lesbian Catholics in the Church,* edited by R. Nugent. New York: Crossroad.

Coleman, J. 1984. The Homosexual Question in the Priesthood and Religious Life. *The Priest* (December): 12–19.

Commission on Social Justice. 1982. Lesbian Women and Gay Men in Religious Congregations/Orders and Priesthood. In *Homosexuality and Social Justice: Report of the Task Force on Gay/Lesbian Issues,* pp. 91–102. Archdiocese of San Francisco: Commission on Social Justice.

Committee of the New England Bishops. 1980. Priestly Formation: Discerning Vocations. *Origins* 9, no. 29 (January 3): 467–76.

Communication Ministry, Inc. 1988. *Nurturing the Gift: Gay and Lesbian Persons in Seminary and Religious Formation. CMI Journal* 2 (Autumn).

D'Arcy, J. 1984. Remarks to the NCCB, Administrative Committee, on Seminary Admission Policy (November 9).

Hickey, J. 1985. Letter to Symposium Endorsers (October 4).

Kelsey, D. 1984. Homosexuality and the Church: Theological Issues. *Reflections.* New Haven, Conn.

Magnano, P., Schau, E., and Tokarski, S. 1985. *Assessment of Applicants to Priesthood.* Chicago: National Conference of Diocesan Vocation Directors.

National Conference of Religious Vocation Directors. 1986. NCRVD Special Report. Chicago: National Conference of Religious Vocation Directors (May).

National Religious Vocation Conference. 1989. *Horizon* 14, no. 2 (Winter).

Nugent, R. 1988. Sexual Orientation in Vatican Thinking. In *The Vatican and Homosexuality,* edited by J. Gramick and P. Furey. New York: Crossroad.

Oddi, S. 1985. You Are All and Nothing, O Priest. *National Catholic Register* (December 1): 5.

Quinn, J. 1987. Toward an Understanding of the Letter on the Pastoral Care of Homosexual Persons. *America* 156, no. 5 (February 7): 92–95, 116.

Ratzinger, J. and Bovone, A. 1986. Letter to the Bishops of the Catholic

Church on the Pastoral Care of Homosexual Persons. Rome: Congregation for the Doctrine of the Faith (Oct. 1).

Senate of Priests. 1986. *Ministry and Homosexuality in the Archdiocese of San Francisco.* In *Homosexuality and the Magisterium,* edited by J. Gallagher. Mt. Rainier, Md.: New Ways Ministry.

Washington State Catholic Conference. 1983. *The Prejudice against Homosexuals and the Ministry of the Church.* Seattle, Wash.: Archdiocese of Seattle (April 28).

21 Lesbian Nuns: Identity, Affirmation, and Gender Differences

JEANNINE GRAMICK, SSND

Joan sat tensely in the folds of the soft brown chair, caressing a Christmas mug of herbal tea more for physical and moral support than to warm her chilled hands and body. Joan appeared to be in her late forties. Over the phone she told me that she was a member of her religious community's committee on women's concerns, which had recently discussed sexuality, including lesbianism. After several meetings, much discussion, extensive private reflection, and prayer, she felt confused, upset, and frightened about her own feelings. How would she know if she was a lesbian? Could we talk?

The following day here was Joan, a confident, professional woman who worked in the health care system but felt vulnerable and fearful of having her suspicions of her own lesbian identity confirmed. Here was Joan with one big question, waiting and longing for a definitive answer: Was she a lesbian or not?

Many times I have searched with women religious who have lived in community for twenty or more years or with young novices or associates aspiring to religious life. I have answered countless letters over the years from nuns desperately seeking information and counsel to grapple with the question "How do I know if I am gay?" I tried to help Joan as best I could, knowing that in the end only she herself could name her orientation.

As women religious venture into new professional fields and caring ministries, rub shoulders with people from varied walks of life, and become involved in the secular and religious women's movement, our care, concern, and interest in women and their needs can naturally cause us to question our own feelings and motives. We live and work with many dedicated, selfless, loving, dynamic women. Isn't it natural that we would admire and love these women tenderly, convinced that we have been gifted by God with their presence in our lives? We may have been extremely close to a few over the years. Or we may have developed a deep friendship with one woman in particular, even lived with her as companion for many years. As these situations are enfolding in religious life, we ask ourselves if this means that we are in a lesbian relationship.

In this chapter I explore the issue of lesbian identity, affirmation, and gender differences between lesbian nuns and their male counterparts. What does it mean to be a gay woman? How can I know if I am a lesbian? If I am, where and how can I find other lesbian nuns with whom to share insights and experiences? How can we institutionally support our lesbian sisters? Are there significant differences between lesbian nuns and gay priests and brothers in the ways they respond to and cope with their sexuality? If so, what are they?

Sexual Identity

For women religious who entered community life immediately after high school or before the effects of the sixties sexual revolution could be felt in religious formation programs, discerning a lesbian identity may take many years. Unlike males, who usually recognize their same-sex orientation in adolescence or puberty, most lesbians do not come to an awareness of their sexual identity until they are about twenty-one years of age (Gramick 1984; Peplau et al. 1978). Like a typical young woman entering religious life in the forties, fifties, or sixties at age eighteen, a lesbian may have assumed she was heterosexual. The young novice probably had no knowledge of the phenomenon of homosexuality, little or no sexual interest in the opposite gender, but perhaps some experience of heterosexual dating as part of the socializing process. She may have experienced the usual crushes on older female authority figures whom she admired; but certainly there would have been no open discussion or exploration of sexual feelings during her convent formation. The young novice unconsciously learned to submerge her sexual energy, usually into productive work or the ministry.

I recall my own novitiate formation on the vows in the early sixties. After several months of detailed instruction on the vow and virtue of obedience, a biology professor delivered three lectures to the novitiate class on the mechanics of human reproduction. With a concluding comment by the novice director that there was "nothing forbidden by the vow of chastity that was not already forbidden by the Sixth and Ninth Commandments," we proceeded immediately to learn about the vow of poverty!

Such was our inability in religious life about thirty years ago to deal honestly with sexuality and celibacy issues. There is little wonder, then, that most women religious today do not consciously consider themselves sexual beings. Many nuns, I believe, properly fall into that 14 percent of the U.S. female population that Kinsey and his associates identified as asexual (Kinsey 1953, 473). An asexual person is one who not only has never engaged in genital sex, but also has never experienced any sexual feelings.

The gay liberation and feminist movements of the late sixties and seventies have affected the lives of women religious in the eighties. Called to justice by the 1971 Synod of Bishops, "Justice in the World," U.S. nuns are beginning to recognize the great societal and ecclesiastical injustices that have been perpetrated against the lesbian and gay community and to sympathize with their plight. Influenced by the women's movement principle that all women must be accorded equal rights, U.S. nuns are learning about and working alongside their secular sisters, some of whom erotically love other women. The issue of sexual orientation is being raised and respectfully addressed. As women religious listen to, champion the rights of, cry with, and deeply love other women, they naturally ask themselves, "Am I therefore a lesbian?"

What Lesbianism Is Not

Before we explore the dynamics of what contributes to one's being a lesbian, it is imperative to consider what does not necessarily indicate lesbianism. Because of a strong identification of women religious with the rights of women, because women religious generally live and work in a female environment, and because most women religious have their emotional and social needs met primarily by other women, I have seen a great deal of confusion in the last decade, even among some leaders in the Catholic women's movement who mistakenly conclude that these women are lesbian. To live and work in a homosocial environment does not necessarily mean that one is lesbian or gay. To have human affectional needs for touching, hugging, and dispassionate kissing met by someone of the same gender is not necessarily an indication of homosexuality, nor is it a display of immaturity. One of the hazards of a celibate life-style is the risk of losing natural warmth and affection through fear of touching others.

Lesbianism is not another name for exclusive relationships. Exclusive relationships should be recognized for what they are: relationships that separate two people in an unhealthy way from the rest of the community, one person often being extremely emotionally dependent on the other. Exclusive relationships can occur between two persons of the same or opposite gender, between two homosexually or heterosexually oriented people, or between a homosexual and heterosexual person. A friendship that allows room only for each other is hurtful not only to community life, but also to the persons involved.

Although it is theoretically easy to describe the divisiveness caused by exclusivity in community life, caution must be exercised to avoid labeling and denigrating healthy friendships that need time to grow. One must also be able to identify feelings of jealousy that may subconsciously prompt criticism or resentment of a wholesome relationship, especially if a closer friendship is desired with one or the other individual. As long as human beings struggle for growth and maturity, we will probably see instances of exclusive relationships in our communities. It is important, however, to distinguish lesbian relationships from exclusive ones and to recognize the practical difference between the two so that healthy lesbian relationships are not mistakenly confused with neurotic dyads.

Lesbianism should be clearly distinguished from same-sex friendships. These have existed and will always exist in religious life. The time of formally condemning "particular friendships" has ceased, and women religious are learning to have a healthy respect for, and to rejoice in, same-sex friendships. A blessing to communities, friendships energize and empower sisters to dedicate their time and talents to serving God's people. To counteract the almost 100 percent professional atmosphere in which most nuns live, same-sex friendships provide a healthy and necessary outlet. It is important to move beyond the faceless masks and formal expression of community toward meaningful adult relationships. Intimate friendships invite sisters to discover who they really are and where their values lie. Providing opportunities to exercise receptivity and independence, close human relationships awaken one's capacity to care and to love.

Simply loving another woman or having a woman as one's closest friend and confidante does not automatically make a woman a lesbian. The fact that many heterosexual women enjoy primary relationships with women is socially acceptable in American culture and in most societies around the world. The crucial difference is that heterosexual women do not face the question of eroticism when they reflect on their female-female relationships. They may have strong emotional ties to their female friends, but their romantic feelings, if any, do not perdure.

Lesbianism is not the situation of living in community with only one other woman. Because of attempts by women religious to minister in far-flung geographical areas where our communities have not been previously established and because of a shift away from large institutional living in favor of smaller, close-knit communities, more and more religious are living as Jesus commissioned his disciples in the gospel: "two by two." Given the social fabric and the ministry goals of women religious as we approach the second millennium, the numbers of such living and/or working teams will only increase. Although some of these couple relationships may be genuine lesbian relationships, it would be a grave mistake to assume automatically that *all* are. Such couple relationships must be accorded a respect for friendship by other community members, and the women so coupled must be careful and conscious about including other community members in their day-to-day life.

Lesbianism should not be equated with the human need for affection, with same-gender friendships, with exclusive relationships, with living or working couple relationships, although a lesbian can find herself in any of these situations. Lesbian nuns experience the same needs for love, touch, and affection as heterosexual nuns. They treasure deep friendships with heterosexual sisters with whom they are not romantically involved. They struggle, as all nuns do, to free their relationships from suffocating domination, control, and exclusivity. Some have a primary relationship with another woman with whom they may or may not live; others do not feel they have a primary relationship. In short, lesbian nuns are similar to heterosexual nuns in all things, except for the fact that they are lesbian.

Lesbian Identity

What, then, is a lesbian woman? In the nineteenth century and until the second half of the twentieth century, sexual researchers defined sexual orientation behaviorally; that is, an individual's orientation depended on genital contact or having sex. Thus, someone who engaged in genital behavior with another person of his or her own gender, no matter how often or how infrequently, was labeled a homosexual. Someone who had engaged sexually with members of both his or her own and the opposite gender was called a bisexual. And individuals who experienced only opposite-gender sex partners were considered heterosexuals. With such a behaviorally biased definition, virgins lacked sexual orientation! With increasing knowledge about sexuality, the old simplistic concepts had to be abandoned. We now know that sexual orientation is determined by inner psychological components, not outward observable behavior. Sexual orientation is not a cut-and-dried, one-of-three-category designation. Our sexual orientation lies on a theoretical continuum, at one end of which is the heterosexual or opposite-sex pole; at the other, the homosexual pole. So it is possible to be "more heterosexual" or "more homosexual" than another person. Although two individuals may have orientations on the heterosexual side of the scale, one may be "more heterosexual" than the other. Many, if not most, basically heterosexual persons experience some degree of same-sex feelings, fantasies, desires, or attractions. What determines our location on this orientation rating scale?

Certainly not genital behavior, as was once believed! More than one-third of lesbian women have experienced marriage and heterosexual intercourse and more than one-half of these women are biological mothers (Bell and Weinberg 1978). In 1948 Alfred Kinsey shocked the world with his findings that 37 percent of U.S. males had homosexual experiences, although only 13 percent were constitutional homosexuals. If genital activity does not determine our sexual orientation, what does?

Sexual orientation is determined by the direction and strength of our romantic feelings, erotic desires, and sexual fantasies. The best guide in determining one's orientation is the answer to the question "With whom have I fallen in love?" If, in the course of her life, a woman has mostly fallen in love with other women, then her primary sexual orientation is lesbian.

Of course, a heterosocial environment is ideal for discovering one's true orientation. Most nuns entered religious life before the age of twenty-one, the average age at which most women discover their sexual orientation. At some period of their lives, most nuns have lived, worked, and socialized almost exclusively in the company of women. It is natural that same-sex erotic attractions, which most people have unconsciously buried, would surface at one time or another in the lives of nuns. If, however, these sexual feelings are extremely strong, perdure over long periods of time, and occur frequently with different women in the course of one's religious life, one's sexual identity most likely is primarily lesbian.

For lesbian women and gay men, erotic desire is not the sole factor attracting them to another individual. We often ask married couples, "Why did you fall in love with your spouse?" The same question can be asked of lesbian and gay couples, and similar responses will be forthcoming. Certainly there is an erotic attraction, the "chemistry is right," but there are other reasons to explain the relationship.

In an attempt to include additional dimensions beyond the physical attraction, Martin and Lyon (1972) state that a lesbian is "a woman whose primary erotic, psychological, emotional, and social interest is in a member of her own sex, even though that interest may not be overtly expressed" (p. 7). Traditionally, the primary psychological, emotional, and social interest of most nuns has been other women. But these elements alone, without the erotic dimension, are not sufficient to define a woman as lesbian. Because of the lack of open discussion of eroticism, romantic or sexual feelings, fantasies, and desires, many nuns may have suppressed or repressed their homosexual and heterosexual erotic instincts. In the absence of an erotic dimension, it is impossible to identify one's sexual orientation.

Erotic attraction, a distinguishing and necessary element in a lesbian identity, is certainly not the most important feature, as the personal testimonies of the lesbian nuns writing in this book demonstrate. Because the quality of the emotional relationship is of primary importance to a lesbian as well as to a heterosexual woman, it may be confusing for many women to determine their true sexual orientation. Because spiritual bonding is central, and physical bonding secondary in a lesbian relationship, many lesbians incorrectly believe that most nuns and feminists are latent lesbians. In the early seventies when the women's movement was embroiled in a controversy about supporting the lesbian cause, Ti-Grace Atkinson coined the term *political lesbian*, which proves useful in explaining the dedication and identification of heterosexual women with lesbian women. A political lesbian is a woman totally committed to all women, even though she lacks any sexual interest in other women.

Whereas erotic interest is a discriminating but subordinate feature of a lesbian orientation, genital behavior is not a necessary one. For this reason, many people, including nuns, mistakenly equate lesbianism with homosexual activity. It is therefore possible that many nuns in our communities would not name themselves lesbian because they do not engage in same-sex genital behavior.

Many ask, "How can nuns know they are lesbian if they are not homosexually active?" Consider the parallel situation: if nuns do not engage, or have never engaged, in opposite-sex genital behavior, how do they know they are heterosexual? In each case the answer lies in an analysis of physical and erotic feelings and romantic or sexual fantasy life. If a woman's erotic fantasies, feelings, and physical attractions continually and repeatedly center around other women, then she probably is lesbian.

What constitutes homosexuality, then, is a deep, innate erotic attraction for persons of the same gender, which translates into strong sexual desire and possibly action when the "right person" comes along. Lesbian and gay people fall in love just as heterosexual people do; the only difference is that they fall in love with someone of their own gender. Being a lesbian does not mean sexual attraction to every woman, just as a heterosexual woman is not attracted to every man. Being a lesbian does mean powerful erotic attraction to some particular woman in one's life and then making a choice of whether or not to act sexually on those feelings. A woman religious who has faithfully observed her vow of celibacy can still know that she is a lesbian. If she has fallen in love with women over the years, if she resonates with what she reads about lesbianism, if she can identify with some of the experiences lesbians relate, she will begin to suspect that these are good indicators of her sexuality. It is not necessary to have a sexual affair to confirm one's sexual orientation. The process of reflection on one's feelings, fantasies, and romantic desires can provide the foundation for the discovery of one's orientation.

Because of the age of entrance into community life prior to religious renewal, most nuns may be middle-aged or older before they realize their lesbian orientation. The ambiguity, meanwhile, may feel extremely uncomfortable. But there is no immediate need to label oneself or to find the right box. It may take many years for nuns to awaken from their asexual identity to a gradual realization, acknowledgment, and acceptance of their sexual orientation. The best advice during one's journey of sexual exploration is: "Don't be anxious; in due time all things will become clear."

Affirmation of Lesbian Nuns

Once a woman religious has discovered her lesbian orientation, what support does she have? Who affirms her goodness and worth? How can and should we minister to our lesbian sisters in community?

The false assumption that everyone is basically heterosexual is painfully oppressive to lesbian sisters. Retreats or workshops that treat of the vowed life automatically presume the participant's heterosexuality and discuss celibacy and sexuality in the context of heterosexual relationships. Keeping lesbian sisters in their anonymous locked closets, because of fear or prejudice, deprives them of some of the ease, relaxation, and joy that community living is meant to provide. If surrounded by a community that neither knows nor wants to know a significant part of her personal identity, a lesbian nun is forced to seek her primary support group outside her community. Returning home to understanding and loving friends should not be a luxury reserved for a few. A lesbian sister anticipates the day when she, who has faithfully served God and God's people for ten, twenty-five, or more years, can freely share with others her lesbian identity and the deepening of love and dedication that her same-sex friendships have brought. For most sisters that day may be long in coming. At present most lesbian nuns, ever cautious and unwilling to risk total rejection, share personal information with only a trusted and proven friend, and some with no one at all.

Because of social misunderstanding and ecclesial apprehensions about homosexuality, lesbian nuns have been forced to remain virtually unknown among us. Most nuns are totally oblivious of the alienation caused by demeaning jokes and derogatory remarks about lesbian and gay persons. For example, derision of homosexual people voiced by community members during a TV program will undoubtedly be interpreted and internalized as self-rejection by a lesbian sister and result in even further loneliness and isolation.

Religious administrators need to validate the topic institutionally by initiating private, informal discussions on a communitywide basis, by referring positively to the reality of homosexuality in community newsletters or communication bulletins, by sponsoring educational events on sexuality, and by generally creating a climate in which their sisters sense a permission to talk about sexuality. Though flawed in a literary and analytical sense, the book *Lesbian Nuns: Breaking Silence* (Curb and Manahan 1985) served as a springboard for discussion of lesbianism in many religious congregations. In this alone the book made a momentous and historical contribution. We hope that the present book will be used by religious administrators to stimulate forums for discussion of the topic.

Particularly in the past ten years, the leadership of women's congregations has been increasingly concerned about its lesbian sisters and willing to be of support, though often feeling at a disadvantage concerning how to proceed. This mounting concern may be due to greater awareness of the issue as more lesbian religious are confiding in their leadership. To the credit of women's congregational leadership, the response of most provincials, councilors, presidents, and the like has been overwhelming solicitude and support. Congregational leaders have provided financial resources to enable their lesbian sisters to attend workshops, retreats, or counseling sessions of the sisters' choosing. They have eagerly sought education for themselves and have provided educational experiences for the larger community. For example, in the academic year 1985–86, more than 150 women's congregational leaders attended a New Ways Ministry–sponsored symposium on homosexuality, priesthood, and religious life. As with parents of lesbian and gay persons, religious congregational leaders show more interest in the subject of homosexuality when they discover that some of their own community members are lesbian.

Congregational administrators may subconsciously fear the possibility of more public disclosures of their community member's lesbianism. Although no lesbian nun is presently contemplating an announcement in the *New York Times* or planning TV appearances to declare her orientation, it may be an eventuality with which some congregational leaders will have to deal in the future. Some administrators may be apprehensive about projecting a homosexual image, both internally and externally. Like parents of lesbian daughters and gay sons, they will be asking a similar version of "What will the neighbors say?" And just as parents of lesbian and gay children must eventually come out to relatives and friends, women's congregations may soon be in the same position of having to decide whether or not they will publicly acknowledge and affirm their lesbian religious family members. Lesbian sisters are asking only for the legitimate right to be open and honest about their sexuality if and when the occasion naturally arises.

Like their lesbian and gay counterparts outside religious life, lesbian nuns need peer-support groups to combat loneliness and isolation and to facilitate the exchange of insights regarding special needs or problems. Lesbian religious need the support of knowing and talking with one another since they develop their sexuality differently from heterosexual religious. Religious administrators can serve as connectors and put lesbian nuns in touch with one another.

In 1984–85 New Ways Ministry coordinated four regional workshops for lesbian nuns in Pittsburgh, San Francisco, Milwaukee, and New Orleans. Although only about fifty nuns attended these workshops, they were important in that they contributed to the nuns' psychological and spiritual growth and formed a basis for a national network of lesbian nuns that has helped reduce their fear, negative self-esteem, and lack of self-acceptance. Some nuns who were confused or unsure of their sexual orientation left the workshops with a greater understanding and appreciation for their own sexuality.

The only existing local support groups for lesbian nuns are located in the San Francisco Bay area, Minneapolis–St. Paul, Boston, and New York City. This serious lack of group support for lesbian nuns illustrates one of the many differences between lesbian nuns and gay priests or brothers. Almost every major U.S. city has monthly support group meetings for gay clergy and male religious. Some congregations of male religious even sponsor gay "caucuses" for their membership. No women's congregation has identified and organized its lesbian members in sufficiently large numbers, even though there are more than twice as many U.S. nuns as priests and brothers.

Gender Differences

There are at least three possible reasons why there are many more support groups for gay priests and brothers than for lesbian nuns. These reasons illustrate some of the gender differences regarding homosexuality in religious life. First, gay priests and religious seem to be much more visible or "out" to one another than are lesbian nuns. This visibility is probably due to male-female socialization in which males learn to be comfortable in more public forums, whereas females are accustomed to small private settings. Such social patterns usually prompt males to organize more readily than females.

Second, the attrition rate for lesbian nuns appears higher than for gay male religious or clergy. Religious women and men, I believe, often make different choices once they establish a close primary relationship with another individual. Religious men have typically been able to integrate a significant relationship into their communitarian and ministerial lives. Perhaps because women usually desire to live with the person of primary relationship and because this arrangement may not always be possible in religious life today, lesbian nuns frequently leave their religious congregations to establish a life-style with a partner. Having witnessed such a scenario many times before, I anguished with a lesbian who sincerely loved her congregation, who cherished every year of her thirty in community, and who stated that in her heart she would always be a sister. Her community leaders deeply respected and valued her and wanted her to remain in religious life. Since there was no viable way to live with the woman she loved, which, she believed, was necessary for her own growth and development, she left the community she considered home and family.

Third, there is probably a greater number of gay priests and brothers than lesbian nuns. In the absence of any reliable scientific data on the incidence of homosexuality among all clergy and religious today, we can rely only on estimates from church workers in lesbian and gay ministry and from church administrators who are dealing with their lesbian or gay members. A 1985 survey by the National Conference of Religious Vocation Directors revealed that 1 percent of the women and 5 percent of the men admitted during 1980–85 into postulancy or residency programs acknowledged a homosexual orientation. These figures pertain only to those in the early stages of religious formation or clerical vocation discernment and rely on knowledge actually shared with authorities. The actual numbers and percentages of lesbian and gay religious or clergy may be much higher. These percentages may indicate a higher concentration of homosexual males than females in religious orders.

The patriarchal nature of ecclesial life may help to explain this concentration. Until the Second Vatican Council, male as well as female religious, and even diocesan seminarians, were schooled in a theology of celibacy and religious life that portrayed the relationship between Christ and the individual priest, sister, or brother as a spousal relationship. This wedding imagery depicted the individual as a bride spiritually uniting with Christ, the Bridegroom. This romantic notion of a heavenly marriage to a divine male figure would appeal to heterosexual women and to homosexual men. Similarly, a conception of God as male, reinforced by masculine God language, would be less attractive to lesbians and heterosexual males. In its extreme form such a patriarchal theology could lead to an ecclesial community of gay men around the altar and heterosexual women in the pews.

If indeed there are fewer lesbian nuns than their male counterparts, several questions naturally arise. Are there more lesbian nuns than heterosexual ones? How many lesbian nuns are there? How does the percentage of lesbian nuns in our convents compare with the general population?

In one informal study of women religious in mid-life transition, 144 religious between the ages of thirty and sixty from approximately 15 active and contemplative congregations in the Midwest, South, and West completed questionnaires to ascertain a variety of issues concerning psychological, sexual, and spiritual adjustment. In dealing with their intimacy needs and related sexual desires, 69 percent of the sample, or 99 women religious, engaged in some form of physical or affectional behavior that they considered to be specifically sexual. Of these, 21 percent indicated a female partner, another 30 percent indicated both female and male partners, and 49 percent indicated a male partner (Murphy 1983, 11, 133).

These data imply that 51 sisters of the sample size of 144 or 35 percent reported sexual experiences with other women, but do not imply that 35 percent of women religious are lesbian or bisexual. There is no reason to suspect that the questionnaires were completed by a random sample of U.S. nuns. In fact, the sample is most likely skewed by including disproportionate numbers of women likely to experiment sexually because they are most interested in interpersonal relationships and personal develop-ment in religious life. A more cautious, though still tentative, conclusion could be drawn from an analysis of the numbers and percentages of women religious who experienced sexual intimacy and those who did not. Of those nuns who have dealt with their increased sexual desires and interests during mid-life, approxi-mately one-third act on their heterosexual desires, one-sixth on their lesbian desires, one-fifth on their bisexual desires, and one-third choose to have no sexual involvement at all. These tentative statistics, however, probably do not take into account the vast numbers of women religious who may be frightened of intimacy and sexuality and have subconsciously chosen to avoid confronting these issues in their lives.

According to the conservative estimates, approximately 13 percent of the American male population and 7 percent of the American female population are predominantly or exclusively homosexually oriented (Kinsey et al. 1948: Kinsey et al. 1953). Since these estimates are generally considered reliable by sexual researchers, gay men are twice as numerous as lesbian women in the general population. The number of gay priests and brothers in the United States, however, currently constitutes only half the number of U.S. women religious. If the percentage of homosexu-ally oriented religious and clergy is consistent with general popu-lation norms, one would expect the number of lesbian nuns to be approximately the same as the number of gay priests and brothers.

If the membership of Communication Ministry, Inc. (CMI), a national network for gay clergy and religious, is any indication of the relative distribution by gender of homosexually oriented persons in religious life or priesthood, then the percentages do not match the general population. Of approximately five hundred individuals on the CMI mailing list, not more than fifty are women religious. Unlike the general population, in which gay men outnumber lesbians two to one, gay priests and brothers may outnumber lesbian nuns by ten to one, if the mailing list of CMI serves as a random sample of homosexually oriented clergy and religious. This may mean that the percentage of gay priests and brothers is much higher than 13 percent in the general male population or that the percentage of lesbian nuns is lower than 7 percent in the general female population, or both.

For women religious, however, all discussion and interest in the relative numbers of lesbian nuns contrasted with the number of gay male clergy and religious may be premature and misleading because women religious, as a group, have not adequately addressed personal sexuality issues. As noted above, Kinsey (1948, 656; 1953, 473) identified 14 percent of the American female population as asexual compared to only 1 percent of the American male population. I believe that more than 14 percent of U.S. nuns have not reflected on their sexual identity. When women religious explore sexuality issues and acknowledge that celibates cannot be fully human with repressed sexual feelings, more lesbian sisters may emerge.

Conclusion

Lesbianism is a sexual, erotic, or romantic attraction more toward women than toward men. A lesbian has not merely *loved* women in her life; she has fallen *in* love with them. Although this sexual attraction is a feature of a lesbian orientation that differentiates it from a heterosexual one, it is important secondarily to other aspects of lesbian loving, such as emotional and affectional female bonds, which heterosexual women also experience. Because what is most vital and valued in lesbian relationships is also of primary importance to heterosexual women, it is often confusing for a woman to identify her true sexual orientation. Because lesbian and heterosexual relationship values are so similar, lesbians often have more in common with heterosexual women than with gay men. There are more elements that unite lesbians with heterosexual women than separate them. This explains why many lesbians feel more committed to the women's movement than to the gay movement.

Many women religious today do not believe they are lesbian because they are not sexually active. Like society in general, they erroneously believe that one cannot be homosexual without overt, genital expression. Compound this myth with the fact that women, unlike men, attach less value or importance to sexual desire or activity in a relationship and greater value to emotional, psychological, and spiritual bonding and one can easily understand how a lesbian nun may not realize her true orientation.

The distinguishing mark of sexual orientation—genital desire— is not the basis of what is most treasured in most females' relationships. This is decidedly different for most males. Unlike females, whose genital organs are internal and whose sexual feelings are more diffused, subtle, and integrated throughout the entire body, males' sexuality is localized in the external genitals. For this biological reason and probably for socialization reasons as well, males may place more importance on sexual desire and specific genital responses. Men may thus be able to determine their sexual orientation more readily because of obvious physical changes during sexual arousal. Women, especially nuns, live with sexual ambiguity longer than men do.

Once women religious realize their lesbian identity, they generally receive support and affirmation from their leadership. Unfortunately, the same cannot be said of the general membership of women's communities. Mammoth educational programs in sexuality and in respect for differences are needed before congregations can become safe and nourishing places where lesbian sisters can grow into the freedom of the daughters of God.

I sat and observed Joan, no longer clutching her half-sipped mug of tea and seeming more relaxed than she had been an hour ago. Instead of the Danish pastry that lay untouched on the coffee table, she had eagerly consumed our conversation. Some of her questions had been answered, some were still unresolved, others seemed irrelevant now. As she closed the front gate behind her,

her grateful brown eyes registered a contented peace. She had promised God that she would be more patient with herself until she could fully understand and accept the sexual gifts with which she had been blessed.

References

Bell, A. P., and Weinberg, M. S. 1978. *Homosexualities: A Study of Diversity among Men and Women*. New York: Simon and Schuster.

Curb, R., and Manahan, N., eds. 1985. *Lesbian Nuns: Breaking Silence*. Tallahassee: Naiad Press.

Gramick, J. 1984. Developing a Lesbian Identity. In *Women-identified Women*, edited by T. Darty and S. Potter. Palo Alto, Calif.: Mayfield.

Kinsey, A. C., Pomeroy, W., and Martin, C. 1948. *Sexual Behavior in the Human Male*. Philadelphia: W. B. Saunders.

Kinsey, A. C., Pomeroy, W., Martin, C., and Gebhard, P. 1953. *Sexual Behavior in the Human Female*. Philadelphia: W. B. Saunders.

Martin, D., and Lyon, P. 1972. *Lesbian/Woman*. San Francisco: Glide.

Murphy, S. M. 1983. *Midlife Wanderer: The Woman Religious in Midlife Transition*. Whitinsville. Mass.: Affirmation Books.

Peplau, L. A., Cochran, S., Rook, K., and Padesky, C. 1978. Loving Women: Attachment and Autonomy in Lesbian Relationships. *Journal of Social Issues* 34, no. 3:7–27.

22 God Calls, Religious Orders Respond

JEANNE SCHWEICKERT, SSSF

I think the most difficult aspect of being gay and religious comes not so much from myself as a sexual person as it does from myself as a social person—a person in need of belonging to a group and acceptance from a group.

—gay religious priest

In late 1985 the National Conference of Religious Vocation Directors (NCRVD) undertook a study called "Who's Entering Religious Life?" They collected data on persons entering religious orders of men and women who came from a variety of life experiences. Since the general pattern of development of American religious orders follows that of the white immigrant church, we asked about experiences with the Caucasian candidate. We inquired further about the incorporation of persons not of the U.S. dominant white culture, namely, those of black, Hispanic, Asian, or Native American origins. Aware that many individuals considering the vowed/ordained life-style today, regardless of cultural background, bring with them experiences different from the pre–Vatican II candidate, we also asked about women and men who were older (forty or more years old), widowed, divorced, alcohol/chemically dependent, self-avowed homosexually oriented, undocumented, physically or mentally disabled.

237

We acknowledge and emphasize that a person is more than any one of these characteristics, and that no one aspect, cultural or social, identifies the totality of that woman or man. Thus it is with caution that we focus on a single distinguishing element or experience of an individual. Unfortunately, however, it is these various characteristics that generate the most concern and discussion among people, and so we respectfully gathered information on the specific experiences named.

The 103 male orders and 251 female orders that responded to the NCRVD study represent 44 percent of the men religious and 62 percent of the active women religious in the United States. This article shares the experiences of these communities with women and men entering religious life who have acknowledged a homosexual orientation. The findings are addressed here by the questions posed in the study.

Survey Findings

1. *Would you* consider *for acceptance into your community a person who acknowledges a homosexual orientation? If so, what are your requirements?*

Almost half (46 percent) of the women's communities expressed openness to considering a lesbian for acceptance into their community. More than a tenth (12 percent) stated a definite no, and the remainder (42 percent) did not respond. More men's communities expressed openness, with almost two-thirds (61 percent) saying yes; however, a larger number (18 percent) of the male orders indicated they definitely would not consider a gay man for acceptance, and about half as many male (21 percent) as female orders made no response.

Communities expressing openness to considering the self-avowed homosexual person for acceptance give greatest emphasis to the requirement of a celibate life-style, including nongenital activity and a "nongay" life-style (for example, frequenting gay bars). The second most frequently stated expectation referred to the individual's personal integration of his or her orientation. Other stipulations called for no public declaration and no participation in advocacy roles.

2. *During 1980–85 how many women and men who acknowledged a homosexual orientation have you* accepted *into postulancy/ residency?*

Over this six-year time span only a small number (3 percent) of the female orders accepted a declared lesbian into postulancy, whereas a fourth (24 percent) of the male orders accepted declared gay men. The 11 lesbian persons and 83 gay men accepted during this time represented 1 percent of the total number of women (1,712) admitted during 1980–85 and 5 percent of the total men (1,820).

3. *How many self-avowed gay/lesbian persons were in the various* stages of formation *(postulancy/residency, novitiate, temporary vows) on September 1, 1985?*

Across the various stages of formation in September 1985 there were 68 men and 10 women who acknowledged a homosexual orientation. Of the total population in the novitiate they constituted 9 percent of the men and 1 percent of the women; in temporary vows they were 3 percent of the professed males and less than 1 percent of the professed females; and in postulancy/ residency they were 8 percent of the male and 2 percent of the female candidates.

4. *Have you been or are you now in* serious discernment *with a self-avowed gay or lesbian person about entry into your community?*

Two-thirds of the men's orders have had some experience discerning with self-avowed gay men. This is almost four times as many male orders as female orders (17 percent) with discernment experience. In September 1985 there were 5 women's orders and 15 men's orders that said they were currently in discernment with 5 women and 25 men who claimed a homosexual orientation. These gay and lesbian persons were 4 percent of the overall male population in serious discernment at that time and 1 percent of the overall female population.

5. *What* worked well *for you in incorporating into community candidates who acknowledged a homosexual orientation?*

This part of the survey, as well as the section on concerns, was a beginning effort to articulate community experiences based on their own perception of the reality. Since their response shared personal experience, there is no assurance that what worked for one order will work for another. Further, in presenting the findings we made no judgment as to whether the community perspective was appropriate or not appropriate. Follow-up reflectors did at times make some comments in this regard.

Some common threads did appear in the responses, and since there was no significant difference between the experiences of men's and women's communities, they are combined in this report. The most frequently stated positive approach for incorporating the gay or lesbian candidate into community revolved around facilitating opportunities for the potential candidate's involvement with the community. Through live-ins, reflection days, volunteer service, and similar events the members come to know the individual first as a person. Such experiences break down the stereotype biases that revolve around various characteristics. This particular approach was addressed as the most effective means of incorporating all persons looking at religious life as an option for themselves.

More directly related to "coming out" in community, it was deemed helpful when the person spoke with council members individually, or acknowledged his or her homosexual orientation to only a small segment of community and received support. Some communities noted that what contributed favorably was the individual's own self-acceptance, noninvolvement in the political aspects of homosexuality, or personal understanding that overt activity was not tolerated.

Various forms of education of the director, administration, and community occurred repeatedly as a significant positive factor. Noted were activities such as keeping up with the latest reading, administration participation in workshops on homosexuality, sponsoring a community seminar on sexuality in general and homosexuality in particular. Specifically for the vocation/

formation personnel, self-education was suggested. Ways of doing this were: making gay and lesbian friends; keeping abreast of the latest studies and insights on homosexuality; meeting the candidate's gay friends; learning how to question respectfully about sexuality, orientation, and behavior; and assessing healthy integration.

Communities also indicated the advantage of clarity of expectations. They spoke to expectations or processes such as allowing the person to be active in such support groups as Dignity, or to associate and socialize with other gay and lesbian persons; requiring a period of celibacy prior to entry and expecting chastity of all candidates; agreeing on a written policy related to these matters.

Attitudes played an important part in positive incorporation of lesbian and gay candidates—for example, appreciation of the individual's gifts, openness and support from members, frankness about possible prejudices to be met in the community, refusal to base acceptance or nonacceptance solely on orientation, an offer of help to the person to feel that he or she is entering as a "normal" person and not running away. In general, these attitudes can be summed up as ongoing openness and honesty.

6. *What* concerns or problems *emerged in working with candidates who acknowledged a homosexual orientation?*

Two major areas surfaced as problematic: (1) misunderstanding and prejudice within the community, and (2) personal issues of the individual candidate. In the realm of community the responses pointed to lack of knowledge, biased attitudes, and prejudicial behaviors of members. In general, homophobia was detrimental to the incorporation process. This was expressed in an uninviting and nonsupportive environment; the community's own discomfort with sexuality; a releasing of latent homosexuality in others; fear of becoming a haven for homosexuals; poking fun at, joking about, and making judgmental statements on homosexuality; and overall lack of education on homosexuality.

In terms of the individual candidate's personal issues, the respondents noted the difficulties arising from the person's concerns about members' reactions; the pain caused by identity problems; the need to reveal orientation in order to find acceptance; the possessiveness, crushes, jealousies in relationships; the "one-issue-only" militancy; and the more central focus on sexual matters.

Advice for Directors and Religious Congregations

In the NCRVD study, homosexual male and female religious and national organizations ministering to gay and lesbian persons were asked to advise religious congregations on how they might more effectively work with lesbian and gay individuals who feel called to the vowed/ordained life. Their suggestions centered around personal awareness and self-education, assessment of potential candidates, and acceptance by community membership.

Those involved directly with gay and lesbian candidates need to consciously name their own biases and fears and work to address them in order to more honestly and fairly deal with the homosexual candidate. Self-education through good theological and psychological sources and through dialogue with healthy lesbian and gay Catholics can help to familiarize directors and members with the experiences, concerns, and difficulties of persons with a homosexual orientation. Congregational leadership needs to support (1) formal and informal education of their membership about sexuality, and (2) acceptance of homosexual men and women into their community membership. Their positive stance is essential to overcoming homophobic attitudes.

The assessment process needs to assist lesbian and gay candidates in focusing on the integration of and comfort with their sexuality—for example, the degree of freedom accompanying their orientation to allow for entering into a community experience and relating effectively with different people; the ability to deal with the challenges of the celibate life-style; the ability to cope with a certain amount of homophobia within the congregations.

Vocation directors need to be sure that leadership and formation personnel are open to accepting a lesbian or gay candidate and that they agree on basic issues related to openness about orientation, degree of public/political activity, and ways of handling homophobic responses of other community members. It is important also that there are enough members who can accept people who are open about their gay or lesbian orientation so that they are not forced into an unhealthy secrecy or isolation.

Observations

In this study it is clear that lesbian and gay persons are being called to religious life. It would be naive to believe that this is a new phenomenon for orders of men and women. We know well that in the not-too-distant past the strong emphasis forbidding "particular friendships" prevailed as a safeguard against gay and lesbian relationships within communities. There is no doubt that women and men with a homosexual orientation were admitted to religious life in the past. To what extent they claimed their orientation even privately and what their actual numbers were remain unknown. Their presence in religious life is a given then, as it is now.

In considering the above data culled from the NCRVD survey it is important to bear in mind that we are talking about the women and men who have "come out" previous to entry or in the process of incorporation. These data in no way take into account the number of men and women who, for whatever reasons, have not yet felt free enough to acknowledge their homosexual orientation. Whether their reasons relate to fear of rejection, lack of personal confidence, a noninviting environment, uncertainty of consequences, personal confusion, or any other rationale, it is reasonable to assume that the picture that emerges from this study underestimates the reality of the situation. It does give some hard data with which to work, but all the reflectors questioned the low numbers. Future studies undertaken may more accurately approximate the true reality, due, one hopes, to the lessening of homophobia and thus a more positive environment.

For now the number of communities expressing willingness to consider the declared gay or lesbian person for acceptance is far greater than those actually accepting them (see Figure 1). Why this is so is not clear. Is it because no homosexual men or women have looked at these particular communities? Is it that lesbian and gay persons have been in discernment and were not accepted or chose

Figure 1. Communities and the Person Who Acknowledges a Homosexual Orientation

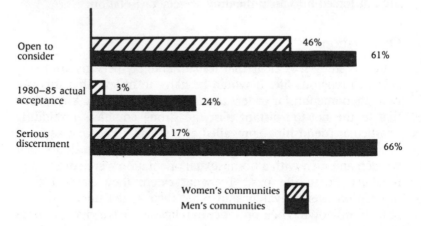

to withdraw for some reason? Is it that communities expressed openness, but the lived reality differed greatly? Is it that individuals have been accepted but have not yet made known their orientation?

Whatever the reasons, it is apparent from this study that respondents have experiences that contribute to positive incorporation of gay and lesbian persons into community. At the same time, it is clear that the "issue" of homosexuality continues to engender misunderstanding, fear, and prejudices; in this sense we are a microcosm of the larger society.

Therein lies the challenge. As religious orders we speak of the ongoing struggle to be missioned gospel communities. Jesus deliberately chose to be with those persons of his time who were most rejected by society. In many ways persons who have owned their homosexual or bisexual orientation as different from the deeply embedded "norm," have faced untold barriers and outright hatred from segments of church and society. If we as faith communities cannot move beyond these tensions and biases, how do we expect the society at large to open itself to the richness of diversity and to seek the unity found in the interdependence of peoples?

As we invite people to join us in our future mission endeavors, we should remember that the fullness of being a person encompasses the totality of the individual and no one characteristic attributed to that person. This belief finds its roots in the fundamental gospel value of the dignity of each human person—the gay or lesbian person along with all others. Today vocation directors are being more skillfully trained to assess the realm of sexuality in all candidates, thus inviting individuals to more honestly face their own reality as it influences their choice of a life direction.

We began this chapter with the words of a gay priest. We end with those of a lesbian sister offering us a challenge:

> I think one of the greatest challenges to religious congregations regarding lesbian, but also heterosexual, members is to provide a community climate where it is possible to explore, learn more about, and be supported in one's struggle to integrate sexuality in healthy ways into a celibate life-style. Another equally important challenge is to understand and free ourselves of the homophobia that affects us as members of the church and of society. Neither of these is an easy challenge quickly accomplished, but both are, I believe, as worthy of our time, energy, and struggle, as are the larger issues of peace and justice in our world. Indeed, I think we are only beginning to understand how closely connected all of these issues really are.

Bibliography

Anonymous. "I Am a Gay Priest with a Community Role." *National Catholic Reporter* 12, no. 23 (April 2, 1976): 29.

Anonymous. "Being Gay and Celibate." *National Catholic Reporter* 16, no. 43 (October 3, 1980): 18.

Anonymous. "A Sacrifice without Growth." *National Catholic Reporter* 19, no. 38 (August 26, 1983): 16.

Barry, William A., Madeline Birmingham, William Connolly, Robert Fahey, Virginia Finn, and James Gill. "The Experience of Phil." *Studies in the Spirituality of Jesuits* 10, nos. 2 and 3 (March-May 1978): 122–41.

Berry, Jason. "Homosexuality in Priesthood Said to Run High." *National Catholic Reporter* 23, no. 18 (February 27, 1987): 1, 16–20.

———. "Seminaries Seen to Spawn Gay Priesthood." *National Catholic Reporter* 23, no. 19 (March 6, 1989): 20–24.

Boswell, John. *Christianity, Social Tolerance, and Homosexuality: Gay People in Western Europe from the Beginning of the Christian Era to the Fourteenth Century.* Chicago: University of Chicago Press, 1980. (See particularly chapters 8 and 9.)

Brown, Judith. *Immodest Acts: The Life of a Lesbian Nun in Renaissance Italy.* New York: Oxford University Press, 1986.

Coleman, Gerald. "The Homosexual Question in the Priesthood and Religious Life." *The Priest* 40, no. 12 (December 1984): 12–19.

Communication Ministry, Inc. *Nurturing the Gift: Gay and Lesbian Persons in Seminary and Religious Formation. CMI Journal* 2 (Autumn 1988).

Curb, Rosemary and Nancy Manahan, eds. *Lesbian Nuns: Breaking Silence.* Tallahasee, Fla.: Naiad Press, 1985.

Gramick, Jeannine. "Cracks in the Convent Closets." *News/Views* (National Sisters Vocation Conference), November-December 1982, 1–7.

———. "Gay and Celibate." *Probe* (National Assembly of Religious Women) 9, no. 4 (January 1980): 5–7.

————. "Homosexuality, Religious Life, and Vocation Ministry." *Horizon* (National Religious Vocation Conference) 14, no. 2 (Winter 1989): 16–21.

————. "Lesbian Nuns." *Probe* (National Assembly of Religious Women) 7, no. 6 (March 1978): 5–6.

Harvey, John. "Counseling the Invert in Religious Life." *Bulletin of the Guild of Catholic Psychiatrists*, October 1962, 210–21.

————. "Homosexuality and Vocations." *American Ecclesiastical Review* 164, no. 1 (January 1971): 42–55.

————. "Reflections on a Retreat for Clerics with Homosexual Tendencies," *Linacre Quarterly* 46 (May 1979): 136–40.

Helldorfer, Martin. "Homosexual Brothers: Sources of New Life." In *Prejudice*, edited by Timothy McCarthy. Romeoville, Ill.: Christian Brothers National Office, 1982.

Hubbuch, Cornelius. "Gay Men and Women and the Vowed Life." In *Homosexuality and the Catholic Church*, edited by Jeannine Gramick. Chicago: Thomas More Press, 1983.

Judith. "Lesbian Nun: Another Perspective." *Sisters Today* 59, no. 6 (February 1988): 344–48.

Kraft, William. "Homosexuality and Religious Life." *Review for Religious* 40 (June-July 1981): 370–81.

Kropinak, Marguerite. "Homosexuality and Religious Life." In *A Challenge to Love*, edited by Robert Nugent. New York: Crossroad, 1983.

McBrien, Richard. "Homosexuality and the Priesthood." *Commonweal* 114, no. 12 (June 19, 1987): 380–83.

Moore, Mary Ellen. "Homosexual Religious in Formation, Some Observations and Reflections." *In-Formation* (Religious Formation Conference) 85 (March-April 1985): 1–5.

Moran, Gabriel. "Sexual Forms." In *Sexuality and Brotherhood*. Lockport, Ill.: Christian Brothers' Conference, 1977.

Morrissey, Paul. "Spiritual Direction for Gay Clergy and Religious: The Integration of Spirituality and Sexuality through the Written Word." D. Min. Diss., Weston College, Cambridge, Mass., 1982.

Murphy, Sheila. "Counseling Lesbian Women Religious." *Women and Therapy* 5, no. 4 (Winter 1986): 7–17.

National Conference of Catholic Bishops, Bishops' Committee on Priestly Life and Ministry. *A Reflection Guide on Human Sexuality and the Ordained Priesthood*, 50–52. Washington, D.C.: United States Catholic Conference, 1983.

Nugent, Robert. "Homosexuality, Celibacy, Religious Life and Ordination." In *Homosexuality and the Catholic Church*, edited by Jeannine Gramick. Chicago: Thomas More Press, 1983.

————. "Priest, Celibate and Gay: You Are Not Alone." In *A Challenge to Love: Gay and Lesbian Catholics in the Church*, edited by Robert Nugent. New York: Crossroad, 1983.

————. "Some Issues of Homosexual Applicants." *Horizon* (National Religious Vocation Conference) 14, no. 2 (Winter 1989): 29–39.

Oddo, Thomas. "Gays in the Priesthood and Religious Life." *Dignity* 8, no. 3 (March 1977): 1–5. Reprinted in *Insight*, Summer 1978, 5–7.

O'Hea, Eileen. "Homosexuality: Perceptions/Misperceptions." *Maryknoll Formation Journal*, "Celibacy/Sexuality," Winter 1983–84, 6–12.

Pennington, Basil. "Vocation Discernment and the Homosexual." In *A Challenge to Love*, edited by Robert Nugent. New York: Crossroad, 1983.

Roberts, William. "The Formation and Integration of the Lesbian/Gay Aspirant." *Sisters Today* 58, no. 7 (March 1987): 404–9.

Sherman, Sarah M. "Lesbianism and the Vatican: Free to Be Ministers of the Gospel?" In *The Vatican and Homosexuality*, edited by Jeannine Gramick and Pat Furey. New York: Crossroad, 1988.

Sweeney, Winifred. *Congregational Policies Regarding Lesbian/Homosexual Candidates*. New York: Intercommunity Center for Justice and Peace, 1980.

Task Force on Gay/Lesbian Issues, Commission on Social Justice. *Homosexuality and Social Justice*. Archdiocese of San Francisco, 1982. See chapter 6. Reprinted in *Homosexuality and Social Justice*. The Consultation on Homosexuality, Social Justice, and Roman Catholic Theology. San Francisco, 1986.

Wagner, Richard. "Being Gay and Celibate: Another View." *National Catholic Reporter* 17, no. 5 (November 21, 1980): 16.

————. *Gay Catholic Priests: A Study of Cognitive and Affective Dissonance*. San Francisco: Specific Press, 1981.

Woods, Richard. "Gay Candidates, the Religious Life and Priesthood." In *Call to Growth and Ministry* (National Conference of Religious Vocation Directors of Men) 4, no. 4 (Summer 1979): 24–43.

Contributors

John Boswell is a professor of history at Yale University. His landmark book, *Christianity, Social Tolerance and Homosexuality*, traces historical changes in public attitudes toward homosexuality in medieval Europe. His most recent book is *The Kindness of Strangers: The Abandonment of Children in Western Europe from Late Antiquity to the Renaissance*.

Eileen Brady, RSM, entered the New Hampshire Sisters of Mercy in 1969 when she was 22. She has worked in schools, parishes, and a variety of social and political ministries, including organizing work with low-income people.

Brother Amos is a Franciscan and an assistant professor of English at a university on the East Coast.

Brother Jonathan served his community in the capacity of local superior, vocation director, provincial, and vicar general. Born on the East Coast of the United States, he now lives and works with people with AIDS in the San Francisco area.

Richard John Cardarelli, OFM Cap., was raised in Cromwell, Connecticut, and has been a Franciscan friar since 1976. He currently directs his province's Office for Peace and Justice.

Father Aelred, who entered the seminary after the eighth grade, completed his studies in Europe where he was ordained. As a parish priest and a diocesan official who has served the church for over twenty-five years, he counsels other gay clerics and lesbian religious as well as lay members of his local Dignity chapter.

Father Paul, a religious order priest, has served as a Dignity chaplain for more than a dozen years and often gives retreats and days of recollection for gay and lesbian groups.

Jeannine Gramick, a School Sister of Notre Dame since 1960, taught mathematics in high school, college, and university. She has worked in lesbian and gay ministry since 1971, and is cofounder of New Ways Ministry.

John P. Hilgeman was ordained in 1969 and holds degrees in theatre, theology, and social work. He has been a parish priest, teacher, chaplain, therapist, and social worker and has been active in the gay community since 1974. With his buddy, Patrick Leonard, he helped organize the St. Louis chapter of the Names Project. He cohosts a radio program for the lesbian and gay community.

Matthew Kelty, OCSO, was born in 1915 in Boston. He was ordained and served as a Divine Word Missionary before entering the Gethsemani Abbey as a Trappist in 1960.

Dan Maguire, a professor of theology at Marquette University, is the author of *Death by Choice, The Moral Choice, A New American Justice, The New Subversives, The Moral Revolution*, and hundreds of articles in scholarly and popular journals.

William Hart McNichols, SJ, entered the Society of Jesus in 1968 and was ordained a priest in 1979. He is an artist and illustrator of books and has worked with people with AIDS since 1983. He shares his personal story in this anthology "for my father."

Robert Nugent is a Salvatorian priest whose pastoral experience includes parish and campus ministry and social work on Philadelphia's skid row. He cofounded New Ways Ministry in 1977 and has written and lectured extensively on homosexuality and Catholicism.

Jo Louise Pecoraro worked at an archdiocesan social service center in the French Quarter for five years. She presently teaches English in an inner-city public high school in New Orleans.

Rosemary Radford Ruether is the Georgia Harkness Professor of Applied Theology at the Garrett-Evangelical Theological Seminary. She is the author or editor of twenty-two books and numerous articles on theology and social justice issues.

Jeanne Schweickert is currently Co-Director of Convergence, Inc. She is the past executive director of the National Religious Vocation Conference and a former vice-president of ministry of the School Sisters of St. Francis.

Sister Linda as a member of her religious congregation for more than twenty-five years engaged in their traditional apostolate of education for most of that time. She currently serves as a province administrator.

Sister Mary ministered for many years as a high school teacher and principal. She has recently served as director of ministry and member of her congregation's leadership team.

Sister Raphaela, with formal education in theology, psychology, and scripture, has engaged in teaching religion, adult education, retreat work, and counseling. She is entirely integrated into the everyday life of her community of about twenty sisters in southeastern United States. Born in 1920, she is preparing to enter a new phase of education and counseling.

Sister Vickie, a member of an apostolic religious community dedicated to the educational mission of the church, entered religious life in the mid 1960's. She is actively involved in bringing the gospel message to all strata of society, especially to the disenfranchised and marginalized.

Mary Louise St. John, OSB, a Benedictine Sister of Erie, was educated at Skidmore College in Saratoga Springs, New York. Her ministries are spiritual direction, liturgical planning, and retreat work. She is now writing a book on "the spirituality of experience."

Judity A. Whitacre, a Sister of St. Joseph for more than twenty years, is currently ministering in the congregation as a member of the General Council and as executive treasurer.